blue
rider
press

HEAD
BALL
COACH

BLUE RIDER PRESS

New York

HEAD
BALL
COACH

MY LIFE IN FOOTBALL

Doing It Differently—and Winning

STEVE SPURRIER

with BUDDY MARTIN

Foreword by Paul Finebaum

blue
rider
press

An imprint of Penguin Random House LLC
375 Hudson Street
New York, New York 10014

Library of Congress Cataloging-in-Publication Data

Names: Spurrier, Steve, author. | Martin, Buddy, author.
Title: Head ball coach : my life in football, doing it differently—and winning /
Steve Spurrier with Buddy Martin ; foreword by Paul Finebaum.
Description: New York : Blue Rider Press, 2016.
Identifiers: LCCN 2016029233 | ISBN 9780399574665 (hardback)
Subjects: LCSH: Spurrier, Steve. | Football coaches—United States—Biography. |
BISAC: BIOGRAPHY & AUTOBIOGRAPHY / Sports. | SPORTS & RECREATION /
Football. | BUSINESS & ECONOMICS / Leadership.
Classification: LCC GV939.S65 A3 2016 | DDC 796.332092 [B]—dc23
LC record available at https://lccn.loc.gov/2016029233
p.   cm.

Printed in the United States of America
10   9   8   7   6   5   4   3   2   1

Blue Rider Press hardcover: August 2016
Blue Rider Press paperback: September 2017
Blue Rider Press paperback ISBN: 9780399574672

BOOK DESIGN BY NICOLE LAROCHE

I am dedicating this book to the very best parents any young boy could have, Reverend John Graham Spurrier Jr. and Marjorie Orr Spurrier.

My dad taught me to compete in everything, and if you are keeping score, you try your very best to win the game.

My mom would simply say before any game, "Stevie, just do the best you can!"

I was blessed to have parents who allowed me to pursue my God-given talents in sports and chase my dreams, wherever that path may lead.

I don't know if I've ever been around a guy as obsessed with winning and perfection as he was. He had a tremendous work ethic. Every day at practice, whether you were in a meeting or on the field or in the stadium—anything associated with football—if you did not give 100 percent or did not play or perform close to perfect, you heard about it. It was the best four years of my life and I was fortunate to play for him.

—Jesse Palmer, ESPN analyst, former Gator quarterback

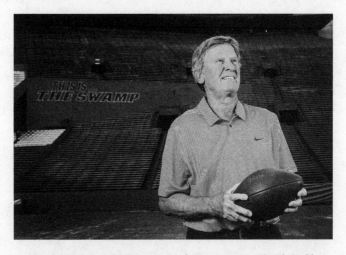

Coach stands on what is now named Steve Spurrier–Florida Field, announced in June 2016. Spurrier is now an ambassador and consultant for the University of Florida's athletic department.

CONTENTS

FOREWORD

Paul Finebaum

When I saw the breaking-news bulletin on my phone the night of October 12, 2015, I sat stunned, unable to move. I stared at the screen for a moment, hoping my eyes had deceived me, hoping against hope it wasn't true. It couldn't be.

But it was.

And it quickly became one of those never-forget, unable-to-breathe kinds of scenes. My first emotion was selfish—I was mad at him. I mumbled to myself: How can you do this? This is not fair. Then I slowly began smiling and nodding my head. The Head Ball Coach had done it again.

One more hidden-ball trick play by him left us all searching for the pigskin while he went racing past us down the field for the winning score. I quickly understood that the announcement that Steve Spurrier was stepping down at South Carolina wasn't an end, but a beginning. He wasn't going to follow the normal path. He was ending one of the most brilliant careers in college football history his own way—putting his own personal imprint on the announcement. It wasn't perfect. But it was typical Spurrier—leaving everyone talking, debating, screaming and hollering, pointing fingers, but also praising him.

In the days that followed, tributes came from all corners of the college football universe, from every major coach in the game, from Saban to Meyer—and then some, from Darius Rucker to Rick Flair—and most, if not all, correctly said the HBC had secured a spot on college football's Mount Rushmore.

But that tells only part of the story, part of what made Spurrier one of the game's most compelling coaches. And personally, my favorite coach of all-time to cover and be around.

Who else could be the greatest coach at two SEC schools?

Who else could win a Heisman Trophy and coach another player who won one?

Who else could be one of the most polarizing figures of the first half of his coaching career—only to become one of the most beloved in the second half?

Who else but Stephen Orr Spurrier?

It is easy to say Spurrier's greatest days were at Florida: the swagger and style, to say nothing of an avalanche of SEC titles—including four in a row. Four in a row! Still hard to believe years later, plus the national championship. But in some ways, his most meaningful accomplishments as a coach were at South Carolina, where he lifted the school's spirits and stature, leading the Gamecocks to the SEC title game in 2010.

Attention was paid and respect was earned after three straight eleven-win seasons—and Top 10 finishes—at South Carolina, mind you—as well as producing the No. 1 pick in the 2014 NFL draft.

I asked him once in a quiet moment at his old office at Ben Hill Griffin Stadium if he agreed with a newspaper ranking that listed him as the best coach in college football. He sat there for a moment, shrugged, and with that all-too-familiar and often-imitated voice—so sharp and often shrill it could pierce a hole through a steel plate—said: "Well, that's their opinion." For the record, he didn't argue or correct a mistake, as he often did with sportswriters. He knew the poll was precise, but to soften the blow, he added: "I'm really just a coach who calls ball plays."

In other words, the Head Ball Coach.

And now the HBC had stepped down. Done. Called it a career.

The next day in Columbia, as the nation watched his emotional press conference—emotional for others, not so much to him—airing on ESPN and other networks and being treated with the gravity and solemnity of a presidential nomination to the Supreme Court, I couldn't help recalling a line written by John Logue of *The Atlanta Journal* about the HBC during his playing days. He had led the Gators to yet another improbable victory over North Carolina State, and Logue wrote of Spurrier's superiority: "Blindfolded, with his back to the wall, with his hands tied behind him, Steve Spurrier would still be a two-point favorite at his own execution."

He did it his way—one reason many today remain so sad for his departure from football, but also so extremely fortunate and grateful to have had a front-row seat to view his greatness.

AUTHOR'S NOTE

Choosing to Do It Differently

I once read that to be successful in life you must do it like everyone else and outwork the competition, or you must do it differently.

If I had talked, dressed, acted, and coached like the other coaches, my record would have been like all the other coaches'.

I'm not that much smarter than anyone else and I don't work that much harder than the other guys. But somehow or another good fortune seemed to smile on our teams for whatever reason.

Sometimes I've had to learn by trial and error, but thankfully when I have failed it has been on me; and when I have succeeded it's not because I have tried to imitate somebody else.

The joy and satisfaction I've had in turning losing programs into winning programs has given deeper meaning to my job as a coach. I have found that throughout my life what really intrigues me and fires me up is achieving new accomplishments at places like Duke, Florida, and South Carolina, where they have never won consistently.

A lot of coaches win wherever they go. Some are blessed to go to the big schools. However, when you go to a big, successful school that already has a winning tradition and attracts the best talent every season, naturally a coach is going to have a better record. And it's far easier to turn the program around if it has slipped.

That's the only thing I can tell people: Here's how it happened. I don't know why it all happened, but here's how it happened for me.

My life story has been a combination of being at the right place at the right time, trying to use common sense in all decisions, doing things the right way for the right reasons, and receiving help from others. Was it a lot of good fortune or God smiling on us and our teams?

Those of us who are Christians believe that all things happen for a reason. We don't always know where our paths are leading, but as Coach John Wooden said, we know they are directed. You could say that maybe God smiles on some people more than others. And I believe that our paths were, indeed, directed. And that's why my life and career have been punctuated with a lot of Thank You, Lords.

—Steve Spurrier

Chapter 1

A GOOD DAY TO FIRE MYSELF

A beautiful, warm fall day in Columbia, South Carolina. A great day for hitting golf balls. Or, for that matter, announcing your resignation. So I did both on Tuesday, October 13, 2015, a day that began like most any other.

I awoke early at my house in Elgin, about a twenty-five-minute drive from the South Carolina campus. I grabbed my two newspapers, mixed some blueberries with my Raisin Bran, ate breakfast, and said goodbye to my wife, Jerri. Then I jumped in my car, plugged George Strait's *Greatest Hits* into my CD player, and off I went to work for the final time as Head Ball Coach at the University of South Carolina.

Arriving a little later than usual, I parked and walked over to our training facility for a quick workout.

I did my usual twenty-five minutes on the treadmill.

Fifteen minutes on the stationary bike.

Got up a good sweat.

Showered, shaved, and prepared for the press conference.

Put on an open-collar shirt with a sport coat.

And went upstairs to formally resign.

On my last official day, I wasn't pondering any great philosophical thoughts, because to me this really wasn't that big a deal. It wasn't like, "Oh, gee! I'm resigning today." I had been preparing for this day for a long, long time. After thirty years, I was completely at peace that my head-coaching career was finished. There was one final official act—the press conference.

This was how it was going to end after more than 400 games as a Head Ball Coach, a position that I had aspired to since breaking into the profession in 1978 at age thirty-three. I knew I would still want to be around football doing something, maybe even at the high school level, so I didn't retire. I resigned.

I had hit a tipping point early in the 2015 season when I felt I wasn't doing a very good job anymore, for whatever reasons. And that became stressful because it bothered me more than anybody else. The stress was beginning to affect me mentally and physically. When you're the oldest coach in the Southeastern Conference ever at seventy and you've had a bellyful, it's time to step aside and give somebody else a chance.

I was aware that I'd be criticized for resigning at South Carolina in mid-season. No matter what, some people were going to say I bailed out on the team. But that's okay. I'd always told Athletic Director Ray Tanner and President Harris Pastides that if and when things started going south, nobody would have to worry about firing me. I'd do it myself. So I guess I fired myself when I began to realize our players weren't getting my message anymore and needed a fresh voice.

I HAD TOLD the players and coaches the night before, after practice on October 12: "I know there's been some rumors and speculation that I may resign pretty soon. And to tell you the truth I'm thinking about it. And I think you guys might be better off without me. But you guys don't need to worry about that. Let's go beat Vanderbilt! That's the only thing you guys need to worry about."

Brandon Shell, the big six-foot-six, 328-pound senior offensive tackle from Goose Creek, South Carolina, came over and said, "Coach, you're not too old to keep coaching!"

"I may have done it long enough, Brandon," I said. "It's not only that. I think you guys would be better off with a new coach here."

The news spread immediately. The players got on their Twitter accounts, Facebook, Instagram, whatever: "Coach Stepping Down." Word got out. I knew it would. That was okay. It wasn't any big secret.

I came home and told Jerri, "By the way, I'm resigning tomorrow. You want to come to the press conference?" She said no, that she didn't plan to go, because she had a class to attend and she was on track to graduate. And I don't think she really wanted to be there, anyway. In fact, she really didn't want me to resign. I kidded her that she wanted me to coach until they put me in the grave.

Jerri just loved going to practice and hugging all the players. Since she was a young girl she had been a true football fan, passionately rooting for her uncle Rip Engle and his Penn State team. She had been my copilot all these years, faithfully attending almost every practice. She was so much a part of our players' lives that some of them called her Mom. She baked cookies on their birthdays. When they were homesick or had problems, she would be there. Believe me, she put way more effort into the job than was required. So she knew all of this was going to be over for her. But in the end, there really wasn't a lot of discussion between us about it.

I'd been a part of a team since I was seven. And even though I knew I'd miss that, I was ready to move on to whatever was next. Quite frankly, at that moment, I had no earthly idea of what "next" was going to be. I just knew this was over.

I had already spoken with "Coach" Tanner, as we referred to our athletic director, and told him several weeks before that this was near the end for me. He had encouraged me to coach through the season, but I felt the time was now.

LSU was going to be my final game. It was an odd place to finish my coaching career—a "home game" in Baton Rouge, Louisiana. The venue had to be changed because of the floods that had hit South Carolina the week before. We played in Tiger Stadium and drew a little over 42,000, but South Carolina got most of the proceeds.

Jerri went jogging the morning of the game, came back, and said, "The people out here are so nice. They had signs, GEAUX GAMECOCKS, and billboards that said WELCOME SOUTH CAROLINA."

The fans were extremely hospitable. Before the game, I always walk around for a couple hours. I said hello to my friend Joe Alleva, LSU's AD. Head coach Les Miles's wife, Kathy, was also out walking. Les and some of his assistant coaches came over. They were just very nice to us. And then the East Baton Rouge Parish sheriff, Sid Gautreaux, came by and gave me an honorary deputy's badge. He said, "Coach, if you ever come back here and need some help, maybe this will help you a little bit." So I said thanks.

I came back to the locker room and told our assistant coaches, "Man, times have changed. And I really like the old times better. When I was coaching at Florida and we came to LSU every other year, they would be shooting birds at us, throwing stuff at the bus, and yelling, 'Arrogant, cocky Spurrier, run up the score!' And now they are really nice to us because they know they are going to kick our ass today. We're going to try and give them a ball game today, but I don't know how we match up." We didn't match up very well. They were extremely confident that they were going to beat us good. And they did, 45–24.

So I made up my mind after my final game in Baton Rouge that it was best for everybody concerned if I stepped down.

Back in Columbia, as the time drew near to make the announcement of my resignation, I had asked the coaches to come upstairs for a quick meeting because "I want to go over some stuff." A few of them might have already had an inkling, but I wanted to break it to my staff gently, including my sons Steve Jr. and Scotty, two of our assistant coaches. We were all in the meeting room with Coach Tanner and Deputy Athletic Director Charles Waddell when I said:

"I'm resigning tomorrow. I've had it, I'm finished. One of you guys is going to be Head Ball Coach tomorrow. And Coach Tanner is scheduled to interview four of you. We have co-coordinators on offense and defense. If anybody else wants to be interviewed, raise your hand and he'll interview you, too, if that's what you want to do. Anybody who wants to be Head Ball Coach."

I didn't recommend anyone over anybody else, but I did suggest that our special teams coordinator, Joe Robinson, be added to the interview list. Later, Coach Tanner actually spoke to the four captains as well. That night he called Co-Offensive Coordinator / Line Coach Shawn Elliott and told him he was the interim head coach.

Shawn really looked forward to this opportunity and embraced it. When I hired Shawn from Appalachian State, I thought he was an excellent choice for offensive line coach. He's from Camden, about thirty miles from Columbia, where he grew up a Gamecock fan. He, his parents, and pretty much everybody in that community love the Gamecocks and have a lot of ties to our state and the University of South Carolina. I was truly hoping he would win enough games to become the head coach and keep a lot of our assistant coaches. This was another reason to step down in mid-season.

Shawn is a very good line coach, an excellent recruiter, and a good person. Even though I thought he would be the logical candidate for Coach Tanner to select, I didn't suggest him or have any input. Jon Hoke, my former D-coordinator at Florida, had been at South Carolina only one year. Lorenzo Ward was the co-coordinator. But the defense was struggling. Steve Spurrier Jr., our co-offensive coordinator, had the wrong last name. So it really added up that Coach Elliott was the best choice and most deserving.

It had been suggested that I stay on another week and "go out a winner" because we thought we could beat Vandy, but I felt that was unfair to the interim coach. I hoped Shawn could turn things around.

A FEW MINUTES before the Tuesday press conference, I met with President Pastides and his wife, Patricia; Coach Tanner; Deputy Athletic Director Charles Waddell; and Steve Fink, our sports information director. The men all had on dark suits and ties. I had on a blue blazer and an open shirt, sort of sporty. It was about 80 degrees that day.

"You guys look like you're going to a funeral!" I joked. "This is not a funeral. Let's just go do this thing!"

We headed upstairs for the press conference, which was being broadcast live at noon on ESPN. I hadn't really taken any notes because I had already thought out what I was going to say. I didn't feel nervous or have any trepidation about the announcement. It was time to move on and let everybody know how blessed I had been to be a head coach for thirty years, and especially the last ten-plus at South Carolina.

President Pastides and Coach Tanner said a few words. And then I told the media: "First of all, I'm resigning and not retiring. I don't have plans to ever be a head coach again . . . but don't say I've retired completely. Who knows what will come in the future?"

Somebody said, "Coach, you're not very emotional." And I said: "I knew this day was coming and I now know I'm finished as a head coach."

I did a few one-on-one interviews right there, including talking with Rece Davis, host of ESPN's *College GameDay*, explaining all the reasons behind it. And away we went.

HINDSIGHT IS ALWAYS 20/20. The best time to walk away would have been after beating Miami 24–21 in the Independence Bowl at the end of the 2014 season. We had won four straight bowl games against Nebraska, Michigan, Wisconsin, and then Miami. I just wasn't smart enough at that time to believe we would really struggle in 2015. As head coach, I took full blame for that losing season.

There wasn't time for me to explain everything at the press conference, so later, in December 2015, I wrote the Gamecock fans an open letter:

"In the last few years when asked how much longer I plan to coach, I have said often that if our team is going in the wrong direction I need to resign and allow someone else to take over as head coach here. After six games, we were 2-4 with two blow-outs by Georgia and LSU. We were behind at halftime against UCF (a team that went 0-12 in 2015). We were definitely going in the wrong direction. I felt that I was doing a lousy job as head coach and a change would help our team become more competitive. I told our team after I resigned that they needed new leadership, new enthusiasm and a new plan." I said that by resigning I would save the University of South Carolina several million dollars, as I forfeited the buyout clause. And I said that I might coach again, possibly as a volunteer coach at a high school.

What I didn't explain was how the losing began to cause more stress for me than normal. I loved coaching at South Carolina, felt blessed to have so many excellent players, and appreciated all the support of the boosters, fans, and administration. But I'd begun giving thought to resigning for more than a year after experiencing symptoms of acute stress syndrome.

During 2014 when our team lost four out of five in the middle of the season, the stress level started to wear on me. In three of those games, we had 13-, 14-, and 14-point leads with six or fewer minutes left in the games. One of the most difficult losses for me to take was to Tennessee, where we were up 14 with four minutes left. They scored quickly, and we got the onside kick but failed to make a first down. I blamed myself for one bad call in the last possession. They scored again and the game went into overtime. We held Tennessee to a field goal, and I thought we had a chance to win it. On first down, we allowed their right defensive end to come in untouched for a sack. On second down, their left defensive end came in clean for another sack. We lost 45–42. After the game, I addressed the media and gave a few comments and then said, "I can't take any questions. I hope you understand."

We had an open date the next week. I couldn't sleep much at all for a week. I saw our team psychologist, Dr. Tim Malone, for a prescription for some strong sleeping pills. He told me I had "acute stress disorder." I was forgetting things like the code to my locker in the stadium and also some common phone numbers that I used all the time. I eventually got over this as we won three of our last four, including the bowl victory over Miami.

I thought we were headed back in the right direction in 2015, but we weren't. My friend Malcolm MacLeod, who I have known and played golf with for more than twenty-five years, said, "Steve, how do you take all that stress on the sideline?"

I began to realize that I had done this coaching gig long enough. I had a team that was really struggling, and I knew that our team needed new leadership, new direction, and new passion. That is when I stepped down.

I decided not to announce that I was retiring at the end of the season, as some other coaches have done. If I had done that, I would have been a distraction throughout the remainder of the season, with all of the attention on my last game everywhere I went. I did not want a "Spurrier Farewell Tour." The players deserve to be the story of each game. Also, it would have prevented Shawn Elliott, a coach who has loved the South Carolina Gamecocks his whole life, from getting a shot to be the interim head coach, with the possibility of becoming the head coach.

LIKE EVERYTHING ELSE in my coaching career, I wanted to handle my resignation differently. When it's time, it's time. Nobody knows better than the coach himself. You get to a certain age and people start asking, "Are you about through?" And if you are through, you might as well move on, then. No sense waiting around.

After my resignation press conference, I went out and hit some golf balls at the golf range at Woodcreek Farms. Then I went home and had dinner with Jerri. That night after dinner at home, I enjoyed a decent night's sleep, convinced that this was the right time to move on.

Little did I know that the floodgates for departing coaches were about to open up in 2015. I just happened to be the second of fifteen Power Five head coaches who would resign, change jobs, or get fired that season. Seems like it had become open season on Head Ball Coaches.

When a coach gets fired, however, the change is often good and helpful to the team. Miami was 4-3 when Al Golden was fired, and the interim head coach, Larry Scott, went 4-1 in the regular season and Miami got to the Sun Bowl before Mark Richt came over to the Hurricanes from Georgia after being fired. Randy Edsall was 2-4 at Maryland when he was fired, and his replacement, Mike Locksley, got the team playing better, handing it off to D. J. Durkin from Michigan.

When Steve Sarkisian was fired by Southern Cal, Clay Helton was picked as the interim, and after the Trojans went 5-2 under his watch, Clay wound up being hired as head coach. Before the dust had settled there was a slew of other changes—among them Kirby Smart being hired by Georgia and Gary Pinkel of Missouri resigning and Missouri promoting his defensive coordinator, Barry Odom. For a while, it also looked like LSU was going to fire Les Miles after eleven years, but the administration pulled back at the last minute, maybe because he had a $15 million buyout.

Head-coaching spans seem to have shrunk. Why? The money has gotten huge. The pressure to win has mounted. Fans and alumni expect more success, and quicker. The fact that I'd lasted thirty years as a head coach sometimes amazed even me.

Losing takes its toll on you. For so long I had just refused to grind year-round like some coaches. I chose to go about it from a different angle. If I hadn't mixed beach, golf, and family time in with my job, I most likely wouldn't have survived those three decades. Even with that, in the end the stress began to impact me in several ways, including off the field. And after I made my decision, I felt a load was off my shoulders.

As my youngest daughter, Amy, says, there really is no exit strategy for coaches: "You either get fired or you have a heart attack." Luckily, after thirty years I read my expiration date and got to pick my time and place, although it wasn't what I had envisioned for my final game.

Storybook endings for coaches are hard to come by anymore. All coaches dream of riding off triumphantly on the shoulders of their players after their final game. One guy who did was Frank Beamer of Virginia Tech, whose team beat Tulsa in the Independence Bowl, 55–52, for his 238th win in twenty-nine years. Coach Beamer was replaced by the young up-and-comer from Memphis, Justin Fuente.

It turns out my last win was against the University of Central Florida, 31–14, on September 26, 2015. We went into halftime trailing 14–8 against a team that would eventually go 0-12. We needed a twenty-seven-yard field goal from Elliott Fry just to make it that close. I'll never forget that game because it was such a wakeup call for me that we were headed in the wrong direction. And if you like symmetry, then how about this? UCF was also the first team I beat at South Carolina, 24–15, at Williams-Brice Stadium on a Thursday night, September 1, 2005.

My farewell at South Carolina was simple, direct, and nonceremonial, without any tearful goodbyes or regrets—and, unfortunately, following a loss to LSU. But I was fine with all that.

As my son Steve Jr. said, "Eleven years! We had a heckuva run."

I RECEIVED LOTS of texts and calls in the next few days after my resignation. Current players. Former players. "Coach, thanks for everything—I am what I am today because I got a chance to play under you," "Appreciate all you have done for me," et cetera. Those kinds of messages are really nice.

John Wooden said, "If you're a good coach, twenty years after you've coached, some of your players will want to hang around you and say nice things about you." It's always rewarding when that happens.

I also received calls from a few fellow coaches—Urban Meyer, Bobby Stoops, and Nick Saban among them. And that meant a lot to me. There may have been a tweet or two. I'm not big on goodbyes, but I really appreciated hearing from those people.

SOUTH CAROLINA ANNOUNCED a new head coach, Will Muschamp, on December 7, 2015. Will was an excellent choice. He got a running start on recruiting and began to shore up some of our prospects right away. I wish Will the best of luck in getting the Gamecock program back to where it was just a couple years ago, and beyond. Retained by Will from my former staff were Shawn Elliott and Jamie Speronis, associate athletics director / football operations, and my son Scotty for quality control.

Someone once said, "To be successful in life you must either do it like everybody else and outwork your competition or do it differently." I'm not smarter than most coaches and I don't work harder than the other guys. But somehow or another good fortune has seemed to smile on me. Sometimes I had to learn by trial and error. When I failed it was on me; and when I succeeded, it wasn't because I tried to imitate somebody else.

EVEN THOUGH I wasn't fired as a head coach, all coaches know the odds are not in their favor. I was not retained in my first two assistant coaching jobs. Kim Helton—my former Gator teammate and father of new Southern Cal coach Clay Helton—and I were the first to be let go when Charley Pell took over at Florida. The headline in *The Gainesville Sun* said "Spurrier, Helton Fired." I clipped it and put it on my bulletin board as a reminder of how quickly coaches can become dispensable. And I kept it for many years, even after I was hired by Florida as head coach. Maybe it was my inspiration for keeping one step ahead.

From the very start, when I landed back in Gainesville at the end of my NFL playing days and hoped to try coaching, I would learn from others but then attempt to always be myself as a coach. Of course, to become a football coach, first you have to get somebody to hire you.

Chapter 2

GIVING POWER TO CIRCUMSTANCES

*The great thing in this world is not so much where
we stand, as in what direction we are moving.*

—Oliver Wendell Holmes Sr.

**My first job was as assistant coach for Doug Dickey at Florida.
(Gold chains were popular in 1978!)**

I had just been cut from my third NFL team. It was 1977. My wife, three
kids, and I were driving north from Miami in two separate cars, uncertain of what future awaited us. We had no game plan. Professionally, I was

at a crossroads. Geographically, we were going back to the place we knew best—our home in Gainesville.

Nine years in San Francisco with the 49ers, one year of playing for the expansion Tampa Bay Buccaneers, and now cut by the Denver Broncos and Miami Dolphins. After ten years in the National Football League, obviously my options as a player were about finished, unless I wanted to try semipro football in Jacksonville. Reality had begun to set in, but it came as no surprise that I was about done playing football. Although I knew the end had been coming, I guess I'd just never given a thought to what I'd do for a real job.

Back then, communication wasn't what it is today. There were no cell phones or emails or faxes. So the news of one team cutting you and another team picking you up traveled at a snail's pace. The Denver Broncos had released me during the 1977 preseason. I drove back from Colorado to Florida not knowing that Don Shula of the Miami Dolphins had already telephoned University of Florida associate athletic director Norm Carlson about my status. When I reached Gainesville, I was pleased when Jerri told me the news. Of course I was pleased, thinking that finishing up my playing career in South Florida wouldn't be so bad, since I played at Florida and was actually born in Miami Beach. Happily, Jerri packed up the kids and we headed to Miami, where we rented an apartment. Lisa was ten, Amy eight, and Steve Jr. six.

After the Dolphins' last preseason game, however, Coach Shula decided they were going with two quarterbacks—Bob Griese and Don Strock. I called Jerri and said, "Guess what! I got released. Let's drive back to Gainesville." So off we went up the highway.

Jerri merely saw this as another adventure. She was well qualified at instant mobilization. In less than a day, she was able to take our three children out of school in South Florida, return their textbooks, and pack up for Gainesville. We loaded the two cars and hustled out of South Florida, starting the 335-mile trek north, windows down, with the ears of the family dog Jippy flapping in the wind.

Some wives might have come apart under such emotional pressure. Having her as my navigator and partner for the past fifty years has been beyond wonderful. She's not only the love of my life and the mother of my children, but my best friend, my roommate, and my adviser. And the best wife that a football player or coach could ever hope to have.

"This is not a race!" Steve Jr. blurted out as we sped up the Florida Turnpike. Turns out he was right. I was pulled over and got a speeding ticket.

Philosophically, I suppose speeding tickets remind us not to get ahead of ourselves and that timing in life is everything. That's certainly been the case for me. A large measure of my success has come from being in the right place at the right time—although it might not have felt that way at various times. The conviction that you will ultimately find your niche in life can stem only from your faith. Even though I struggled with finding my path at times, I've always believed there was a higher power involved. As one of my favorite coaches, John Wooden, once said: "We may not know where the paths may lead, but we know they are directed somehow."

Me as a coach? Only when I was done with the NFL and had moved back to Gainesville after a year out of football as a spectator at Florida Gator games did it dawn on me that coaching might be my true calling. In fact, I hadn't yet arrived at the conclusion that I might even want to be a coach, let alone that I could be successful at it. Turns out there was a bigger plan.

We moved back into our house in The Valley, a subdivision on Hogtown Creek, and started our so-called normal life. I needed to find that job. I'd had exactly one offer, from Gator alumnus Whit Palmer Jr. He knew I needed work. This was something in sales at Dixie Lime & Stone Co. in Ocala. I told Whit I wanted to wait and see what happened with football. When a player gets cut they tell you to wait a month and see how things shake out. So for a while I held on to a flicker of hope that an NFL team might call during the 1977 season.

Thankfully I was in good physical shape after ten years in the NFL, because I played the equivalent of only about two seasons during that time. That's why, as I've told many people, backup quarterback in the NFL is the best job you could have.

While waiting to see if a team would call, I played a lot of golf with my buddies at the Gainesville Country Club. One Saturday I went to watch the Gators play, where, unknowingly, I would be glimpsing my future. The stadium was not yet named the Swamp, or even Ben Hill Griffin Stadium. The University of Florida was my home turf, where eleven years prior I had played my college football career and had been fortunate enough to be an All-American, win a Heisman Trophy, and participate in two major bowls.

Sitting in the stands instead of playing on the field or watching from the sidelines seemed to give me a fresh perspective, and it piqued my interest. That season I saw maybe five or six games, including Florida–Georgia in Jacksonville. I must admit: The notion of my becoming Head Ball Coach at my alma mater and winning a national championship one day certainly seemed unrealistic at the time.

> *The circumstances of our life have as much power as we give them.*
>
> —David McNally, *The Eagle's Secret*

ONE DAY at the country club, I was talking to my friend Henry Gray, a lawyer from Gainesville. "Steve, what do you think you want to do?" he asked. And I said, "If I could get into coaching somehow, I think that's something I'd like to do." My first inkling was, "Well, if I can be on a team coaching, that's something that sounds like fun and not so much hard work." That's when the desire to become a coach really hit me.

Henry was very good friends with Florida coach Doug Dickey, ex-Gator quarterback and SEC championship coach at Tennessee. They had gone to high school together at P. K. Yonge in Gainesville. Coach Dickey asked for me to come see him, maybe thinking a former NFL quarterback could share some new thoughts on the passing game, despite the fact that the SEC was predominantly defense- and run-oriented back then. Florida was operating out of a wishbone, but a new trend was emerging. Everybody wanted to start throwing the ball.

I'd been around a lot of good coaches and some not-so-good coaches. I was about to discover that coaching could be challenging. And rewarding. You always hear that if people can't wait to get to work every day, then they have the right job.

Back then, once their careers were over, NFL players didn't consider coaching to be a glamorous profession. Coaches didn't make a lot of money. They supposedly had to work until midnight—a lot of hours. I could not see myself doing that, but when you don't have a job and you need one, your thinking changes. Today the money is better, and lots of former players want to get into coaching! So times have changed.

We all want to make our family proud of what we do. My prime motivation was the need to support a wife and three kids. I'd lost some of my fire because I hadn't gotten to compete much in the NFL. I not only needed to find a new career, I needed to regain the passion that I had lost somewhere along the way in the pros.

Just getting that first job is sometimes very tough. You've got to find somebody who believes in you and what you might stand for as a coach. So I was fortunate to have a connection with Coach Dickey, a former Gator quarterback who knew something about me, and to land a job at my alma mater. I will always be thankful to him for hiring me as the quarterback coach for the 1978 season. But I had a lot to learn. And I was about to find out a lot about how much I didn't know—especially about the new recruiting rules. I don't think Coach Doug Dickey realized how green I was, because I didn't realize it myself.

THE NCAA RECRUITING regulations had changed dramatically since I'd been recruited in 1963.

Offensive line coach Kim Helton and I flew down to Miami to check out a running back at Carol City High School. We rented a car. Went to the high school. The recruit talked to us awhile. I said, "You got a ride home?" He said, "No." I said, "Come on, hop in, we'll give you a ride." First NCAA violation.

We stopped at a Burger King. I bought him a Coke and maybe some french fries. That was another violation.

We drove the recruit home. The Tennessee coaches were also coming by—they met with him awhile and we waited. Then we met with him awhile and went to a sports bar with former Gator player and assistant coach Jerry "Red" Anderson, the Carol City high school coach and a friend. I paid for his. That was another violation.

I came back to Gainesville and was turning in my receipts when one of the ladies in Administration said, "You know you're not supposed to do this!" And my friend on the coaching staff also said, "You can't do that! You can't pay for stuff. It's against the rules."

I said, "Nobody told me! And everyone did it for me when I was in high school! Well, my bad, then. I'm learning!" And then I added, "Well, what CAN we do?"

Luckily we didn't suffer any consequences for my missteps. Clearly there was a lot for this rookie coach to learn.

ANOTHER THING I learned early was the necessity of giving every player a chance. One of the first players you have to settle on is your quarterback. And then give him the ball. My first quarterback was Johnny Brantley of Ocala, whose son John IV later played for the Gators from 2007 to 2011.

Picking the quarterback who would become the centerpiece of our offense was a critical decision. Teaching him proper fundamentals, good judgment, and leadership were all vital, but mostly what I wanted to see from our quarterbacks was commitment and courage. Over the years, as they would progress—or not—I was never afraid to make changes on the fly. Just like in baseball, when one pitcher isn't getting it done, you have to bring in another guy.

Brantley could take his steps properly and get the ball out on time, which was key to timing routes that would become the staple of our offense. During spring football, however, Brantley had been playing baseball. Cris Collinsworth was even playing a little quarterback. That summer we moved Cris over to wide receiver. We were pretty ugly. The spring game score was something like 6–0.

In fall preseason, Johnny finally came around. One thing I've always coached is to take your steps and throw the ball. If you've got an area to throw it, you gotta throw it over there on time. Teaching that is a lot harder than people think. You can tell a guy to take seven steps, hitch, and fire it right in there, but they want to hesitate. Johnny had no hesitation. He'd take his steps and let it go. He actually played very well from about the third game on, and he became the starter. Meanwhile, Collinsworth had his best year at Florida as a receiver, catching ten touchdown passes in 1978.

You want to see the players you coach play well. You want to prepare them as best you can. Teach your players to execute at a high level. Watch your team and players become successful. That's what it's all about.

After the 1978 season, the Gator program was struggling and Coach Dickey was in the hot seat. We lost to LSU, Alabama, and Georgia, but we were decent. Then we lost our starting quarterback to injury. And we lost our last two games of the season to rivals Florida State and Miami to finish 4-7. Because we didn't win enough, we were all fired.

CHAPTER ONE of my coaching career was in the books, but what now? I had no idea. It became clear, however, that if I was going to coach I needed to figure out my own way of doing it.

I had stepped out on the pathway as a coach and with that came a great deal of uncertainty. Mostly things would just fall in line, but not without an ensuing struggle. No coach gets to say where he's going to live and work forever. It's a nomadic profession. You wind up going wherever fate and the game take you. Jobs are hard to come by. When you're out of work, you have to hit the road again.

Looking back, I can see that every experience was preparing me for a lifetime in sports. It began when I was growing up in East Tennessee. There was one clear message: As a young boy I was taught that in life there are winners and there are losers. I just always thought there were alternative routes to winning.

Chapter 3

UNDERNEATH THE VISOR

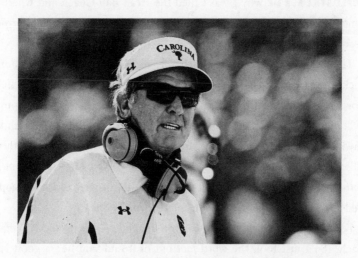

The HBC on the sideline at Williams-Brice Stadium.

The decision to wear a visor on the sideline, when nobody else did, was a point of emphasis: We do things differently around here, and we intend to have fun playing this game of football. That applied to everything: How we practiced and prepared; my attitude about enjoying life; the style of offense we ran and the attacking mode were stayed in right up to the final whistle. We wanted to score every time we had the ball if possible. If the opposition wanted to complain about us running up the score, then have at it.

Our statement was about how we played and what we won: the seven SEC championships and a national title. (Even though the official record book says six SEC championships, I count 1990 as well. We had the best conference record, but an NCAA penalty from 1986 and Florida's decision to take the penalty that year precluded us from being awarded the trophy for 1990. It went to Tennessee instead.)

PEOPLE STILL ASK ME why I was called the Head Ball Coach and where it came from. Although maybe they'll have to refer to me now as the Former Head Ball Coach, or FHBC.

The nickname Head Ball Coach sort of evolved over the years and stuck. In Johnson City, Tennessee, where I played youth and high school sports, the term "ball coach" just described someone who loved sports and taught or coached ball of any kind. A group of us guys in high school played three sports under three different coaches. We just called them ball coaches. "He's a good ball coach," we'd say. We dropped the *foot* in *football* because there were good coaches in other sports. A lot of people used it—not just me—instead of using the word *football*.

Football coaches overuse the word *football*. "He's a good *football* coach." So I just took the word *foot* out of it and said he's a good *ball* coach. If someone coached basketball, he or she would still be called a good ball coach. I once was asked if I could have been a good basketball coach, and I think I could have been, because I think I would have learned how to do it. I used to always tell Pat Summitt, the Tennessee women's basketball coach, that she would have been a heckuva good *football* coach. And she would have been, because she inspired her players. Encouraged them. And demanded they play their best. And that's what good ball coaches do.

At some point I started referring to myself as just a ball coach. Later at Florida, someone referred to me as Head Ball Coach. I'm not sure who started it, but a guy named A. J. Vaughn from Jacksonville, a friend of sportswriter/broadcaster David Lamm, brought me a shirt with HBC on it, and the nickname seemed to stick.

Of course, anybody can adopt the title Head Ball Coach. Matt McCall, the son of my former Florida teammate Wayne McCall, was hired as basketball coach at Tennessee Chattanooga in 2015 and called me to leave this message: "Now I'M a Head Ball Coach, too!" Yes, Matt, you've earned that title!

HBC had become part of my so-called brand, to a point where it was the label they put on my headset and sometimes used to refer to me in our football offices. I even got into social media just a little bit and my Twitter handle was @SC_HBC. But I don't expect I'll be tweeting much anymore.

THE VISOR THING sort of began with a superstition about a white cap. In 1989, Duke beat Clemson, 21–17, in a drizzling rain and I was wearing a white baseball-style hat. I said, "I'm going to wear this until we lose." I hardly wore a visor at Duke—maybe at practice every once in a while. A lot of times I didn't wear any kind of hat at all, unless it was a cold or rainy day. Well, I wore that hat that day against Clemson and we didn't lose the rest of the season. That hat was on my head when they carried me off the field at Kenan Stadium in Chapel Hill after Duke became the Atlantic Coach Conference champions. But the visor didn't become a permanent fixture until I moved to Florida as the Gators Head Ball Coach. Prior to becoming a head coach in Florida, I'd only worn a visor while playing golf, a game I've always loved, and a couple times when I was the head coach of the Tampa Bay Bandits. I used to buy visors at every good golf course I played and wear them during my round. So I've collected a rather large stack.

Back in 1990 there were no deals with Nike or Under Armour or Adidas. Schools had their own arrangements. Larry Habegger from North Carolina had a company called Coaches Choice. Larry had a wonderful idea and should have gotten the rights. When he visited the Florida campus, he offered to make us visors, hats, shirts, et cetera. They made blue visors and white visors. I usually wore the white one.

When I started wearing a visor as Gator coach, I had no idea it would start a trend. I just decided, "I'm going to the Sunshine State, the Florida Gators, so I need to start wearing a visor on the sideline." I liked the fact that it was different, but I also liked it because in Florida it was much cooler than a cap.

I'd like to think that's not the only thing that the Head Ball Coach is known for doing differently. However, the visor was definitely symbolic—part of a plan to break with some traditions and do it my own way. Now numerous coaches around the country wear visors. These Visor Coaches are all just a little bit different.

WHETHER YOU'RE a coach, a teacher, or the CEO of a large company, you should develop your own brand. If you are going to be a coach, be unique—but be yourself. Dress the way you want to dress. Coach the way you want to coach. Say the things you want to say—the way you want to say them. If you say all the things other coaches say, then you are going to be just like them. You can't separate yourself from others if you copy them. Coaching is such an individual thing. There are a lot of good coaches you can learn from. And there are some who can show you what not to do. If you choose to be different, as I am suggesting, you can rest assured that others will take notice and often comment.

I have been criticized for my unorthodox coaching style. Early in my career, critics assumed that I wasn't serious about coaching and accused me of not wanting to work hard enough. I never bragged about how hard I worked like most coaches do. I've never bought into the idea that to be a successful coach you must spend long hours at night in your office studying tape.

I tailored my coaching career to fit my lifestyle, not vice versa. I tried to work smart and have fun—to find the joy in winning football while doing things the right way. No doubt players picked up on it. But you have to earn the right to have that fun. Sometimes that means a little restraint is in order. One morning at 6:30 an NFL scout came by the Florida coaches' office while I was in there watching tape of our opponent that week. He said, "Coach, you're going to ruin your reputation of not working hard." I said, "You're right, so please don't tell anybody."

I always encouraged our team to keep competing at all times, right to the end of the game, and never take our foot off the pedal no matter the score—whether you're winning or losing. Don't start celebrating until the game's finished. That's a problem a lot of people have. In fact, our usual pregame and halftime speeches are "Just keep playing hard and competing. Don't relax until the game is over."

Getting your substitutes in the game and letting them take part is important. Winning is to be shared, and it's a much happier locker room when everybody gets to contribute. It helps build the team. That was one of the keys to our success at Florida—getting a big lead and letting the backups log in some playing time. Allowing your team to score a touchdown late in the game when you are ahead is part of rewarding your walk-on players, your backup players who haven't had a chance to play much.

At South Carolina the last few years, because most of our games were close, we weren't able to get the guys in that much. But at Florida, our backup quarterback, Brock Berlin, threw a touchdown pass in each of the first seven games in 2001.

I've always believed you want to encourage your backups to give a good effort in a relief role, so sometimes that will result in tacking on touchdowns. I will admit there have been a few times when running up the score was meant to send a message. But mostly it's giving your reserves a chance to show what they can do when they get their chance to play—and not just in a mop-up role.

Some of these so-called unwritten rules in the mythical coaching handbook are thinly disguised as Emily Post etiquette.

I want to score as much and as often as possible until our backup players are in the game. And if the shoe is on the other foot, I don't mind the opposition doing the same thing. If coaches don't like a lopsided score, then the best thing to do is stop the other team from scoring. The really good coaches never complain about the final score because their main focus is winning the game.

The first time I was ever accused of running up the score was when I was at Duke. We played Georgia Tech following a very, very tough loss at Maryland, where we blew a big lead. We had gone up and down the field and when we got inside the five-yard line we kept trying to run it in with two tight ends and two backs. And we had to kick a bunch of short field goals. This was purely my fault. We were up 22–7 in the fourth quarter and Maryland scored two touchdowns and tried two two-point conversions and, unbelievably, they made them both. And they beat us, 23–22.

So when the game was over I told our players, "Fellas, I'll take full responsibility for this one. There was some dumb-ass play-calling down on the goal line and I guarantee you I'll try my best to never do that again! From now on, when we get on the goal line, we may be in a spread formation. We're not getting in any more two tight end formations. That's history!"

The next week we played Georgia Tech—they came to Wallace Wade Stadium. In the fourth quarter with eight minutes left we learned that our quarterback, Steve Slayden, had tied the ACC record with five touchdown passes. We were sort of struggling that year with only three or four wins. So I said, "Steve, I'm going to give you a shot at the record, but you've got to do it in the normal course of the game. We're not going to call time-out." We had time for maybe one more drive. We got the ball at about our 20 and we go driving down the field and, sure enough, on second and eleven Steve hit the touchdown pass—a seam route to Bud Zuberer. And we ended up beating them 48–14 and Slayden set the ACC record.

Bobby Ross was the coach at Georgia Tech. He might have been a little upset, I don't know. But a writer in Charlotte, North Carolina, named

Tom Sorensen wrote an article saying, "Steve Spurrier of Duke ought to be ashamed for running up the score on Georgia Tech. With the game safely in hand and a minute fifty left, he threw another touchdown pass."

Sorensen called Tom Butters, the AD at Duke, and asked him, "How do you feel about having a football coach who ran up the score last week against Georgia Tech? Do you believe in that?"

And Mr. Butters told him, "Let me tell you something. I've been the athletic director here for twenty-two years. And this is the first time anybody has accused my football coach of running up the score. And to tell you the truth, I sort of like it!"

So I encourage new, young head coaches to do it differently, whether it's your style of coaching, talking, or what you choose to wear. Don't be afraid to do your own thing.

IT'S A NICE TRIBUTE when a coach comes up and says, "Coach Spurrier, I wear the visor because you wore one." I've had Gus Malzahn of Auburn tell me that. Hugh Freeze, Ole Miss coach. Gary Andersen, formerly of Wisconsin and now of Oregon State, and Dan Mullen of Mississippi State.

When Coach Bobby Stoops came down to join us at Florida in 1995 before becoming head coach at Oklahoma, all of our staff was voluntarily wearing visors. Bobby said it made sense because they were a lot cooler to wear in the hot sun than hats. And then when Kevin Sumlin joined Bobby's OU staff, he began wearing one—and still does as head coach at Texas A&M.

I was deeply honored when some of them—Coach Malzahn and Coach Stoops, as I remember—paid tribute to the HBC by going visorless in their games that followed my resignation. And I especially appreciated the gesture by South Carolina interim coach Shawn Elliott when he waved his visor at the camera before the Gamecocks took the field to play Vanderbilt.

What's interesting is that the Visor Guys are usually offensive-minded coaches, with the exception of Coach Stoops.

PEOPLE MAY HAVE this idea that I throw my visor a lot, but not so much the last few years. I will admit, however, that I've tossed a few. The first time I recall throwing my visor was in 1990, my third game ever as Gator coach. We had beaten Oklahoma State, 50–7, in our opener. And then we went to Alabama and beat them in a huge game, 17–13.

In our third game we played Furman, a small but good and tough opponent at that time. We'd just enjoyed two big wins in our start at Florida, but our guys were a bit down and we didn't get them as ready for Furman as we should have.

Our defense played super and we ended up beating them 27–3. At one point, the ball was on Furman's 15-yard line and we had the perfect play called—a corner route to the split end. Furman played man-to-man and the defensive back was playing hard inside. So it should have been a gimme touchdown. But our receiver ran a bad route. I watched in disgust as the pass fell incomplete. It really frustrated me. Our guys had run that play in practice numerous times. It should have been an easy touchdown, but we just didn't execute the play correctly.

I took my visor off and fired it to the ground. And the camera got me as I did. And we had to settle for a field goal. It wasn't because we won or lost or that I had a disagreement with an official. It was because we hadn't done a good job as coaches of teaching that guy how to run that route. I was mad at the player, but even madder at myself.

After a couple more times, as I became more experienced as a visor-thrower, I also found out that firing a perfectly good new white visor to the ground causes a grass stain and can ruin it. Those stains are almost impossible to wash off. I made a note to myself: "I gotta quit doing that!" And so I didn't do it as much. I started flipping the visor up in the air and catching it.

———

AS FOR DOING things differently, one thing we all have in common as coaches is knowing the will to win trumps just about everything. I side with the experts who say success can be learned, taught, and adopted.

For coaches, it all starts with the commitment to becoming a winner. That means getting yourself and your team in order, to give fate a chance. And no matter your coaching style, timing is a key to being a winner. Most successful people are also in the right place at the right time. Coach Wooden of UCLA certainly was. And for me, that has also been the case. I have found the wisdom of Coach Wooden's words most helpful throughout my years of coaching and have collected ideas from many books and articles in formulating my coaching philosophy. But for me, the heart of the matter started at home, where my father taught me the valuable lesson of why they have a scoreboard.

Chapter 4

WINNERS AND LOSERS

I was pretty happy at the Sugar Bowl after Terry Jackson's
touchdown made it Florida 45, FSU 20—and
then Terry added another to make it 52–20.
A memorable night!

Winning is what makes it fun for coaches and players because it creates memories that last forever. I look back fondly at every one of the 228 college victories and 47 pro football wins as special moments to remember in my coaching career. But it's beating rivals and winning the championships that I cherish most—especially in a powerfully competitive league like the Southeastern Conference.

The first rule of thumb, corny as it may sound, is that individual awards and recognition won't fulfill you like team accomplishments. It's far more rewarding to share an achievement with a team than it is to celebrate your own personal success. I told many of my former players at Florida that they should always value those SEC titles very highly.

I know I take great pride in those SEC titles as coach of the Gators. We were never able to accomplish that dream of winning the SEC at South Carolina, but we did win an Eastern Division title and finish in the Top Ten in 2011, 2012, and 2013.

Any personal accomplishments for me pale in comparison to achieving team goals that are more enjoyable when shared with those who helped achieve them. The idea is to celebrate being winners together. Championships are forever. Everybody will always remember that the 1991 Florida team was the first school in history to win an official SEC championship. And most everybody will remember the 1996 team was Florida's first national champion. (I still say our 1990 team was our first to win the SEC. We simply were not recognized by the conference.)

Much is made about SEC rivalries stirring the passion of fans in what is considered the best college football conference in America. Truthfully, fans are passionate in the Big Ten or Big Twelve and all of the Power Five conferences. But because we pack our large stadiums down South, more weight seems to be given to the SEC. We might be shortsighted about that. But rivalries inside your division and conference are the most intense because that's the ticket to winning the conference title and ultimately the national championship.

I have said many times that it's often as difficult to win the SEC as it is to win the national championship. Back in 1996, when there was no playoff, the SEC schedule then was certainly tougher than any other conference. At Florida we were usually battling Tennessee for the Eastern Division supremacy when the Vols had some of their highest-ranked teams. And when we were also playing our instate rival, Florida State, they were at the peak of their run, ranked among the Top Five teams in the country thirteen of the fourteen times we played.

Our 1992 Florida team was fortunate enough to play in the first SEC championship game, which we lost to Alabama on an interception for what we hoped would be the game-clinching drive. The SEC title game created another level of competition for our league. I'd always been in favor of it, just as I supported the idea of a national tournament. Now there is a four-team playoff, which I feel is a step in the right direction. But it needs to expand.

AT FLORIDA AND SOUTH CAROLINA we were able to hold our own pretty well against rivals. We were able to win more times than not against the likes of Georgia, Tennessee, and Clemson. Maybe we didn't do as well against Florida State, but we won our fair share and will always have that 52–20 Sugar Bowl victory over FSU that led to Florida's first-ever national championship.

When it came to the Gators playing Georgia—still considered by many fans as their fiercest rival—we were fortunate to win eleven out of twelve against a team that had always dominated us in the past. And when we added on the five wins the Gamecocks were able to gain over the Bulldogs, our sixteen wins over Georgia were the most ever by any other coach. Coach Ralph (Shug) Jordan of Auburn beat them fifteen times.

SPURRIER BY THE NUMBERS VS. RIVALS

At Florida
Tennessee, 8-4
Georgia, 11-1
Florida State, 5-8-1
Miami, 1-1
Total: 24-14-1

At South Carolina
Tennessee, 5-5

Georgia, 5-6

Clemson, 6-4

Combined at Florida / South Carolina

Georgia, 16-7

Tennessee, 13-9

LEARNING HOW to win is a process, but certain people have the leadership qualities and vision to advance the cause quicker. Wisdom can be gained through experience, but it can also be acquired from others.

I found that wisdom in several places—starting with my own dad's words, as well as reading books and adapting the philosophies of others to my own style. Plus, experiencing the trials and errors of my own journey. However, while you listen and learn from others, it's ultimately your decisions you must live and die with. That's why I cannot emphasize enough the importance of coaches putting their own fingerprints on their program and a team—doing it their own way and trusting their own choices.

Are winners born or made? Some people will argue both sides. For certain it takes courage to be a winner. Over the years I have compiled wisdom from many sources in lists—including my list of Winners and Losers, and how to know the difference between them. One my favorite sources is Sydney J. Harris's book, appropriately titled *Winners and Losers*, which tells you how winners act and talk. A winner says: "This is the best way to do it around here." A loser says: "That's the way we've always done it around here."

When I began my fifth head coaching job at age sixty, my goal was to be South Carolina's winningest coach. I said that at the outset because I wanted Gamecock fans to know I was going to be there at least ten years or so—not just coach for a couple years and then leave when some big-time school came calling. I needed to win sixty-five games to do it, and by the end of year eight (2012) that goal was reached.

I began goal-setting with my teams at Duke in 1989. At South Carolina I continued to reach out for new goals, some of them very intriguing and challenging for our teams, coaches, and fans. In 2015, while writing this book, it was brought to my attention that I needed only sixteen more wins to become the only FBS coach with one hundred or more wins at two schools. But it wasn't to be.

Still, we wound up 86-49 overall and 44-40 in the SEC after ten-plus seasons. In the previous decade at South Carolina, the Gamecocks were 46-64 overall and 28-51 in the SEC.

And then there was that "expiration date" I should have heeded.

EVERYBODY WANTS to be a winner in life. Nobody wants to be called a loser. As a coach, it's more than just your record. Simply adding more wins just to enhance your résumé and your own personal legacy was never what it was all about for me. My satisfaction was in charting new territory and going where the programs had rarely, if ever, been before.

I was asked by a reporter several years ago at our SEC coaches meetings in Destin, Florida, if I thought I'd ever catch Coach Bear Bryant for most victories in the SEC. Coach Bryant was 159-46-9 in SEC games while at Kentucky and Alabama. Somebody had calculated that I would need to average a little more than seven SEC wins a season for the next four seasons back then to catch him. "Had I wanted to break that record, I would have stayed at Florida," I said to a reporter. And I meant that. However, for other reasons I have to admit in retrospect that I left Florida four or five years too early. All the pieces were in place to keep winning more championships—conference and national.

FLORIDA BEFORE SPURRIER, 1933-1989

1. SEC Titles: 0
2. Most Wins in a Season: 9

3. Ranked No. 1: One week, 1985

4. Final Top Ten Rankings: 3

5. SEC Record: 148-166-15

6. Most SEC Wins in a Season: 5

7. Most Points Scored in a Season: Under 350

FLORIDA WITH SPURRIER, 1990–2001

1. SEC Titles: 7 (counting 1990)

2. Most Wins in a Season: 9–12 over 12 years

3. Ranked No. 1: 29 weeks

4. Final Top Ten Rankings: 9 out of 12 years

5. SEC Record: 87-14 (.867 percentage)

I KEEP a long list of players and coaches I've admired as winners, all the way back to my youth. Being a winner is reflected in how you act, how you talk, how you compete, what you stand for in your principles, and how those core values impact others in your program and around you. Over the years I have compiled lists of wisdom from many sources. I've mentioned Sydney Harris's *Winners and Losers*. Harris, a Chicago columnist and author, talked about the subject of winning in broader terms than just sports. If you know the difference, it's easy to say: "If you act and talk like a winner, you've got a chance to be a winner. If you act like a loser and talk like a loser—good chance, you'll be a loser."

I have also studied the work of behavioral experts like Dr. Charles A. Garfield, who I came across when Jerri found a *Success* magazine article on "What Successful People Have." Dr. Garfield, a computer analyst for the first Apollo mission to the moon, has studied and written about peak performers extensively. He talks about characteristics and traits of peak performers—highly successful people.

The most interesting thing was, he said: Almost anyone can acquire these traits. So I wrote these traits down and began to make sure I'd acquired them, or would, and I tried to get our coaches and players to acquire them, too.

1. Attitude. We all know what a good attitude is and what a sorry attitude is. Always positive.
2. No excuses.
3. Be responsible for your actions. Accountability.
4. Effort. Persistence. Determination.
5. Courage. Confidence.
6. Preparation.
7. Creative risks.
8. New ideas.
9. Bouncing back from adversity. (Almost every year we won the SEC we lost a game at some point.)
10. Transcend previous accomplishments.
11. Love to compete.

WHEN I FIRST got into coaching—and especially when I became a head coach—I was curious why some coaches and teams won more than others. Vince Lombardi was known as the best to ever coach in the NFL. In the NBA, the Boston Celtics were the best team. The New York Yankees were the best in baseball. The Yankees won with different managers—Casey Stengel, Ralph Houk, Billy Martin, and later Joe Torre. Those guys knew how to win.

And, of course, Jack Nicklaus was the best in golf. He won eighteen majors, more than anybody. He knew how to concentrate, focus, and pay attention. You never saw him when his mind was not on the game. John Wooden was without a peer in college basketball. In tennis, it was Chrissie Evert and Björn Borg.

Coach Lombardi said: "Winning isn't everything—it's the ONLY thing." He also said, "When you're on a winning streak, you've got to stay on players' butts, because they can become complacent. You've got to find something to chew them out about a little bit. If they're on a losing streak, you've got to lighten up a little, maybe shake things up." When we lost four out of five in 2014, we adopted the theme of the Taylor Swift song "Shake It Off." We did, and won three of our last four.

Doing it differently? When I say "differently," it doesn't mean you ignore history or that you can't learn from proven winners. I mean that you study successful people and see how it fits what you do. You can't outright replicate somebody else's success, but you can sure learn from them and put your own twist on things. It's not a given, however, that because you are around highly successful people you can soak up all the knowledge and do it yourself.

In the South during my lifetime, we looked up to Coach Bear Bryant as the best, and his record proved it, as he was the third-all-time winning-est coach, with 323 wins. I was recruited by Coach Bryant and competed against his team when I was at Florida. He knew about winners and winning and was a big proponent of passion. Coach Bryant was a planner, as you can see in this version I obtained of his "Three Rules of Coaching":

1. Surround yourself with people that have a passion, desire and attitude that they cannot live without football.
2. The ability to recognize, identify and know winners. They come in all sizes, shapes and forms.
3. Have a plan for everything, every day—and make it work.

I really like number 2. So many coaches look for size, speed, strength. But the real coaches look for the guys who know how to play the game, make the plays when the game is on the line. Effort. Smarts. There are all kinds of other identifiers for winners.

As for number 3, you do need a plan for everything, every day, and need to make it work. I think Coach Urban Meyer is one of those guys who has a plan for everything. When he watched Auburn run that missed field goal back against Alabama, he said, "We never worked on that. Now we work on it every week, just in case. If the other team tries a field goal, it can be run back."

SOME OF THE BEST SOURCES for me have been great books, including *Leadership Secrets of Attila the Hun* by Wess Roberts and *The Art of War* by Sun Tzu. I started reading Coach Wooden's books in the early 1990s. And I have an old tape recording of one of his speeches where he talks about his pyramid of success and his philosophies about coaching. I've incorporated a lot of his wisdom in what I tried to teach.

I consider Coach Wooden to be as wise as any coach ever. Why was he so successful? It wasn't because he was more intelligent than the other guy. He did his share of hard work, but he didn't waste a lot of extra hours or work longer than his competition.

These are some of my favorite Wooden-isms:

1. Try to never be better than someone else; never cease to be the best you can be.
2. Don't become involved in what you have no control over; be involved in what you CAN control.
3. No excessive jubilation; no excessive dejection.
4. Don't look ahead. Don't dwell on how well you did last week.
5. Respect all opponents, fear no one.
6. Definition of success: Peace of mind and self-satisfaction in knowing that you have done your best to be the best you can be.
7. The greatest ally a coach can have is the bench. Coaches must put players on the bench if they are not striving to play their best within the framework of what's best for the team.

Number 7 is one of my favorites, and I have used it many times over the years. People wonder why I have often substituted quarterbacks. I once benched a guy who was going to win the Heisman—Danny Wuerffel. I even rotated quarterbacks every other play at Florida with Doug Johnson and Noah Brindise back in 1997.

When people criticized me for frequently changing quarterbacks, I always said that they change pitchers in baseball all the time, which is why they have a bullpen. Some days maybe a guy just doesn't have his best stuff. I've also used the bench to send a message to a player who was not playing his best "within the framework for what's best for the team."

High-fiving quarterback Doug Johnson after we beat No. 1 FSU at the Swamp in 1997. Doug alternated with Noah Brindise in one of the most exciting games ever played on Florida Field.

THERE ARE ALSO times in defeat when you can learn something that will make you and your team better down the road, or as it is said by Attila the Hun, "Live again to fight another day." That is one of the many principles of Attila, whose strategies I have studied—as have other coaches and many prominent businessmen and businesswomen. Attila, a ruthless and aggressive warrior born around 406 A.D. in what is now Hungary, became the king of the Hunnic Empire and terrorized the Roman Empire by devastating lands from the Black Sea to the Mediterranean.

I often refer to other Attila strategies, but the one I like most from him is: "A leader must use and apply massive common sense in solving every problem."

I had a guy ask me: "How have you lasted so long?" I said, "Well, I don't irritate the president or the AD if I can help it. I try to get along with everybody." Obviously, you gotta win. But I try to use common sense in every little situation. It was key to my lasting as long as I did in the coaching profession.

There are many more excellent Attila-isms I have referred to over the years, even early in my coaching career. Some my other favorites are:

1. Leaders must want to be in charge. (This inspired me to go after the head-coaching job of the Tampa Bay Bandits when they called and asked if I was interested in the job as offensive coordinator.)
2. Good morale and discipline are a must for unity.
3. Reward your workers (players) for character and integrity. (Our favorite players are usually the ones most well conditioned and unselfish.)
4. You must aim high, going after goals that will make a difference rather than seeking the safe path of mediocrity.

The Art of War by Sun Tzu is also popular among many coaches, and most of us have pored over the wisdoms of the famous Chinese general. Some apply, some don't, but I think we can all agree that the simplicity of his wisdom is most refreshing.

YOU MAY GATHER wisdom from around the world, but you can't beat the homegrown teachings of your coaches and parents. I always hearken back to my days as a young athlete when my dad taught me that the goal is to win. I have told the story many times about what my father said as the head manager of our Thomas Products Babe Ruth baseball team after our first practice, because it underscores my core value about Winners and Losers and has remained close to my heart ever since I was a teenager: The reason they keep score is to determine who won and who lost. Much of my desire to be a winner was instilled in me by my dad, the Rev. J. Graham Spurrier Jr.

A commitment to the principle of winning is pretty much why and how I have lived my life as an athlete and a coach. Yes, there are times when you have given your best, and the other team was just better that day. But what my father was saying was that the purpose of playing is to win—not just to try hard. When you compete, winning must be the priority for winners. If you have committed to giving everything you have and still lose, then you have to acknowledge that the other team was the winner that day. And as I look back at my life, growing up in Tennessee and winding up choosing Florida as my college, I know for sure my path was being directed. My friends predicted I would play baseball and basketball, as I did in high school. In football, I developed more slowly. I wasn't even a quarterback at first. Raised a Tennessee football fan and having lived most of my life about a hundred miles from Knoxville, by rights I guess I should have been a Vol. But other forces were clearly at work, because none of it turned out that way.

Chapter 5

FLORIDA BORN, TENNESSEE RAISED

Reverend J. Graham Spurrier Jr. didn't believe we should be playing ball on Sundays. He got a little mad at us boys one time and felt compelled to point out, "Sunday is a day of rest!"

My dad was a really committed, sincere Presbyterian minister who believed the Bible from the front to the back. He also loved all sports, especially baseball and tennis. He would shoot basketball with us and toss the ball around. But he had some strong feelings about when we played or practiced. My brother, Graham, and I would go to church and Sunday school and then head down to the park to play ball.

Church was important to us. But us kids didn't go around preaching to other kids, or begging them to come to church. We were not religious zealots, but ours was a family of strong faith. I was proud to be awarded my thirteen-year perfect attendance Sunday School pin. The whole family went to Sunday School, church service Sunday morning and Sunday night—and prayer meeting every Wednesday night.

I can still hear my brother, Graham, saying, "Mom, we go to Sunday school and we go to church . . . we go to Sunday-night church . . . we go to prayer meeting. We go to all those. Don't you think maybe we could go down to the park Sunday afternoon and play ball?" Mom said, "I'll talk to your dad about that." And she did. She said to him, "Graham, I don't think the Lord will mind if those boys go and play ball Sunday afternoon as long as they're going to church three times every Sunday."

So Mom got us the free pass to play ball on Sunday afternoon.

MOM AND DAD met in youth group in Charlotte, North Carolina. She was as wonderful a mother as any young man could have, but Marjorie Orr Spurrier did not have an athletic background. She and her whole family loved music and played the piano. Mom also played the organ in church. She did the bulletins. She did it all. Sometimes Mom, along with Graham and me, even had to clean up the church when the janitors didn't show up.

Mom made my brother, sister, and me take piano lessons. I would rather have been down at the park playing ball, and my dissatisfaction soon became apparent. After three or four lessons, Mom finally said: "Stevie, you're not musically inclined. You don't like this, do you?" I said, "No, Mom, I really have no desire to play the piano." She said, "I can tell that. You can go on down to the park and start playing ball." And I didn't have to take piano anymore.

While my father was a huge influence, providing structure in my life and fostering passion for sports, it was also my mother's tender, compassionate touch and common sense that kept us balanced. She had a unique ability to make a nice home for us wherever we lived. And we lived quite a few places. Presbyterian ministers seem to move about, so in the early years we changed locations a lot as my dad changed churches. He was always pastor of a small church.

My mother was one of the most calm, passionate, helping-others individuals I've ever known. I never saw her mad. She would get her point across without raising her voice. But the thing I remember most is that every Friday, about four hours before a football and basketball game, she would cook me a baked potato and green peas. Back then they thought eating steak was good. So I had a little $2 steak. Maybe it was a dollar. Usually at four o'clock, my brother and sister were out doing whatever they were doing and Dad was out preaching somewhere. So it was just Mom and me. We would have conversations. I was a little overconfident and cocky, like a lot of high school athletes, and would say stuff like, "Mom, how many points you think I'll score tonight?" And she'd say, "Steve, just do your best—that's all we can ask for." I'd say, "How bad you think we'll beat these guys?" She'd say, "Steve, just do your best and the score will take care of itself." It was never about results, unlike Dad's zest for winning. Just, "Do your best."

Back then we would never even hug after games. She would stand in the background. Nowadays, everybody hugs after victories. But we weren't a real hugging family, for some reason. I guess because a lot of people didn't do that in those days. But we should have. I probably hugged her more in her latter days after I was fifty or so. She lived to the age of eighty-seven, had a wonderful life, and she was ready to go to heaven and be with my dad.

MOM GAVE BIRTH to three children, three years apart, in three different places. My brother, Graham, was born in Eudora, Arkansas, three years before I arrived. My sister, Sara, a year older than me, was born in St. Albans, West Virginia. During World War II, Dad was hired by a church in Miami Beach, Florida, which is where I was born—at St. Francis Hospital on April 20, 1945. The previous pastor had gone off to be a chaplain in the Army, and when the war was over he returned.

You might wonder: Three years apart, three different birthplaces—how in the world did this occur? Why did he leave some of these churches? I'm not sure. Some people said maybe he was a little overbearing. He had a tendency to go overtime when he preached on Sunday morning. Maybe the congregation didn't want a minister that was as passionate and as gung-ho as my dad.

I've said many times that my father was the most passionate Christian man that I have ever known or met. And he believed that he was on this earth to spread the gospel and to win as many people for Jesus as he possibly could. He would introduce himself to somebody on the street and ask them if they were a Christian. And if not, he would explain to them how they could accept Jesus Christ as their savior and gain their path to heaven. Very seldom did he ever meet someone without an attempt to witness to them. I guess that's what they call an evangelical, but that was just his way. So maybe some of the congregations thought his evangelical approach was a little aggressive—I'm not sure. Or maybe it was just time to move on.

SOMETIMES DAD HELPED coach our teams. And he let everybody know right away that in organized sports, the purpose was to win the game. Effort alone in organized sports wasn't enough. We needed to achieve a result. Of course, winning was part of the fun. So playing football, basketball, and baseball and trying to do my best to help our teams win every time was very important to me.

From Florida, our family moved to Charlotte, North Carolina, to live with my grandmama, Willie Austin Spurrier. She actually had two duplexes around downtown. She rented out one side. Mom, Dad, and we three children lived with her in the other side. It was a two-bedroom. I was still an infant and I'm told my crib was in the living room. So we had tight quarters, but we didn't stay there very long.

It was when we got to Athens, Tennessee, that my interest in sports began. Dad became pastor at Mars Hill Presbyterian for about five years. Just two blocks away from the church was Tennessee Wesleyan College, where, ironically, quite a few years prior to that, my college coach, Ray Graves, had played for the Bulldogs before transferring to the University of Tennessee.

I really didn't have any kids to play with in my neighborhood. At Tennessee Wesleyan, Graham and I would sort of throw or kick the ball around with some of the players. And I still have some photos of myself with one of the players, Doak Willett. They sort of adopted me as a team mascot.

Later when I was coaching at Duke, I met one of my all-time favorite players, Charlie "Choo Choo" Justice. He was an All-American running back at North Carolina. My dad and mom, both being from Charlotte, were big fans, and Choo Choo was a big hero in that part of the country. When I was six years old, I got my first football uniform for Christmas, Choo Choo's number 22. Choo Choo went on to play for the Washington Redskins.

While living in Athens, Tennessee, my dad was very involved in youth sports. As a youngster, he'd played baseball and tennis. He won the Independence Park tennis championship in Charlotte as a teenager. His brother Bob Spurrier played at Presbyterian College and was a well-known amateur tennis player in North Carolina back in the forties and fifties. Uncle Bob won several tournaments and was the best athlete in the Spurrier clan at the time. And Uncle Bob was the athlete all us young Spurriers who loved sports looked up to.

Athens was a fun place and we have fond memories, but once again it was time to move on. My dad was hired by the First Presbyterian Church in Newport, Tennessee, in what could be characterized as a better job.

Newport was a neat little town on the Pigeon River in East Tennessee, approximately forty miles from Knoxville. My dad would get tickets sometimes to see the Tennessee Vols play football at what was then Shields-Watkins Field. So we got a chance maybe once a year to go over there. I was ten when I saw my first game, on November 5, 1955. Tennessee played Georgia Tech to a 7–7 tie. Johnny Majors was a triple-threat tailback at Tennessee, one of the last schools to use the single wing. Buddy Cruze was the tight end. John Gordy the tackle. Bill Anderson was the wingback. Bowden Wyatt was the head coach. That 1955 Tennessee team posted a 6-3-1 record.

The 1956 Vols squad won an SEC Championship, going 10-1 and finishing the season ranked No. 2, but lost to Baylor in the Sugar Bowl. That year, UT achieved one of its greatest victories, a 6–0 win over Georgia Tech in Atlanta. The Yellow Jackets were ranked No. 2 nationally and the Vols were No. 3. Majors was an All-American and runner-up for the Heisman Trophy in 1956.

Little did I know I would later coach in Neyland Stadium numerous times while at Duke, Florida, and South Carolina—including twice when Majors was head coach of the Vols. In fact, our team at Duke beat the Vols 25–24 in the opening game of the 1982 season at Neyland Stadium and later, when I was head coach in 1988, we won 31–26. Before both games, I had goose bumps. I really got fired up when the announcer said before the game, "It's football time in Tennessee!"

Or little did I know that I would one day be named the winner of the General Robert Neyland Award, which would be given by the Knoxville Quarterback Club in April 2016.

I attended elementary school in Newport through the fifth grade, so we went to school with the same kids all the time. We loved Newport. Loved the sports. Loved the school and the teachers. My fifth-grade teacher was Miss Reba Williams. Everybody wanted to be in Miss Williams's class because she was so positive. Miss Williams always said, "If any of you ever grow up to be a millionaire, remember your old fifth-grade teacher." I never forgot her. And sent her a $100 bill one day with a note, "I remember what you said!"

My athletic skills started to develop as we began to play a lot of pickup basketball. And it appeared basketball was going to be my game. We played a ton of three-on-three, four-on-four, and a game where after eleven buckets the winner got to keep playing, or else you'd have to sit over there and watch the other guys for fifteen minutes or so. I did not like to sit. That's where I learned the importance of competing constantly.

I was beginning to realize I had been blessed with good eye-hand coordination, and around fifth grade I began to separate from others. I could dribble around most kids at the time. I could never run fast, but I had a quick step and could find myself an open shot, layup, or reverse layup.

My dad knew a preacher from nearby Morristown who also had a son in the fifth grade who played basketball. My dad said: "Why don't we get eight or ten of your kids in the fifth grade and put together a team and we'll put together a team over in Newport and play each other home and away, and have a little game? These kids have no team to play on."

The Morristown preacher brought his basketball team over to Newport. They played man-to-man defense. We beat them 44–28, or something like that. I scored 40 of the 44 points in my first competitive game. And, I shot almost every time I got the ball.

The next week we traveled to Morristown and they had those short goals, eight feet high. I'd never played on those. Morristown went with a zone defense. And it was a little more difficult the second time around, but we still managed to beat them. I think I scored about twenty-five. I did most of the shooting and had probably earned my nickname of "Gunner" after only two games of organized basketball.

In Athens and Newport, we had an outdoor goal at the house. I'd shoot out there, even if it was freezing outside. I'd play one-on-one with Graham, or I'd just go shoot by myself.

Graham was a starting guard on the eighth-and-ninth-grade basketball team. They didn't have many girls' sports then, so all my sister, Sara, had was church league basketball. About all the girls could go out for in those days was cheerleading. She was a pretty good athlete who didn't get a chance to participate.

During my time in Newport, my dad had a friend who gave him an autographed Mickey Mantle baseball. We put it up on the mantel in the living room. It stayed there for maybe two or three weeks. And then one day Graham and I needed a baseball to throw around. "All right, now, it can't hit the ground," we declared. We played catch with it. No grounders, just catch. And then we started firing it harder. And the Mickey Mantle baseball hit the ground. Then it began to get dirty, so we started playing with it regularly—even hitting it. Pretty soon the Mickey Mantle baseball was in the woods. We knew it was a good baseball and we didn't have many. When a preacher makes about $4,000 a year he doesn't go buy a sack full of baseballs. We had to use what we could. The Mickey Mantle baseball served us better as a tool than a trophy, I guess.

My dad teamed up with a couple other men in town to organize a Little League baseball. Dr. Hobart Ford, our dentist, applied to Little League headquarters and got it started in Newport. There were only four teams: the Yankees, the Cardinals, the Giants, and the Indians. I was on the Giants. With only four teams, we didn't get to compete in tournaments or anything like that. But I loved getting ready for the games.

Then one day came the news: We were moving to Johnson City. It was the summer of 1957. We all cried. Little did we know what a good move it was going to be for our family. I'd asked Dad again why we had to keep moving and he would just say, "It's an opportunity for another church." Or maybe it was time to find a new congregation that hadn't heard his sermons.

WE WOULD REALLY be blessed in moving to Johnson City. It was one of the Tri-Cities—at the time the sixth-largest city in Tennessee with a population of about 25,000, near the North Carolina and Virginia borders. (The other two Tri-Cities were Kingsport and Bristol.)

Moving to Johnson City in 1957 was like hitting the jackpot for youth sports, because it was a higher level of competition and it came at a perfect time for a young boy who would eventually make a lifetime of playing or coaching competitive sports.

We had a beautiful baseball diamond at the Veterans Administration facility in Johnson City. In my teen years, baseball would get even more competitive. Dad would get more involved in coaching Babe Ruth.

I had big dreams and, in Johnson City, the opportunity was there for a young boy to achieve just about all of them.

Chapter 6

JOHNSON CITY DREAMS

1962 Tennessee High School Baseball Champions, Science High School of Johnson City. I'm in the top row, second from the right, next to one of my all-time best buddies, Lonnie Lowe. We pitched every other game throughout the playoffs.

1963 Tennessee High School State Champions, Science High School. I'm kneeling, first from the left. Not everybody was present for the photo, but in the front row, from the right, are Jimmy Sanders, Bud Oxendine, and Tommy Hager—we played football, basketball, and baseball from grades 6 to 12.

Kiwanis Park was a block away from our house in Johnson City, right across the street from Calvary Presbyterian Church. We won lots of imaginary championships in that park. It was near a Little League baseball diamond with an outfield where we could also play pickup football. Close by there was also a nice open-air basketball court, concrete, full length. It was the scene of so many of my wonderful youth sports experiences.

"Let's go down to the park and see who's there," we'd say. And the games were on, whatever season it may have been.

Sometimes I would just go down to the park and kick the football by myself or dribble and shoot the basketball. Those days in Kiwanis Park laid the foundation for us in organized sports. Having friends and the ample space of the park gave us freedom. It was an ideal place to hone our athletic skills. No doubt that led to me becoming a decent athlete, and I was fortunate enough to make all-state in football, basketball, and baseball.

Early on I played with my brother, Graham, and some of his buddies, or just some guys in the neighborhood—whoever showed up. Most of my pals I went to school with were in another part of town. We were in West Johnson City, not the high-income part of town.

My first year in Johnson City, Dad drove me out to a Little League baseball park where tryouts were being held. They'd hit you a few grounders to pick up and fire to first. Aspiring pitchers threw from a mound. Then we had batting practice. I did pretty well and it was helpful to be able to measure my abilities against those of others. So it was a nice tryout. Must have been twenty to thirty kids out there that day.

The next day, the team's head managers bid on the players who had tried out. The coaches of twelve teams had a set amount of points. My dad was asked to become an assistant coach for the Steinway Bears. I wasn't there that day, but as the story goes, somebody said, "Okay, we've got this kid named Steve Spurrier and we'll start the bidding at five hundred points," which was the minimum. When a couple coaches started bidding on me, J. Ross Edgeman, owner of the Steinway plant and sponsor of the Steinway Bears, allegedly said: "Wait a minute! Just to let you guys know, Steve's dad, Reverend Spurrier, is one of my assistant coaches. So I get him for the minimum five hundred points."

Everybody looked around and they said, "He's right! His dad's a coach—they get him for five hundred." Hearing about that, I guess that was the first time I understood the importance of "recruiting."

So I went to the Steinway Bears, Mr. Edgeman's team. His son Jimmy was on the team. We proceeded to win nineteen of our twenty games. We lost one game, 5–4, to General Finance, and I still remember it like it was yesterday. The umpire missed a call on a key play. Our guy slid into second and they tagged him out, but the ball was kicked out of the second baseman's glove. The ump had seen the base runner get tagged. But he turned his back to the play and didn't see the ball pop out. And of course we were all yelling, "He dropped the ball!" The ump wouldn't change his call. We still lost. But we won the Little League championship. I pitched and played shortstop. I never lost a game pitching in Little League that year.

When I wasn't playing ball, I made a little spending money keeping score. When I was thirteen years old, I had a lot of responsibility as the scorekeeper. People would holler up, "Steve, was that a hit or an error?" I'd get to choose which, but I was always fair. Did that for two years. I was paid a dollar a game for keeping the books on two games each night. So Monday through Thursday I could make $8 a week. And every night I'd ride my bike about ten blocks downtown to the *Johnson City Press-Chronicle*, where I'd drop the box score in a little slot, and then ride home. One of my sportswriter friends later suggested that since I reported on the games, perhaps I was an official member of the media at age thirteen! But I wouldn't go that far.

AFTER LITTLE LEAGUE, I played Babe Ruth baseball. My dad became the head manager of Thomas Products and I was on his team. Before our first game, Dad gathered the team down the right field line and asked the thirteen- to fifteen-year-olds, "How many of you boys believe in that saying, 'It's not whether you win or lose but how you play the game'?" All the kids raised their hands—except me. I'd heard him ask this before. And I knew what response my dad would have, which was:

"I believe you are supposed to do everything you can within the rules to win the game. We're going to be keeping score. And anytime you keep score, you're supposed to try your best to win. So that's what we're going to do. If we're fortunate enough to get ahead, maybe everybody will get to play. But if it's a real close game, some of you guys might not get in. Hopefully we can get way ahead and everybody plays."

The importance of winning was ingrained in me my whole life, and in all those boys on that team. Even as a college coach, I kept Dad's words in my heart and mind. And so did many of my teammates.

Dad's dedication to teaching that winning was important had an impact on more people than just me. My real good friend Ralph Cross, who was on that Thomas Products team and attended a lot of our South Carolina football games, talked about it. My high school teammate Joe Cowell did as well. Joe would come to South Carolina every spring game, and a few in the regular season.

When we'd win it was a huge sense of accomplishment. Dad didn't celebrate by hugging or anything like that. It was just, "Hey, we did a good job today, and enjoy it a little bit, but get ready for the next game." Dad did not like losing, however—especially if you'd goofed around. He believed strongly in playing the game to win. As the Bible says, "Run your race to win."

THERE WAS a nice, orderly fashion to the sports seasons back in those days. When one ended, the other started. Nothing like today when seasons overlap and some kids play only one sport. I loved playing many sports and I always suggest young boys and girls try playing several—then maybe pick out one or two they enjoy most by the time they get to college.

In Johnson City, my interest in sports was at an all-time high, but football wasn't my best game until later. Basketball and baseball came more naturally for me. I was simply a lot better at them.

When we played sandlot ball down at Kiwanis Park, we'd choose sides for football and tried to make them as even as we could. We were twelve to fifteen years old and we'd always play tackle without pads. Later in high school we quit playing those tackle games for obvious reasons—we were bigger.

Sometimes I played quarterback and sometimes I played receiver. If an older kid was there he played quarterback. I had just as much fun playing either. I loved trying to get open and catch the ball. I never could run very fast, but I could sort of give a little juke and get a step on a guy. To me back then, it was more fun making a diving catch or catching a touchdown pass than throwing one.

Basketball had been my best sport. There was a basketball team at Henry Johnson Elementary. We won the elementary school championship there. I was the most valuable player in the sixth grade and got a trophy from the superintendent of public schools, Howard McCorkle.

I also played sixth-grade football, but we were just sort of so-so as a team. My buddies would say, "You're no good in football, but you're pretty dadgum good in basketball and baseball." I was just another guy out there on the field, but I was slightly bigger and taller than most. Back then I wasn't a quarterback. I played linebacker or fullback or running back. And I just never quit football. I could have been shooting hoops and getting ready for basketball season but, no, it was football season.

One of my most memorable basketball games occurred my sophomore year. We were down two points against Bristol. They were shooting a free throw with five seconds left. It looked like it was over. I told our center, Red Miller, who was about six-four—tall back then—"If he misses, I'll be out there at half court. Fire it to me and I'll throw it up at the basket." The guy missed. Red didn't get the rebound. One of their guys got it, shot it, and missed. Now there's about three seconds left. Red got the rebound, fired it to me at half court; I took one dribble and threw it up. Swish! Nothing but net. It was scary! I'm sure it was the longest shot I ever made in my life. In 1961 it was good for only two points! But we went on to win the game in overtime.

After my sophomore year I started taking snaps at quarterback. Had it not been bred in me to always do my best and hang in there, I might have quit. Clearly I had a long way to go because of my lack of speed, but I made it a point to begin working on my agility and strength. Luckily, I started to grow as well. And I got better.

We had an outstanding football coach at Science Hill High School in Kermit Tipton, and I was fortunate to play for him all three years. The football stadium at Science Hill is now named after him. Coach Tipton taught me a lot—including how to think big. He was a tremendous influence on me and on my style of coaching later on.

After my sophomore season in football, there was something called the Preaching Mission at East Tennessee State, which was located in Johnson City. They'd bring in ministers, preachers, and athletes, and invite all the area high school and junior high kids and so forth. Chicago Bear quarterback Bill Wade was one of the speakers. Someone invited him to come by and watch Science Hill spring football practice. Wade pointed me out to Coach Tipton: "You see that tall kid over there"—I was one of the taller kids at Science Hill High School; most of my teammates were five-seven to five-ten. "He can throw the ball pretty well. You've got a few good receivers. I'll give you a few passing ideas and see what you can do." And so he gave Coach Tipton some passing routes that we added to the offense.

I wasn't really a decent quarterback until that fall, but Coach Tipton saw something in me. He would allow me to call the plays. In our passing attack, we'd mostly do a half rollout, with some dropback. And eventually my decision to stick with football began to pay off. This goes to show you how one coach can change everything, and Coach Tipton was about to help me prepare myself for big-time college football.

Originally at Science Hill, we played the full-house backfield or Dead
T: two tight ends and three running backs. But Coach Tipton opened it up
some. Our tight end was Ronnie Pelfrey, a good player who caught a lot of
passes. Sometime we would throw out of the backfield to our backs. But
for the most part it was not a pass-oriented offense. Jimmy Sanders was
our best wideout. Later we added a couple more receivers.

We won the Big Seven Conference one year, but we lost a lot of close
games. My senior year we were actually 2-4 at one point—lost back-to-
back 20–19 games. But Coach Tipton kept us hanging in there and we
managed to win four in a row. I was being recruited by a number of
schools. Because I fought back and we won a bowl in my final game, it
helped draw more interest. The folks in Kingsport hosted a postseason
game called the Exchange Bowl and invited Science Hill to come play
against Church Hill, a school in the area about thirty miles away.

The game was put together late in the year and we probably weren't as
prepared as we should have been. A couple of us had already started practicing basketball. Anyway, we got off to a bad start. Church Hill was kicking our tails. I went back to punt and it was a low snap. I tried to sort of
kick the ball off the ground and instead I kicked it right into one of their
guys and they picked it up and scored. We were down 21–0 with about
three minutes left in the first half.

So Coach Tipton said, "Steve, you can throw every down!" I said,
"Okay, let's do it!" We started throwing and throwing and throwing. I
ended up passing for four touchdown passes and close to 300 yards. And
we beat them, 28–21. In the sixties, that was unheard of for a high school
quarterback.

They say in sports you're only as good as your last game. That was my
last one in high school. More college recruiters started calling after that.

IN BASKETBALL, we won our Big Seven Conference championship my junior and senior years. Our biggest conference rival was Dobyns-Bennett

High School in Kingsport. We seemed to win the district every year. And then Kingsport would come back and beat us in the region. So we never got to the state tournament. But we won a lot.

Elvin Little was a wonderful basketball coach. He arrived at Science Hill before my sophomore year. He was very enthusiastic and energetic on the sidelines. He yelled and screamed, but he was also always patting us on the back. He was just into it—a tremendous competitor. I thoroughly enjoyed playing for Coach Little. He got the most out of his players. Tough man-to-man defense most all the time. We dove for loose balls. He did not allow loafing by anyone. And our guys were always ready to play. I think the best thing he did was get the most out of his talent. I held the career scoring record at Science Hill for a while, but I think I'm down to about number 15 on that list now.

As far as state championships go, baseball was our sport, because we won back-to-back state titles in open classification. Our baseball coach was John Broyles, known to us as Mr. Broyles because he was also our history teacher. Mr. Broyles was a gentle person. I don't ever remember him raising his voice. We didn't do a lot of fancy bunting or sacrificing or anything like that. But for some reason—none of us knows why—it was hard for us to lose. We simply could not lose. And I really mean that when I say it.

My sophomore year I didn't play much. I wasn't quite good enough, but we had an excellent team and we went to the state tournament. You have to win your district and then region and then go to state. And in the 1960s in Tennessee all high schools were in one classification. There was one champion in basketball and baseball. There were no football playoffs back then. My sophomore season we won the district and the region and went to Chattanooga, but we did not win the state baseball title. My brother, Graham, played on one of the baseball teams that also went to the state tournament, and they did not win it.

My junior year we lost only two regular-season baseball games—to the same team, Kingsport. And amazingly, they beat us by the identical scores of 13–1, home and away. They were by far the best team in the state. Their team batting average was almost .400. They were not in our district, but we'd meet them in Knoxville for the region.

Our ace pitcher was Lonnie Lowe. I'd pitched a little in high school but never started a high school game before. Because I played basketball and started a little later with the team, I didn't rotate pitching with Lonnie until midseason. When the regional tournament came, Mr. Broyles told Lonnie, "You pitch in the first game, and if we win, Steve's gonna pitch against Kingsport." Lonnie had struggled against them the first two times. So, sure enough, we beat Knox East. Kingsport, of course, clobbered its opponent. So the next night we're playing Kingsport and the winner of that game would go to the state tournament in Nashville. Mr. Broyles gave me the ball to pitch against Kingsport in one of the most memorable games of my life.

In the fourth inning, tied 2–2, they had the bases loaded when their batter hit a fly ball down the left field line.

Our left fielder, Tommy Hager, ran over and—thinking it was going to land about a foot foul—let the ball hit the ground instead of catching it. Catching a foul ball would have allowed their runner to tag up and score. When the ball hit, the ump apparently never saw it because he was still watching for the tag and the catch. Since it wasn't ruled foul, the two Kingsport runners scored and put their team ahead 4–2. And they had guys on second and third—getting ready to blow this thing wide open. I walked the next hitter unintentionally. The next batter hit a one-hopper right to me and I threw home, our catcher, Choo Tipton, threw to first, and we got the double play. Then I struck out the next guy to end the inning.

We put a little rally together to tie the game 4–4 going into the seventh and last inning. Our leadoff man, Tony Bowman, got on with two outs. I was batting fourth that night and hit one of my patented little squibblers right over the first baseman's head down the right field line in fair territory—it had a little slice spin and rolled toward the light pole out there. The first baseman and right fielder almost collided. It was the perfect distance between the two of them and Tony was able to score from first base.

So now we were up 5–4 and we needed three outs to win. A Kingsport runner reached third base in the last inning, but I got the last batter to fly out to center field. We beat Kingsport 5–4, and we won the region—and we were going to the state tournament!

It was a wonderful bus ride home from Knoxville to Johnson City, about 100 miles.

Next up was Nashville and the state. I pitched the first game and we won. Lonnie Lowe pitched the second one and we beat Memphis Messick 1–0, and we won the state championship my junior year.

My senior year, Bud Oxendine and I would rotate pitching. It was almost identical to the year before: We won the district and beat Bristol in the region finals, which was played in Kingsport. We returned to the state tournament in Memphis again and won the first game 7–6. In baseball we always seemed to win the one-run games. In the other sports we'd lose the close ones, but on the baseball diamond, the Lord would smile on us and we would win. The first game was extra innings and I pitched all the way. Since it was double elimination, I would have one day off before we played again.

Then we had the challenge of playing the favorite, Memphis Christian Brothers, where Tim McCarver went to high school. McCarver went on to become a two-time All-Star major league catcher. Later in 1978, the minor league stadium there was named after him. And he became a Hall of Fame broadcaster on CBS and Fox. Memphis Christian sent a lot of players to the major leagues.

Bud Oxendine pitched the first game and we got beat 12–3. I actually had a sore arm, which I very seldom ever had—maybe pitching into extra innings two days prior had something to do with it. Before the finals, our team manager, Lennie Fortner, rubbed my arm with some hot liniment. I started warming up and I said, "Yeah, I can pitch! I can pitch, let's go!"

The only way we could get the hitters from Christian Brothers out was to get them to pop up, which is what I tried to do. I believe our guys made eight errors behind me that afternoon. Christian Brothers would leave two men on base about every inning, and we rocked back and forth. They had guys on second and third when I finally got a guy to pop up to right center again in the final inning. We finally beat Christian Brothers 7–5 in the last inning and won the state championship! They left twelve runners on base in the seven innings. I've still got baseballs from those games.

Johnson City threw us a big parade. We rode in an open-air bus down Main Street. Looking back now, it's just flat amazing. I don't know how it happened that we could win back-to-back state high school champion- ships in open classification. And to think I never lost a game pitching in high school. If you were never going to play baseball again—and I did not—what a good way to go out! Pitch your last game and win the state championship! The Lord continued to smile on our baseball teams and we were all thankful.

Years later, at our fiftieth reunion, I remember talking with the base- ball guys and saying, "Can you guys ever remember us losing a one- or two-run game?" Nobody could. I don't think we ever did, especially our last two years. It was something . . . just amazing.

My dad always thought I should have been a baseball player, even after I became a head coach at Florida. Sometimes I would visit him in nearby Green Cove Springs. One day while we were watching a baseball game on TV, he asked: "Steve, do you think maybe you'd have done better playing baseball?" And of course I told him no.

I loved baseball, and in the back of my mind, I thought I might want to play baseball in college. But I decided if I was going to be a quarterback, I needed to participate in spring football and work on getting better.

IT WAS TIME to officially pick my college. Recruiting was going on and there were a lot of people who wondered why I didn't attend the big state school, Tennessee. I had seen the Vols play several times when my dad would get tickets, but they were still committed to running the single wing, which was not a good fit for me. Nobody threw the football around much back then.

I was fortunate to have a number of offers, but had been a late bloomer in football, and I had a tough time deciding where I wanted to go to school. All during the spring I had been taking visits to various other colleges, trying to sort out where my future was going to be. Finally, it came to me, but it wasn't exactly what my parents and some of my friends had in mind.

Before Florida came into the picture that January, I thought Ole Miss was where I wanted to go. However, for some reason I decided to hold off on my decision. I also visited Kentucky, Vanderbilt, Alabama, Clemson, Duke, and North Carolina. There was no limit to the number of "official" visits back then. So I took my time and took full advantage of seeing the college football world outside the state of Tennessee.

My dad wanted me to go to Alabama to play for Coach Bear Bryant, who had told me he thought I was a good enough athlete to play safety if it didn't work out at quarterback. Joe Namath was Alabama's quarterback then. Steve Sloan was his backup. And Kenny Stabler would be along the next season. My mom wanted me to go to Georgia Tech because of academics. Bobby Dodd was just winding down as coach and Tech would eventually leave the SEC after the 1963 season. Quite a few other schools were calling us regularly, I think—among them Ohio State. I was in no big hurry to make my decision, because I was taking trips everywhere. Quite a few other schools were calling regularly.

Sometimes the coaches would visit Johnson City. Coach Johnny Vaught of Ole Miss showed an early interest and came up to watch me play basketball against Elizabethton. So my first visit was to Ole Miss. The first plane ride of my life was from the Tri-Cities to Memphis on the now-defunct Southern Airways, and then on to Oxford, Mississippi. Ole Miss sent a pilot and airplane to fly me to the campus about seventy miles away. Traveling in that single-engine airplane for the first time ever was an experience I will never forget. It was like being a copilot, sitting right

I'm on the far left, standing with Coach Johnny Cain, teammate Jimmy Sanders, Coach Johnny Vaught of Ole Miss, and my dad on the right, in 1962.

up there in the seat next to the pilot. He let me steer it a little bit. "Just aim for that water right over there," he said. So on my second flight ever I got to fly the airplane.

If there had been a National Signing Day like today, I would have been an Ole Miss Rebel. In 1962–63, Ole Miss had the best passing attack of any SEC school. The quarterbacks—Glynn Griffing and Jim Weatherly—were the best in the SEC. And Coach Vaught was right up there with Coach Bryant as a winner, having won six SEC titles at Ole Miss, three of them in the previous four years. He was also coming off a 10-0 record in 1962.

I had a wonderful trip to Nashville. One of my teammates, Jimmy Sanders, was also was being recruited by Vanderbilt. We got to visit Governor Frank Clement at the governor's mansion. There was a helicopter in his yard. Governor Clement asked, "You boys want to go up for a little ride?" We said, "Sure!" We went straight up and flew over the city of Nashville, so that was breathtaking. Jimmy loved it and he wound up accepting a scholarship to play for the Commodores. He went on to become a very successful attorney in Nashville and a senior member of Neal & Harwell. In fact, he's noted for being instrumental in the Exxon *Valdez* oil spill case in Alaska.

When I visited the University of Tennessee I was also able to bring some teammates with me to Knoxville. Of course, there was pressure for me to sign with Tennessee, then considered an SEC powerhouse. If they had run the T-formation and had been throwing the ball around, it would have been different, because where I grew up most of us pulled for Tennessee. These were the final days before Coach Bowden Wyatt was replaced by his staff member, Ohio State grad Jim McDonald, for just the 1963 season, and Coach McDonald would then step aside to become assistant athletic director at UT. Ironically, the person they hired next was the person who gave me my first coaching job: Doug Dickey. But by then I was already enrolled at Florida. At the time, Tennessee wasn't getting a lot of the top players in the state. Between that and their run-oriented offense, it was not the best place for me to go. But Coach Dickey quickly turned that around in Knoxville, where his Vols teams won two SEC titles and he was recognized as SEC Coach of the Year twice.

Tennessee basketball coach Ray Mears also offered me a scholarship at our basketball banquet. He said, "Steve, if you want to come up I'll give you a basketball scholarship." I said, "Coach, I really appreciate it, but I think my best sport is football."

I also went down to Tuscaloosa and watched Alabama beat the University of Miami during that 1962 season. Alabama was down 3–0 at the half and won 36–3. They won two national titles over the next six seasons and lost only six times. The only loss by the '62 Crimson Tide team was to Georgia Tech, 7–6, one year after Coach Bryant and Coach Dodd had gotten into a feud. It was about a forearm used by Alabama's Darwin Holt on Yellow Jacket running back Chick Graning, who suffered a broken jaw, a broken nose, a concussion, and multiple facial fractures. Eventually the two schools stopped playing each other and it wasn't long before Tech— for whatever reason—dropped out of the SEC.

I visited with Coach Bryant that Sunday morning, but Alabama seemed a bit crowded at the quarterback position. Later, Coach Bryant said a lot of wonderful things about me as the quarterback at Florida. But when Coach Bryant was recruiting me, he said he felt maybe he probably "cussed" too much for me to go to school there, since my dad was a preacher.

On my visit to Clemson, I went to a game in Memorial Stadium— talked to Coach Frank Howard. Then I traveled to Georgia Tech in Atlanta to meet Coach Dodd and watch LSU beat the Yellow Jackets 10–7. I also visited the University of North Carolina. You talk about a strange coincidence! I visited Chapel Hill in 1962 when Duke beat Carolina 16–14 in Kenan Stadium to clinch the ACC title. Bill Murray was the coach at Duke at that time. Twenty-seven years later I was the head coach at Duke. We beat North Carolina in Chapel Hill at Kenan Stadium Hill for Duke's next ACC title—and only one in the last fifty-four years. So I was at Kenan Stadium for the last two ACC championships (through 2015) for Duke University!

Then I visited Duke later on when North Carolina played the Blue Devils in basketball. We had played high school basketball on a Friday. I drove over there on a Saturday night and I got to see one of the most famous Duke players in history—Art Heyman. He was a six-foot-five guy who would lead the Blue Devils to their first Final Four that March. Heyman had a reputation for brawling. In 1961, he was involved in a fight with Larry Brown of Carolina that lasted about ten minutes. Brown later played in the NBA and became the first and only person to win both an NBA title (with the Detroit Pistons) and NCAA title (with Kansas). Heyman wound up becoming the national player of the year and was drafted

No. 1 overall in the NBA by the Knicks. Even though Duke finished third, Heyman was also MVP of the 1963 NCAA tournament.

Florida started calling me that January. Coach Ray Graves telephoned to ask if I was interested in Florida. I had just watched the Gators beat Penn State in the Gator Bowl, 17–7. Quarterback Tommy Shannon was the game's MVP. So Florida was an up-and-coming program.

Coach Graves had gotten a note from his brother Edwin, a postmaster in Knoxville, after we beat his old school, Knoxville Central, that year. "You ought to get this tall kid," Edwin said in his note. Coach Graves came up to see me play a basketball game in Greenville, Tennessee.

The next week I enjoyed a wonderful visit to Gainesville. It was beautiful down there—temperature in the seventies. And it was about 32 degrees back home.

THE NEXT DAY I was sick as a dog. I came down with mononucleosis and had to spend some time in the doctor's office. Coach Graves was very attentive and checked on me regularly, which I appreciated. His kindness and consideration were among the things that attracted me to Florida— along with the wonderful climate. He came into the picture late, but one thing I always appreciated about Coach Graves was that he didn't promise me anything except that Florida wanted to pass the ball more and I'd have a chance to earn the job. Other coaches talked about me being the starter as a sophomore.

David Bludworth of Palm Beach, then a current Gator player who would go on to become a lawyer and state's attorney, took me out to the University of Florida golf course. "We play all the time down here, and it's free," Bludworth said. Of course what he didn't say was that they snuck on the course most of the time instead of waiting for a tee time.

Coach Graves always liked to tell the story that as soon as I found out there was a golf course on campus I wanted to become a Gator. (It didn't hurt!) He had come up to Johnson City two or three times and sometimes would bring his wife, Opal. Back in those days a coach could take a recruit out to dinner. We've got an outstanding restaurant in Johnson City, one of the best in all of Tennessee—The Peerless Steakhouse, now known as The Peerless Restaurant—and it has been around since 1938.

To this day when I visit Johnson City I make it a point to go to The Peerless and see owner Jim Kalogeros. Coach Graves set up a sort of a signing party for me and my family at The Peerless. So I managed to get the coaches to take me and my parents to The Peerless several times.

One of the stories Coach Graves told later was about us all sitting down to the table to eat when he heard my father note that we hadn't yet blessed the food. Years later, looking back, Coach Graves told a writer that he feared, "I've come all the way up here and I'm going to lose him because we didn't say a blessing?" He apologized that night. After all, he was the son of a Presbyterian minister, too.

It became entirely clear one fine spring day, March 28, 1962, in Gainesville when the temperature was about 75 degrees: I wanted to become a Florida Gator.

One of my buddies said, "Why are you going to Florida? You don't even know anybody down there." And I said, "I know one guy—and he's the Head Ball Coach."

In the end, I just felt like Florida was the best place and the best opportunity for me. It was also a school that had not accomplished much. And I thought perhaps we could achieve some things that had never happened there before.

Chapter 7

BECOMING A GATOR

Signing with the Gators and Coach Graves in 1963.

Going to the University of Florida was one of the best choices of my life, and I continue to thank the Lord for directing my path to Gainesville. I loved the school, loved the coach, and loved the opportunity, which prepared me for becoming an NFL football player and later a coaching career.

The beautiful Florida weather was better for throwing the ball—not to mention playing golf and going to the beach. Florida felt very much like home, a place where I wanted to spend most of my time someday. As a Gator, I got to play with some special people as teammates and win some big games. Most of all, it led to my meeting a young coed named Jerri Starr, who changed my life forever.

Coach Ray Graves had started the program in the right direction his first season in 1960. In only his third game, he defeated his former boss, Coach Bobby Dodd of Georgia Tech. The Florida Field crowd went into a frenzy when the Gators' first-year coach elected to go for two points and his team converted for an exciting 18–17 victory.

I came to Florida with a group of good guys who were highly skilled, competitive teammates. By 1963, the team consisted mostly of Coach Graves's handpicked signees, and with that recruiting class he began seeing the fruits of his labor. Up until then, All-Americans had been rare at Florida.

In the 1960s there was no limit on how many players a school could sign. We had about 150 players overall. The B team consisted of some upperclassmen not on varsity, and freshmen who weren't allowed to play varsity. Florida brought in about thirty-five to forty signees my freshman year. Some schools signed fifty or sixty. The freshman team played four games, usually FSU, Auburn, Georgia, Miami—two home, two away—and traveled by bus.

Although I never had a single regret about becoming a Gator, I wish now our teams had been more focused on winning the SEC championship, because I think we were good enough. I wish as players we were all more committed—that I had been in a little bit better physical and mental shape for some games. At the time we didn't really realize how important winning a championship would be: a memory for a lifetime. As one of the leaders of the team, I wish I could have helped set and achieve those goals.

That regret definitely helped me later in coaching at Duke, Florida, and South Carolina.

I ENJOYED a very close relationship with Coach Graves; his wife, Opal; and his family. To this day when I say the blessing at home before dinner, I sometimes say, "Thank you, Lord, for bringing Coach Graves into our lives." Coach Graves brought me to Florida to run a passing offense, let me call the plays, and even let me make up some of them. And he let me kick a field goal every now and then.

So it was a very sad day for me when his health began to fail in 2015 and he took a turn for the worse at age ninety-six. I telephoned his daughters, Becky, Katherine, and Beth, at the hospice in Tampa and asked them to put the phone up by his ear, even though he couldn't respond to anything. It was a one-way conversation. I told him I loved him. Thanked him for bringing me to Florida and all the wonderful things that happened in my life because I had gone there. And then I said, "I'll see you someday." It was sort of neat, being able to say goodbye. He had a wonderful life. If we could all live ninety-six years like that, we'd be happy.

WHEN I ARRIVED in Gainesville in 1963, I think there were six quarterbacks on the freshman team.

I wanted to wear number 11, since that was my number in high school, but I didn't get it until several weeks into my freshman year. Allen Kelly, another quarterback from somewhere up in Tennessee, had enrolled early for summer school and got jersey number 11. So when they took the freshman picture I was actually wearing number 16. I made a deal with Allen that whoever got to be starting quarterback would get to wear number 11. He said, "That's fair enough with me." So I beat him out and got number 11.

Our freshman class stayed all four years. Coach Graves encouraged us to complete our degree. Players didn't flunk out much back then. And they certainly didn't transfer! They didn't get mad at their coach because they weren't playing, the way they do now.

I arrived at the end of the era of one-platoon football and the use of two-way players. After 1964, the NCAA allowed teams unlimited substi-

tution, which meant we could have separate offensive, defensive, and special teams as we know them today.

Our 1964 defense was ranked No. 1 in the SEC and was one of the best in the nation. The following year when we could specialize, it allowed us to take more advantage of our talent and that produced a number of All-Americans. A big reason for the All-Americans was that Norm Carlson, our sports information director, was one of the best in college football.

We also had some excellent assistant coaches. I had a pass-oriented quarterback coach my sophomore season, Pepper Rodgers, who would leave the following year for an assistant's job at UCLA under Tommy Prothro. At UCLA, Pepper coached quarterback Gary Beban, who would win the Heisman Trophy the year after I did. Coach Pepper was later my boss at Georgia Tech. In addition to becoming head coach at UCLA, Kansas, the CFS Memphis Mad Dogs, and the USFL Memphis Showboats, he had become my friend. After Coach Pepper, Ed Kensler took over as Florida's offensive coordinator, with Fred Pancoast as backfield coach. In 1965, Bubba McGowan was added as receivers coach.

We had some of the best defenses in the nation under Gene Ellenson, a terrific defensive coordinator who should have probably succeeded Coach Graves. But it didn't work out that way. It's a shame he didn't get to become a head coach because he would have been a super one. Coach Ellenson was a strong father figure to many Gators and a World War II hero who fought in many battles in the European theater, including the Battle of the Bulge. He won the Bronze Star, the Silver Star, and the Purple Heart. He was a very smart man and one of the best motivators in football ever. He knew exactly how and when to motivate a team, but did it only about twice a year. In fact, he was so effective that in future years as a head coach I would use him as a motivational speaker for my teams on occasion. Coach Ellenson loved his players and was beloved by many, as evidenced by the large turnout for his funeral at Florida National Cemetery in March 1995 in Bushnell, Florida.

We had several former two-way players. Tommy Shannon had been a defensive back and quarterback. He and I took turns starting my sophomore year but I would always play at least a half. I was okay with that because he was the senior and deserved first consideration.

Alabama and Coach Bryant had never lost in Denny Stadium up until our 1963 team beat him 10–6, although I didn't play in that game because freshmen weren't eligible. We went back to Tuscaloosa in 1964 for the second straight year—imagine that!—and I got my chance. Tommy Shannon and I were good friends and he had been starting, with me coming in the second half and playing the remainder of the game. Shannon had been the winning quarterback against Alabama the year before, but Coach Graves said, "It's time for you to go ahead and start." He had been telling me he was going to start me in that game and he kept his word.

It was Alabama's homecoming. Their kicker David Ray hit a fourth-quarter field goal, and we were behind 17–14 when we put a drive together. I was making up some plays that were working. The defensive back was playing way inside in front of Charlie Casey. So I said, "Just go ahead and run about a little ten-yard corner and I'll hit you in between those two guys." Then *boom-boom-boom*, right down the field we went.

We had the ball at about the 7-yard line with forty seconds and no time-outs remaining. But I somehow thought we were on the 2-yard line so I called a quick running play to our fullback John Feiber. When I finally realized where we were, there was no way to stop the clock. I should have spiked the ball or grounded it. We never even threw it in the end zone. I was calling the plays all the way down there and I didn't do a good job. I should have just kept throwing. I should have pitched it to Casey in the end zone. Fade, slant . . . anything! But I messed that up.

The clock was ticking down when we rushed the field goal team into action and only ten of them showed up on the field. Jimmy Hall's kick was wide. Alabama won and went unbeaten the rest of the way to win the national title but lost to Texas in the Orange Bowl. Back then they didn't count the bowls in the final rankings. Arkansas actually went 11-0 and beat Nebraska in the Cotton Bowl, but the Associated Press and most other polls gave it to the Crimson Tide.

In the end, it was just a lack of preparation on my part in those kinds of situations. Here we had the eventual national champion on the ropes at home and we couldn't finish them off. That was a shame, because that '64 Florida team was first in the SEC in total defense. It was really a bunch of good defensive players. One of the best was tiny Jack Card, a blitzing specialist at middle linebacker who stood all of about five-seven and didn't weigh even two hundred pounds. He was ferocious and his timing on the blitz was impeccable, and despite his size, he was strong and could make tackles all over the field. Coach Ellenson loved Card's spunk, his style of play, and his heart. Still, we wound up losing three games somehow in 1964. Offensively, we should have done a lot better, but we didn't.

Just to show you how uneven and sometimes unfair college sports was back then, I remember asking Coach Graves: "Why did you go to Tuscaloosa two years in a row and they didn't come to Gainesville?" And he said, "That's the only way the Bear would play me. I wanted to play Alabama and we couldn't get them on the schedule." Back then each team made their own schedule. And all you had to do was play six conference and four out-of-conference games. Obviously, Coach Bryant was a very smart man. He'd play one or two good teams out of conference, but another two or three that were pretty much sure-fire victories. He even scheduled his own SEC teams. Alabama did not play Georgia much at all during that time.

In my junior season we had a decent team but continued to let games get away from us. We lost to Mississippi State, but still had a shot at the SEC until Auburn came back and beat us 28–17 on some big plays by their linebacker from Orlando, Bill Cody, who forced some key turnovers. So we lost to a .500 Auburn team and there went our shot at the SEC, but we did win seven games and were invited to play Missouri in the Sugar Bowl.

That Sugar Bowl was a winnable game, but we gave it away because we kept going for two points and missing. Missouri had a strong running game, featuring the Big Eight's leading rusher, Charlie Brown, and two-way back Johnny Roland, who was the first African American captain of any sports team at Missouri. They also had a big offensive tackle and future NFL top draft pick, Francis Peay. One of their backup quarterbacks was Lloyd Carr, born in the East Tennessee area of Hawkins County, who would later become Michigan's head coach.

Missouri ran the ball very well, especially in the first half, during which we had maybe four possessions and we didn't do anything with them. Missouri was very good on defense. They played an eight-man front and basically rushed eight while playing a three-deep zone. Our pass protection was not designed to block four from the side. They had a guy running free at me on almost every down. No wonder we were behind 20–0 at the end of the third quarter. We needed to do something.

In the third quarter, I went to Coach Kensler, our offensive coordinator on the field, and asked, "What are we going to do?" He said, "We don't have a protection to block that guy." And so I said, "Is it okay if I start making up some plays, then?" He said, "Sure!" So I told our halfback Jack Harper, "Just line up there and go straight to the flat"—we didn't have a shotgun back then—"and I'll angle back and hit you. There's nobody there, so I'll just lob it over to you."

We hit a bunch of those. And Missouri started backing off, so I hit Casey with a couple. And we scored with ten minutes left. And all of a sudden they said, "Go for two!" One of the coaches convinced Coach Graves that maybe 20–8 looked better than 20–7—which doesn't make a lot of sense to me. So we went for two and didn't make it. The second time we scored they put defensive back Allen Trammel in with the extra-point team and ran a fake. That didn't work. The third time we scored I tried to throw it to tight end Barry Brown, and that one didn't work. So we lost 20–18 in Florida's first major bowl. I wish we'd taken those three extra-point tries. I also wish we'd had some better plays available, but it wasn't to be. I was awarded the Miller-Digby Trophy, the first Sugar Bowl MVP award ever given to a member of the losing team—but that wasn't much of a consolation prize.

THERE WERE a couple wins over FSU that were pretty good. Especially in 1965 (we had become the first Florida team to lose to the Seminoles in 1964). FSU had taken a one-point lead, 17–16, with about three minutes left. We went about eighty yards. I hit Casey on the out and up. That was probably one of the loudest reactions to a play during my career at Florida. We went ahead by six. We had a ten-yard out called. The defensive lineman jumped in the neutral zone right before "set, hut!"—we go "down, set hut . . . down . . ."—and he jumped. I knew I had a free play. Casey was on a ten-yard out and I waved him toward the end zone and I had to hit him. Somebody said, "That was a good play you all called." And I said, "I called it on the go." It was time to take the shot in the end zone. And Charlie ran a beautiful route. And caught it. And then Trammel picked one off and scored to make it 30–17.

The game against Auburn in 1966 probably won the Heisman Trophy for me. We were returning home after four straight road games to play Auburn and we were in a position to win the conference. Florida Field, which held just over sixty thousand fans, was at capacity that day.

My friend Gene Peek of Ocala, a receiver who played a little bit but didn't start, was always joking around with me at the pregame meal throughout my senior year. Gene was a fun guy to be around and he kept things light. It seemed like I'd always find a way to sit next to him and joke about something. So before the Auburn game I said, "I'm going to kick a field goal maybe to win the game. Maybe it'll come down to the last minute." Of course, I had said that four or five times before, but this time it happened! So it makes for a good story.

The score had gone back and forth. Auburn's Gusty Yearout ran a midair fumble back ninety-one yards and they also returned a kickoff back one hundred yards. In the fourth quarter we drove seventy-one yards and I scored on a short touchdown run as the Gators went up 27–20. But Auburn came right back and their quarterback scored on a short run.

Our defense really played super that day, but the score was 27–27 with about two minutes left. We had fourth down on their 23-yard line, so it would be a forty-yard attempt. We took a time out with 2:12 left in the game. Coach Graves said later he still wasn't sure what to do. And apparently Auburn thought it might be a fake. I was actually the long-distance field goal kicker but I'd attempted, and made, only two other kicks in the first game of the season, against Northwestern. I went over to the sideline and said, "Coach, let me have a shot at it." And he said, "Field goal!"

I laced up my square-toed shoe made especially for kicking. It had a zipper on the side in case there wasn't time to tie the shoestrings. But what

a lot of people don't know about that winning field goal was that my holder Larry Rentz placed the ball down with the laces facing me. Fortunately, I hit the seams as well as I could, and the kick was a dead-on line drive. The ball barely cleared from about forty yards out and landed about three rows in the south-end-zone stands. I was happy to have made it and won the game, especially because Coach Graves had believed in me. Although I wasn't the regular kicker, that was my third field goal of the season. Besides the two I made in the season opener against Northwestern, I later missed one against North Carolina State.

Many years later, in my first season coaching at South Carolina, we were playing Tennessee in Knoxville, and I found myself in a similar situation. We were down 15–13 late in the game and thinking about going for it on fourth and four on a forty-nine-yard field goal attempt. I was standing there trying to figure out what to do and all of a sudden our field goal kicker, Josh Brown, came running up and said, "Field goal, right, coach?" And just like Coach Graves, I shouted, "Field goal!" Josh knocked it right down the middle and we beat Tennessee for the first time ever in Knoxville, 16–15. Déjà vu! Just like Coach Graves would have said, "When a guy wants his shot, let him go take it."

Most everyone says that kick in 1966 won me the Heisman, even though the game wasn't even on TV. In fact, we were rarely on national TV at all. I was on TV twice in three years prior to the Orange Bowl game on January 1, 1967—the Sugar Bowl in 1966 and against SMU in the opener my sophomore year. Nobody but our fans in Florida Field saw my field goal live against Auburn—just the replays. They did film the games so they could show highlights, but we rarely made it on live TV. I tell people all the time, "You know how many games my senior year were on TV? The Orange Bowl. That was it!"

Winning the Heisman Trophy was all about the timing. Back then they took the vote before the season was over. The voting began while we were still 7-0, but we didn't get the results until after we lost to Georgia and beat Tulane. If they would have voted after the season I may not have been the winner. However, our sports information director Norm Carlson had done an excellent job with preseason publicity, teaming up with the state of Florida to send out a few clips. Norm said the quotes after the game by Auburn coach Shug Jordan also helped.

"Coach Jordan was such a gentleman," Carlson said. "In his statement after the game he said some of his assistant coaches were telling him, 'Watch out for the fake.' Coach Jordan said he turned around and said, 'You better hope it's a fake, because if Steve Spurrier tries this field goal he'll make it in this situation.'"

I've still got the game ball from that win over Auburn, but it's not the one I kicked. A new ball was put back into play after the kick, but we got back in on offense before the clock ran out and I took a knee and I carried the ball off with me.

The next week we lost to Georgia, but then we beat Tulane the following game. They tallied the Heisman votes and announced it right before my last game, which we lost to Miami. I finished first with 1,659 points, but well ahead of Bob Griese of Purdue. Notre Dame halfback Nick Eddy was third, followed by Gary Beban of UCLA and Floyd Little of Syracuse.

We beat Georgia Tech, 27–12, to win the Orange Bowl in Tech coach

At the Orange Bowl in 1967 with Georgia Tech quarterback Kim King.

Bobby Dodd's last game, which was the first major bowl win ever for Florida. So our Silver Sixties alumni group does have that lasting memory, including Larry Smith's famous ninety-four-yard touchdown run in which he almost lost his pants.

With the help of Carlson, our players began to win top honors. Up until then, Florida had managed only five first-team All-Americans. In 1964, halfback Larry Dupree became the first of our All-Americans in the sixties. Five of us made All-American following the 1965 season: safety Bruce Bennett, wide receiver Charlie Casey, offensive guard Larry Gagner, defensive end Lynn Matthews, and myself. Then Bill Carr and me again in 1966. Bill was my roommate and our starting center, born in Gainesville, also the son of a minister. We played together all four years. Bill later became the nation's youngest major college athletic director at Florida in 1979 when he was only thirty-three.

After I was gone, two of my former teammates, running back Larry Smith and offensive guard Guy Dennis, were All-Americans. They went on to enjoy successful NFL careers—Smith with the Rams and Redskins, and Dennis with the Bengals and Lions. Tight end Jim Yarbrough went to play with the Lions, Larry Gagner with the Steelers and Chiefs, and offensive tackle Randy Jackson with the Bears.

Casey, who played briefly for the Atlanta Falcons, was Florida's first All-American receiver. My sophomore and junior season, Charlie and I had a good amount of success on simple curl patterns and out-routes because the defense gave it to us "off-coverage"—a sort of soft man-to-man. If they'd played bump-and-run, we couldn't have done what we did. But everybody played a three-deep back then.

Charlie was Mr. Reliable—great hands, not great speed, but he ran excellent routes and could adjust on the fly. He made some big catches, leading the SEC in receptions both my sophomore and junior years, and wound up his college career as the SEC's all-time leading receiver during that time.

Richard Trapp was a fast, quick, big-play receiver who caught a bunch of passes (fifty-three) my senior year and made people miss with his jitterbug style on runs after the catch. Before he graduated, Richard had eight games with one hundred or more yards receiving. Which is why he made All-SEC in 1966.

I remain good friends with several former teammates, including All-SEC defensive back Allen Trammel, who played briefly for Houston in the NFL and was also an outstanding Gator baseball player, though not to be confused with the Detroit Tigers star. He holds the NCAA record for RBIs in one inning, with nine against Kentucky in 1965.

I also became good friends with running back Graham McKeel, or "Whitey," as we called him because of his white hair. Whitey invited me to join the ATO (Alpha Tau Omega) fraternity, where I met my future wife, Jerri, a little sister of the house. Long after our playing days, I would often visit Whitey in Lakeland during the summer. He introduced me to Jim Wellman, a big Gator booster, and we used his corporate jet to fly us up to New York for the Heisman ceremonies. Sadly, Whitey passed away in 2008.

Wayne McCall and Gene Peek helped us stay together through the years by organizing our alumni group, the Silver Sixties, which has met many times through the years. So much life has passed in between. We've watched families change and grandkids grow up. I just wish we'd had some championships to talk about. That's why they are so important—they are forever.

We didn't get all the way to the top, but we did take some steps in the right direction and cleared a path for future Florida teams. Three years after my class graduated, Coach Graves went out a big winner. He led the Gators to a 9-1-1 record, including a 14–13 victory over the SEC champion Tennessee team and Doug Dickey—his successor to be—in the Gator Bowl. Then Coach Graves stepped up to be the athletic director, having posted the best record of any Florida coach, 70-31-4. When I was coaching at Florida and we won our seventy-first, we asked Coach Graves to come to the locker room and I gave him the game ball. He had started it all.

WHILE I WAS PLAYING at Florida, Dr. Robert Cade came up with a strange concoction. In 1965, Dr. Cade asked Coach Graves if he could experiment on the football team. Drinking this liquid was supposed to replace the nutrients that you lost sweating. And certainly we were sweating a lot down in Gainesville. So on our break they'd have these little milk cartons full of Gatorade—I don't even know if they called it that back then. A lot of it tasted pretty bad. But eventually they started adding Kool-Aid or lemon or something to it and it was pretty good. It was a cold drink. Obviously everybody was very thirsty out there. Nobody in sports did anything like it, and Gatorade was a revolutionary discovery for athletes. Back in those days coaches thought water or liquid was bad for the players. So we were the first team to experiment with it. Obviously, the Gatorade people now say it helped us in the fourth quarter. And maybe it did.

There is some evidence it probably helped, but a few mythical stories also emerged—such as the one about our supply of Gatorade being hijacked by Georgia before our 1966 game in Jacksonville. As far as I know that never happened, as much as many Gators would like to have an excuse for us playing so lousy in the 27–10 loss. It was more of a case of being overconfident. And I doubt Gatorade would have cured that.

Coach Graves was ahead of the curve in a lot of ways. Back then, teams ran the ball and rolled out to throw a pass here and there. Play action. But it was mostly about running the ball. And if it's third and eight, maybe you throw it somewhere! So Coach Graves allowed us to throw the ball around a lot more than many schools did. I wished we would have opened the game up even more with the no-huddle—the way everybody does it now. Today a lot of schools come out firing it all over the place. I would have loved a chance to call the plays in the no-huddle.

But we achieved the highest national ranking in Florida's history up to that point, along with Florida's first major postseason appearances in the Sugar Bowl and the Orange Bowl. I was fortunate to be named SEC Player of the Year and chosen United Press International National Player of the

Accepting the 1966 Heisman Trophy in New York.

Year, as well as the Walter Camp Outstanding Back of the Year, All-American, and, of course, Heisman winner.

The Heisman Trophy presentation was a lot different back in '66. Contrary to how it's done today, there were not any finalists sitting in a room in New York on live TV. I never got to hear them call my name as the Heisman winner. I was watching film for the Miami game when they called my wife, Jerri, at home—we got married at the beginning of my senior year—and asked about my whereabouts. She said, "I don't know where he is right now, but he'll be here soon because he never misses lunch."

I was told by Norm Carlson that I should report to the office of University of Florida president J. Wayne Reitz. "Something about the Heisman" was all he would tell me, but I figured maybe I had won it. We had a brief, short press conference. I thanked my coaches, offensive line, running backs, receivers, and defense, and several weeks later I flew to New York to receive the trophy, which now sits in a case at the University of Florida. A TV broadcaster friend from Jacksonville, Dick Stratton, suggested I give the original trophy to my school and ask the Downtown Athletic Club to issue me another one. They did that and it has been a policy for every Heisman winner since then.

As the proud thirty-second winner, I have been back to the Heisman black-tie dinner every year since 1977. I was there in 2015 when Derrick Henry of Alabama became the eighty-first Heisman winner. He was a good choice. Derrick is a fine young man from a very humble background who gave a wonderful acceptance speech and interviews. Some of the Alabama coaches said, "We've never heard Derrick talk this long!" He's a big fellow at six-foot-three and 240 pounds. I was standing right behind him and can tell you this: You don't want to have to try and tackle this guy.

We do enjoy going to New York and doing all the Heisman stuff with the grandkids. Jerri is our leader. She knows where to get on the subway and when to get off. We took our grandson Gavin in 2015 and went to the

Statue of Liberty and the Empire State Building. It was a very, very foggy, overcast day. But it was starting to clear and you could see the top. When we bought our tickets there was hardly anybody in line. We walked right on up and one of the girls taking tickets said, "You know, you're not going to be able to see anything today." But by the time we got up there it had cleared off and so we got some good pictures.

I began to notice that the older Heisman guard is thinning out. Only about twenty-five people were at the black-tie dinner. A lot of my old Heisman buddies weren't there. Texas A&M running back John David Crow, a former teammate of mine with the 49ers, passed away in 2015. Former Auburn quarterback Pat Sullivan is in ill health. UCLA's Gary Beban (1967), who sits next to me, and USC's Mike Garrett (1965), who sits on my other side, were there.

One of the most fun things we Heisman winners got to do is the commercial campaign for the Nissan Heisman House in Pasadena, California. The writers are very clever and come up with skits outside the box. In early July 2015, before I resigned from South Carolina, we flew out to Pasadena. In this one commercial, Roger Staubach was supposed to be shaving and I was blow-drying my hair—with a visor on! We were paired up with Marcus Mariota, the 2014 winner from Oregon. When they brought me a Gator visor, I told the director, "Hey, I'm the head coach of South Carolina. I won the Heisman at Florida, but I can't wear that Florida visor right now." They had just a plain white visor there, so that's what I wore.

We had our lines down pat. They did ten, twenty takes—over and over and over.

The script called for Mariota to walk in and ask who opened up all the windows in his room.

And I say, "You know this house is haunted, don't you?"

"By who?" asks Mariota.

"Jay Berwanger, the first Heisman winner," I say.

"University of Chicago guy," says Staubach.

Horns sound, lights flash, and weird things are happening before Roger finally goes to the window and says, "Hey, Jay, cut the crap!"

Then it gets quiet.

And I sort of holler, "Jay! You gotta let it go!"

Then we did another one in which George Rogers of South Carolina got all dressed up. Robert Griffin III was sort of the head guy at the cocktail party, dressed in his tux, and he said of George's outfit, "George, that's too much." Next they had me come in with my tux and no shirt on and Griffin says, "Not enough, Coach, not enough!" We must have done that one twenty times. I said to the director, "Show me exactly how you want me to do that." I thought I was doing it exactly the way they wanted. So he coached me up. I guess just like in football, repetition helps.

Anyway, it was a lot of fun. Roger Staubach is a fun guy. We were up in the hallway doing a commercial. He grabbed a football. "Hey, Coach!" he said, and he zinged me a pass. He was really firing that thing and not just sort of lobbing it. He told me he played one-on-one half-court basketball until he was seventy or seventy-one when he hurt his Achilles. So he had to quit doing that. But he's an active guy.

So even though the Heisman House isn't real, it does give us all a chance to have fun and bond a little bit.

I ran across Tim Tebow in New York City and told him, "Now that I'm freed up, I'll be hanging around you and Danny Wuerffel a little bit more." He got a big smile on his face. I noticed he was wearing glasses. I said, "Do you really need those glasses?" He said, "I'm just wearing them for style." Maybe it makes him look smarter. And speaking of smarter, I'm proud to be part of the answer to a couple good Heisman trivia questions.

1. Who is the only person to win a Heisman and coach a Heisman winner? I coached Danny Wuerffel in 1996.
2. Who were the three Heisman winners at Florida? That's easy: me, Danny, and Tim Tebow.

3. But this one is harder, so let's see how smart you are. I am
   also one of only three Heisman winners born in the state of
   Florida (Miami Beach). Can you name the other two?

If you said Tim Tebow again, you're wrong because he was born in the
Philippines. Danny (Fort Walton Beach) and Derrick Henry (Yulee) are
the others.

Tim, Danny, and I have several other things in common besides winning a Heisman at Florida. All of us have at least one national championship to our credit as a player or coach. And none of us had long, successful
NFL careers as a starter.

Chapter 8

MY NFL PLAYING DAYS

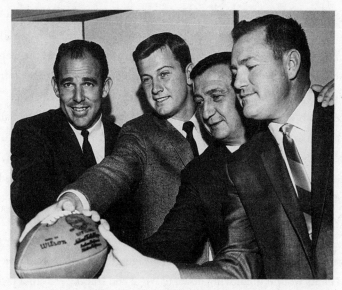

John Brodie, me, 49ers GM Lou Spadia,
and coach Jack Christiansen in 1967.

Professional football can be a crapshoot when it comes to what team is going to draft you. For a Johnson City kid who grew up winning imaginary championships in Kiwanis Park, just being drafted by the NFL and getting paid for playing football was almost beyond my wildest dreams. So after winning the Heisman Trophy and being projected as a first-round pick, I was even more thrilled and optimistic about playing professional football.

Instead of getting an agent, I worked with my Gainesville attorney and friend Bill ("Uncle Willie") O'Neal in sorting out what kind of money could be expected. Uncle Willie was good friends with almost all the Florida football players and helped a lot of us without charge. We would go out to his lake place or to his house for dinner or parties, as players and also after our college careers were over.

Once, when I was a freshman, I told Allen Trammel I needed a car and he said, "Uncle Willie will let you borrow his." Sure enough, Uncle Willie did and I got it back in one piece. Nowadays that would be a big NCAA violation. You can't borrow cars from boosters. Back in those days that was normal. But Uncle Willie was a special person who loved the Gators. He told somebody he had a $4,000 phone bill one year, presumably from calling NFL teams, scouts, coaches, and others to seek information.

Meanwhile, prior to the draft, I visited with the New Orleans Saints. At that time, it was believed New Orleans had the first pick as a new franchise in the league. I had briefly met with minority owner Al Hirt, the famous jazz trumpet player, on one occasion when he performed in Gainesville.

Apparently, the league was worried that in the muddle of the merger, the New York Giants might lose their first overall pick which they had earned by being the worst team in the league the year before. However, the Giants wound up moving down to No. 2 and trading that first pick to Minnesota in exchange for the first pick the following year, 1968.

So Uncle Willie became my "agent" and my lawyer. On draft day I was sitting down at his office in Gainesville. They didn't showcase No. 1 picks on national TV like they do today.

On March 14 and 15, 1967, the American Football League and the National Football League conducted a common draft at the Gotham Hotel in New York City as part of the merger agreement of June 1966.

It was one of the most confusing NFL drafts ever, marked by trades and special dispensations that were granted because of the merger. So much horse-trading broke out that, looking back all these decades later, it's still tough to even track now what actually happened then, and it almost makes your head spin.

Eventually, Bubba Smith of Michigan State would go No. 1 to Baltimore, which had wrangled the New Orleans Saints' first choice. A week before the draft, the Saints picked up center Bill Curry in the expansion draft and traded him to Minnesota for quarterback Gary Cuozzo, former backup to the legendary Johnny Unitas. The Vikings sent Cuozzo to the Saints and would wind up picking Bubba Smith's Michigan State teammate, running back Clint Jones, at No. 2.

Then the Giants traded their three top picks to Minnesota for quarterback Fran Tarkenton and a player to be named later.

The third pick belonged to the Atlanta Falcons. Some people thought because of Atlanta's affinity for Southern football they were going to draft me. Instead, the Falcons made a deal with the 49ers for three players— wide receiver Bernie Casey and two offensive linemen, Jim Norton and Jim Wilson. Casey, an actor, said he was going to retire, which he did the next year. Wilson and Norton only played a combined twenty-eight games for Atlanta during their careers.

With the third pick overall, the 49ers chose me. I had never been to San Francisco and all I'd heard about it then was the song "I Left My Heart in San Francisco." Imagine my surprise when I was drafted in the first round by a team that already had two quarterbacks, John Brodie and George Mira. But I was pleased to be picked third overall. Mira was with the 49ers only one more year and then they traded him to Philadelphia. The fourth pick was the Miami Dolphins', and they chose Bob Griese of Purdue.

Somebody suggested the merger wound up costing me a lot of money, estimated up to maybe a quarter of a million dollars, but I don't know about that. The year before, Joe Namath signed a four-year, $427,000 contract with Sonny Werblin, owner of the Jets, and that was considered maybe the last big deal. But I wasn't really worried about money at that point. I wound up with a four-year, $225,000 deal plus a $25,000 bonus—and no agent's fee. Not too bad for a guy whose Johnson City buddies had predicted he wouldn't even keep playing football in high school.

Jack White was the general manager of the 49ers. Jack Christiansen was the head coach at the time, but he was let go after one year. Dick Nolan, a former defensive assistant with Tom Landry in Dallas, was head coach of the 49ers the last eight years I was in San Francisco. While Coach Nolan was there we won three straight NFC West titles and missed the Super Bowl twice by one game in 1970 and 1971. After that he was head coach at New Orleans.

So how did I fit in? Basically as part of the old Four- to Five-Year Plan. "Steve, we're going to get you ready for five years from now," Nolan said. "We've got Brodie for another four or five and then you'll be ready." In reaction to the Five-Year Plan, I said, "Really?" That wasn't exactly music to my ears. I lost my "Give a Dang," and a little get-up-and-go right there, subsequently lacking ambition to push myself to play as hard as I should have. So I wound up having high expectations as a player that I was never able to reach—partly because of the hand I was dealt and partly because I lost some fire and motivation.

Five years came and went and I was still a backup, throwing only 204 passes. I finally got a chance to play in my sixth year, 1972, after Brodie suffered a severe ankle sprain. I started nine games that year and we went 6-1-1 to make the playoffs. But I didn't play very well in one of those games and Brodie was healthy for the playoffs, so he became the starter again. I understood that.

I had thrown five touchdown passes against the Chicago Bears, my best game statistically. And I was the quarterback when the Dallas Cowboys lost their first game in Texas Stadium that season. All that happened in about five days. We played the Bears on Sunday and won, 34–21. We played Dallas on Thanksgiving and won, 31–10. We finished 8-5-1 in the regular season and won the West Division. But then we played the Cowboys again in the playoffs and lost a heartbreaker. After falling behind us 28–13 in the third period, Roger Staubach brought the Cowboys back for seventeen straight points and beat us 30–28. Their onside kick hit one of our players right in the chest but the Cowboys recovered it. Dallas then lost to the Washington Redskins, who went on to lose to the Dolphins in the Super Bowl.

As a backup, I learned a lot about football watching from the sidelines, where I would take note of what the defense was doing, which later helped me call plays from that vantage point in college. Every experience we have, good and bad, prepares us for a situation that could come up later in life.

So my role was limited. In addition to punting, I also tried to stay involved by studying the other team's defense as another set of eyes for the 49ers and Brodie. He would come off the field and ask me, "What do you see?" Mostly I paid attention to what the opponents were doing in their secondary. Brodie called his own plays and occasionally would improvise, so any additional info was helpful to him.

I started four games in 1972, during which I completed passes 108 for 1,232 yards with 18 touchdowns and 6 interceptions. But with Brodie still firmly entrenched as the starter, it would be a long time before I'd get a real shot. So I geared down, started playing a bunch of golf and enjoying life. Therefore, I didn't totally prepare myself as an NFL quarterback. Basically, I lasted ten years, eight of those as the backup. Out of the ten years in the NFL, I probably played the equivalent of about two and a half seasons, all told. There's no doubt sitting out so many games took away some of my competitive fire. Looking back on it now, maybe if I had been a little more intense and demanding of myself, things might have been different. But that was not to be.

Would I have liked to have played more with the Niners? Of course. But as I have said all along, stuff like this happens for a reason. Now I feel very fortunate and blessed that I was a backup quarterback for eight of my ten years in the NFL. I'm positive that being a backup prevented serious injuries and lengthened my career. And it gave me a chance to study NFL defenses.

It was always interesting. Once in the preseason against the Cleveland Browns they were playing what everybody now calls the "Cover Two" defense with deep safeties. Brodie could throw the quick-out beautifully— "One-two-three, throw!" If they rolled the coverage one way, he'd throw it the other way. "One-two-three, throw!" When Cleveland rolled one way and he threw the other way, it almost got picked off.

"What's going on there?" Brodie asked me.

"Brodie, they got both the corners up short with two safeties back there," I said.

"That's stupid, they can't do that!" Brodie said.

"That's what they're doing," I said again.

So later when we started watching on film he said, "Well, I'll be danged, they are doing that!" It felt like there was a lot of room out there, which there was. To play that coverage you have to keep people from going into the middle and deep corner areas. So that's the first time, around 1970, the Cover Two ever came into the game.

Then we were playing the Detroit Lions one year when Hall of Famer Dick LeBeau blitzed from his cornerback position and the safety ran over there to cover his receiver. It was an early version of the zone blitz—the first time we'd ever seen that. Now people use the zone blitz all the time— something that LeBeau basically invented and has relied on for more than forty years as a defensive coach in the NFL. It's always interesting to be there and see something creative for the first time.

In 1975, my last season as a 49er, I was still sitting on the bench and decided to go to Coach Nolan to ask for a chance to start the next week against a team we seldom seemed to beat: the Los Angeles Rams.

That turned out to be maybe my best game in pro football or, at least, my favorite game. I had been seeing a little action. Veteran quarterback Norm Snead and youngster Tommy Owens were doing most of the playing. Our record was 2-5. And the Rams were 6-1. They owned us. Brodie had beaten them once, in 1970.

I went to Coach Nolan early in the week and said, "Coach, I've been here nine years and I've never played against the Rams down there in L.A. We're 2-5 and we have nothing to lose. I'd like a shot to see if we can beat them."

I just kept telling him, "Coach, let me play, we don't have anything to lose." I wanted to see if I could get myself and the guys fired up and see what we could do.

Coach Nolan would respond: "Well, Steve, just keep working, get yourself ready. You never know when somebody's going to go down.'"

And I said, "Nah, nah, nah, Coach—I'm just asking you. I've been here nine years. Never asked for anything. I'd just like to go see if we can put together a game plan, go down there and beat those guys. I've never played against them in L.A. They've owned us ever since I've been here. And I want a shot at them." In eight years, our record against the Rams was 1-15. One win and fifteen losses!

"Well, you never . . ." Nolan said.

"Nah, nah, Coach . . ." I kept saying.

"Well, let me think about it," he said.

The next day Nolan consented: "Okay, you got it. You're going to start and play the game. We got nothing to lose."

I said, "I'd also like to call the plays. I'll be ready." He said okay.

Right before the game, Coach Nolan informed me that our quarterback coach was probably going to start out calling the plays.

And I said, "Coach, I'm ready to call them!" So the quarterback coach called them the first couple possessions. Nothing good happened and we weren't going anywhere. I said, "Let me try to call 'em." He said, "Okay, you go ahead and call 'em." So about the third or fourth possession he let me. And we started moving the ball.

That was probably the most inspired game for me as an NFL

quarterback—I was motivated to see if we could go beat those guys. We threw to our All-Pro and Hall of Fame wide receiver Gene Washington, one of the NFL's all-time great wide receivers. The Rams double-teamed the outside guys. The Rams couldn't cover our quick little halfback, Delvin Williams, who we hit for a touchdown. On a third and one, I hit Gene Washington on a sixty-five-yard play-action touchdown pass, my second touchdown pass of the game. That put us ahead, 21–17.

The Rams put a drive together, but we stopped them on about the 30. They had a field goal kicker, Tom Dempsey, who was born with a clubfoot and wore a special metal shoe with a flattened and enlarged toe surface. He had worn that shoe to kick a then-record sixty-three-yard field goal as time expired to give the Saints a 19–17 win over the Detroit Lions on November 8, 1970. Now he was a big weapon for the Rams.

Our defensive back, Ralph McGill, rushed around the corner and reached out to block the kick. But Dempsey's metal shoe hit McGill right up the side of the head. Full go. McGill was out for a long time. Back then they'd drive that ambulance out to midfield. When they put him in it he was still out—a scary moment. We didn't know how bad McGill was hurt, if Dempsey had killed him, or what. But he wasn't moving.

Printed reports later stated McGill did not regain consciousness on the way to the hospital, where a preliminary examination showed he suffered a severe concussion. McGill kept playing that year and appeared to be okay, but a few games later in the year he blacked out on the charter flight from Philadelphia and our team plane had to make an emergency landing in Chicago, where he was taken to a hospital and remained for four days. He went on to play four more seasons—two with the 49ers and two for the Saints. He died in 2015 at age sixty-four.

They called roughing the kicker on McGill, the guy who got kicked in the head and who was being hauled off on a stretcher. The Rams got a first down and went on to score for a 23–21 lead on a short run. But Dempsey missed the extra point, probably still thinking, *I may have killed a guy.*

McGill's status was on all of our minds. Dempsey sort of jabbed at it and missed it right.

We got the ball with about four minutes—plenty of time, dinking and dunking to their 37-yard line with fourth and four. Our kicker, Steve Mike-Mayer, was looking at a fifty-four-yarder with fifty seconds left. We called our last time-out and were over there thinking: *Kick it, or go for it?* Well, we said, he had been able to reach from there before, so why not? And I was the holder. I got it down, Mike-Mayer nailed it, and we won 24–23.

We had pulled off a rare win over the Rams and only our second in the last eighteen meetings. In my nine years against the Rams we were 2-16. I felt a tiny bit of redemption. I had gotten the chance to show what I could do as a starter calling my own plays. I had a fairly good day passing, 240 yards, three touchdown passes, no interceptions.

Now we were 3-5 and the Rams were 6-2. San Francisco sportswriter Ron Fimrite, then at the *Chronicle* and later of *Sports Illustrated*, paid me a nice compliment. He wrote: "I've been watching Spurrier play for a long time. I've never seen him throw spirals like he did that day. Never seen him come close to that." Fimrite wrote that this 49ers team hadn't done anything to that point and after we beat the Rams we suddenly looked pretty good. He said it was amazing—"You'd have had to have been there to see it to believe it."

So that was my favorite NFL game of all the ten seasons. That night, Jerri and I got a babysitter and went to Lake Tahoe to celebrate because we were off Monday. The following week we beat the Bears, 31–3. The next week we knocked off the Saints in New Orleans, 16–6, for our third win in a row, to pull up to 5-5. But then the bottom dropped out: We lost our last four in a row. After that I went back to being my old self.

This was going to be Nolan's last season with the 49ers.

As a player, I still needed someone to push and challenge me. Later, as a coach, I tried to push, encourage, and demand that our players were up for every game.

When you really, really want to try to achieve something and put the work in, you've got a chance. Without it you've got no chance at all. And I think maybe that prepared me for coaching. I always tried to have our players ready—especially to inspire the quarterbacks to play their best game every week, striving always to improve and play our best football in the next game. And I hoped that best effort would result in a win the last game of every season.

My time was running short as an NFL player. First, though, there was a penance to be paid with an expansion team in its first year of operation. In San Francisco I had been the punter and backup, playing only sparingly.

On April 2, 1976, the 49ers traded me to a Tampa Bay expansion franchise for wide receiver Willie McGee and linebacker Bruce Elia—from the Rams and Dolphins, respectively—and a second-round draft choice. And I was thrilled at the idea of finishing my playing career in Florida.

I played for John McKay of the Tampa Bay Bucs, a legendary coach from Southern Cal, and we went winless. He was a feisty, outspoken guy. After one game when we got booed, he called the fans "a bunch of idiots." He was known for his colorful quotes—some funny, some of them not so funny.

Coach McKay came from Southern Cal with a big track record and reputation—fifteen seasons, four national championships, nine bowl games, and a record of 127-40-8. Obviously he had been an excellent recruiter. The Trojans were known for their running game, pulling linemen and running sweeps, which was called "Student Body Left, Student Body Right." And he had bigger, better bodies. However, very little of that success in college would transfer to the NFL, where the talent is more equally divided by the draft.

NFL teams kept coming after him until he said yes to the Bucs, who reportedly quadrupled his salary. I was about to find out what it was like to play for him. I was also going to get sacked a bunch of times every game and become the quarterback on a team where the coach would insist his son be the starting wide receiver—and therefore expected to be the primary target. Still, I was thrilled to start over with a new team.

Coach McKay brought the same offense without the same talented roster of players, so we struggled quite a bit. But his defense was very good. Wayne Fontes was his defensive coordinator and defensive end Lee Roy Selmon from Oklahoma was world class. The one year the Bucs were first or second in league defense they almost went to the Super Bowl. But in the early years there was just a lack of talent on offense. We didn't have the players to run that offense. And that was something you learn as a coach: You have to do whatever your talent level can allow.

When you're the starting quarterback and your team is losing, they go with somebody else. So Parnell Dickerson of Mississippi Valley State University, drafted in the seventh round, started against Miami in game seven at home and he got hurt in the second quarter. Parnell played one season with the Bucs. I played the entire second half of that game. We picked up Terry Hanratty, who had been the backup quarterback to Terry Bradshaw with the Pittsburgh Steelers, and he started against the Steelers, but I played the entire second half of that game. So I played in all fourteen games of the 0-14 season in 1976.

John McKay Jr. had been drafted in 1975 as the sixteenth pick by Cleveland and he didn't make the team. After leaving Cleveland, John Jr. played for the Southern California Sun of the World Football League. The next year his dad took the Tampa job and brought in his son. Most of the guys on the team thought, *Well, you know he'll probably make the team as a backup receiver. Hey, his dad's the head coach, so no big deal.* Not only did Junior make the team, he became the starter. And then a first primary receiver. He wasn't a terrible player, but he wasn't real fast. We didn't have much protection from the offensive line. It was an expansion draft, so we were all "down-the-line" guys. The reason we were there was that our teams hadn't protected us in the expansion draft, sort of saying, "This is an excess player—one we don't need." Rejects, if you want to say it that way.

John Jr. actually became the first Buc to be announced over the public address system when we took the field at Tampa Bay Stadium for the first time.

We had two or three games we could have won. Seattle beat us 13–10, and they blocked a field goal at the end of the game that would have sent us to overtime. We lost to Miami 23–20 and to Buffalo 14–9. Against New England the last game of the year, we had 'em 14 to nothing and we got beat 31–14. So we were close a few times, but maybe we weren't quite good enough. And that's how my year ended at Tampa. I was uncertain about the future, but hopeful. Clearly we needed help all over the offense, and especially at wide receiver.

In the off-season, the LPGA Tour was playing at Bent Tree outside of Sarasota. They invited me to come down, spend the night at a Sarasota hotel and play in the pro-am. So Jerri and I were down there, not really knowing if Coach McKay or anybody else from the Bucs was playing in it. At two a.m. the fire alarm goes off. Startled, we rolled out of bed and went outside with all the guests. One of them was Dick Beam, the Bucs' director of operations and Coach McKay's right-hand man. As he was standing next to me, we started making small talk.

"You think there's really a fire?" I asked.

He asked how things went the past season. I replied: "You know—okay."

I've always been one to be honest with my opinions, so I told him about my concerns regarding John Jr.

"Some of the guys are a little concerned that Coach McKay has a son starting at wide receiver. There's a feeling among some that maybe other players on the team are a little better than him. But coach has his son out there starting. I'm just telling you that's what the players think."

I don't want to make excuses or throw off on John Jr., who was a decent player, and a pretty good guy—and didn't have it easy playing for his dad.

So Beam went back and told Coach McKay what I said. The next week he sent me packing.

I was named the MVP of the offense in 1976 by the Tampa Bay Booster

Club, but I was cut—which has to be a first. And after two more tries, in Denver and Miami, my NFL career was over in 1977.

When Coach McKay died, his ashes were spread in the Los Angeles Coliseum. Years after his father's death, John Jr. said coming to Tampa Bay was his dad's "worst professional move he could have made" because he'd arrived there as one of the best coaches ever in college football. And since his NFL record wound up being 44-88-1, that was obviously not the way he wanted to be remembered.

Looking back, I am so thankful that I got cut by him. And I'm thankful Miami and Denver cut me. It forced me to make up my mind about my profession. I was able to sit up in those stands in 1977 and watch the Florida Gators play football. And I thought to myself: *I've been around a lot of good coaches, and maybe some not so good. So if I treated our players fairly, the way they deserve to be treated, and gave them some ball plays where they can be successful, then maybe I could become a coach.*

There are good plays and bad plays. And good players and bad players. Every player's gotta have a chance. You gotta look at them all and realize they might be a diamond in the rough. And when I did become the Head Ball Coach at Florida, I often dug deep down on my roster to see who could play—just as I did my first year at Florida, when we found a guy named Shane Matthews, who was on the fifth string and had just never gotten a chance to play.

SOME PEOPLE MAY WONDER if I considered my NFL career to be a disappointment, or feel that I failed because I never caught on with the right coach or right team. When you play on teams that don't win, they usually get rid of the quarterback pretty soon. I stayed around for a decade, but didn't get to start as many games as I would have liked.

This may sound strange, but in the end it worked out well for me because I had two of the best jobs in the game—backup quarterback and punter. That gave me the longevity and health needed to walk away from the game of pro football after ten years with my body intact and a pension to my credit. And once you get to age sixty-five, those NFL pension paychecks are pretty nice.

It was a good time for our family, even when we were commuting between San Francisco and Gainesville. Jerri has fond memories of San Francisco and being young marrieds and making lifelong friends with my 49ers teammates, their wives, and their families.

"In the NFL, no one thinks it's going to end. All you think about is the next game, like it's going to go on forever," she once said.

There were some excellent takeaways from the NFL, right down to the week before I was cut. A guy named Billy Nelsen, who had played at Southern Cal for McKay, came along as the quarterback coach.

Billy was a quarterback with the Steelers and Browns in the late sixties and early seventies. He was an excellent teacher of passing fundamentals and I learned more about the mechanics of throwing in that one week than in all my other years of playing football. After that I could pass the football better than at any time in my life.

Even though I never got to use those tips from Nelsen as a player, they certainly trained me as a coach. I could also throw the ball really well in practice, which I continued to do into my mid-sixties as I demonstrated passing fundamentals to all my quarterbacks. I used them on every quarterback I ever coached, including talented freshman Ben Bennett, who was the key man in the first version of my own offense at Duke.

Chapter 9

NEXT STOPS: GEORGIA TECH AND DUKE

O nce I'd had a taste of coaching at Florida, I really loved it. But one
year after I started, I found out the trick was to stay employed. Charley Pell took over the program after the 1978 season and changes were
under way. I met with him briefly, but he said he needed a quarterback
coach with more experience. "I understand" was about all I could say.

So I went back home and told Jerri, "I don't have a job here anymore."

"What are you going to do?"

"I don't know."

"Well, do you want to coach, or not?"

"Yeah, I think I'd like to keep coaching, but I don't know anybody else
to call and find out about possible openings."

I was out of work. So I was playing golf, messing around, and following
up on leads. Some semipro team in Jacksonville wanted me to come over
and be the quarterback and player/coach—said I could make $500 or so
a game.

In January of '79 I got a call from former Florida Gator Jack West-
brook, who was working at Georgia Tech with my former quarterback
coach, Pepper Rodgers, who had played at Tech and was now Tech's head

coach. He said Coach Pepper wanted me to call him. Tech's former quarterback coach, Dave Fagg, had taken a job in Hawaii with Dick Tomey, who would later become head coach at Arizona and San Jose State.

So I went up to Atlanta and hung out for a day or so with a couple guys on the Georgia Tech staff. Larry Travis was a former All-SEC guard at Florida who later became assistant head coach/offensive coordinator at Tech and went into administration before becoming head coach and then AD at Kansas State. The offensive line coach was Les Handley. And after a bit, finally, Coach Pepper said, "Steve, I'm going to hire you. But I want you to go back and bring Jerri up for another interview. You two can stay at my house." I guess he wanted to make sure Jerri was comfortable with the move.

Jerri and I flew up to Atlanta and had dinner with Coach Pepper at the Capital City Club. About eleven p.m. we went for a nightcap at a nice little place in Buckhead called Billy's. About two hours later, at two in the morning, we went back to Coach Pepper's house and chatted for a bit. It was sort of like renewing a friendship. We played tennis together. We played golf together. And that made it pleasant to work for him. He didn't treat me like an assistant coach. I was thinking, "He's treating me like one of his good friends." He's still a wonderful friend and would have a role one day in my becoming an NFL head coach.

So I was the quarterback coach for one year at Tech, in a system where we'd usually run the ball on first and second down and then they'd say to me up in the press box, "All right, Spurrier, whatta ya got for third and nine or third and seven?"

We lost to Alabama in our opener 30–6—Coach Bear Bryant's last undefeated national championship team—and then tied Florida 7–7. That was Charley Pell's only scratch—tie or win—that year in his 0-10-1 inaugural season. Just think of it: I was in the Swamp (yet to be named that) for Coach Pell's only tie that year.

Ironically, in that game against the Gators, my former quarterback Johnny Brantley and his brother Scot—an All-SEC linebacker and future starter for the Tampa Bay Bucs—were both injured, ending their college careers. Scot was knocked out for quite a while with a concussion and never played again as a Gator. He went on to play eleven years in the NFL. After the game, I went by Florida's training room to check on them, having no idea how serious the injuries would be.

In game three of the season, we were struggling, trailing William & Mary 7–6 at halftime. I had been on the phones upstairs in the first half. Coach Pepper came in at halftime and asked me, "What do we need to do?"

I said, "Coach, we need to throw on first down."

"We're not throwing on first down?" he asked.

"No, we're not. The play-action passes we got are good on first down, but on third and eight it's no good because they're sitting in a big ol' soft zone back there. But I'm the third-down play-caller, so I can't get it in."

Coach Pepper said, "Dang it, get it called! Get it called!"

So we finally got a few of those plays called and beat William & Mary 33–7, but we still couldn't get things turned around that season. It was beginning to get frustrating because I was not the play-caller as most quarterback coaches are.

So I went out jogging one day, came back, went into Coach Pepper's office, and said to him: "Coach, I'm asking you if you'd let me come down to the sidelines and put in the offense for the game against Duke. Because I think I can help you, help our team. I think we've got a chance to win some ball games. But I'm not any good up there calling third down passes."

He thought a minute and said, "Okay, you got it!" He told the other coaches, "Steve's going to put in the offense and call the plays." And away we went. Fortunately, we were playing Duke, Air Force, and Navy, and we won three in a row with the emergence of quarterback Mike Kelley and wide receiver Kris Kentera.

We beat Duke, 24–14, hit some passes and did some things on offense in what would turn out to be a very important "audition" game for me. The Duke coach, Red Wilson, noticed that we had been moving the ball and was apparently impressed. I had no idea I'd be calling him in late December for a job.

We lost in our final game to Georgia, 16–3, finishing with a record of 4-6-1. But listen to who we lost to: national champion Alabama, Auburn, Tennessee, Notre Dame, and Georgia. It was a tough schedule as an Independent (Tech wasn't in the Atlantic Coast Conference yet).

Tech fired Coach Pepper and hired Bill Curry, who met with all of us assistant coaches and said we were "all free to look around . . . and I'll get back with you in a day or two."

When I got home Jerri asked me: "Do you have a job?"

"I'm not sure—I don't think so."

"Well, what are you going to do? Why don't you go ask the guy if you've got a job or not, and if not you'd better find one if you want to coach."

"You know what, that's a good idea."

So I went in to see Coach Bill Curry and asked him, "What's my status here? Am I going to be quarterback coach next year or not?"

He said, "Right now, I've got to interview one or two other guys and you're a candidate."

"Okay, that's all I need to know," I told him.

I had heard Duke was looking for an offensive coordinator. I called Eddie Williamson, the line coach at Duke, who recruited a lot of the high schools in Atlanta that I had. Eddie asked if I was interested in the job and, of course, I said yes. He suggested I move fast because he thought Coach Wilson was about to hire a coach from East Tennessee State. Eddie was meeting with Coach Wilson that night so I asked him to pass along my number. I received his call that same night. Oddly enough, Eddie and I had run into each other that spring and I got to meet Coach Red Wilson that day back in May. Back then head coaches could go out in the spring. So I just happened to be at Dunwoody High School one day when Eddie brought his head coach.

I flew to Raleigh-Durham on a Monday morning and met with Coach Wilson and Duke athletic director Tom Butters, who was going to make this call as well. While I was in Coach Wilson's office, there was a nice-looking kid sitting on the sofa. Coach Wilson introduced him to me as Ben Bennett, a top quarterback recruit from California. Ben just happened to be on his official visit when I went there.

Keep in mind, I had no job, I was just a candidate. I asked Ben why he was still there on a Monday and he said he'd gotten into North Carolina late Saturday due to the time change from the West Coast and would be leaving that night.

So we started talking and he sort of knew who I was, since he was from California and I had played for the 49ers.

I said, "Ben, are you coming to Duke?"

He said, "I'll come if you're coming—are you coming?"

I said, "I'm coming if Coach Wilson hires me."

Then I asked Coach Wilson, "Have I got a chance to be here as offensive coordinator?"

Coach Wilson said, "I think so, if Mr. Butters says you're okay. If you are approved by our athletic director, then I'm hiring you." I was approved and I became an offensive coordinator at a major college in my third year in coaching.

I said, "Thank you, Lord! Let's go do it! Well, let's go make Duke football a winner!"

So I went back home, packed, and left for Durham immediately to work for Coach Red Wilson. Some people thought my brief coaching career would end at Duke University, since they'd had very few winning seasons in the past ten years, but it did the opposite and paved the way for me to advance as an offensive coordinator and Head Ball Coach. On the staff with me at Georgia Tech was Norm Van Brocklin, an NFL Hall of Fame quarterback who won championships with the Rams and Eagles and then became the first head coach for the Minnesota Vikings, and later head coach of the Atlanta Falcons. Coach Pepper had hired Van Brocklin as the running backs coach in 1979. When I told him I was going to Duke, he said: "Steve, you can't do that!"

I said, "Why not?"

"Steve, you can't win at Duke! When is the last time anybody ever won at Duke and got a better job? You need to go somewhere where you can win. Tennessee. Georgia. Ohio State . . . a team that has a strong tradition of winning."

"Well, that's a great idea," I said. "But guess what: None of those schools are asking me to come coach. The only one in America that's asking me to come coach is Duke University. So I'm either going to make it or not make it at Duke University."

What turned out to be the beauty of the job was that I had control of the offense. When I got there, I asked Coach Wilson, "Is there any terminology or numbering system you want me to learn?"

He said, "We don't have an offense here. You can create the one you want."

"You mean I can make up the numbering system, the words and everything else?"

"Yeah. I want to throw the ball and I like trick plays, so have a go at it," he said.

I said, "Man, this is my third year ever as a coach and I get to make up the offense!"

Very few head coaches would give a third-year assistant that kind of freedom. Again, sort of scary. So Eddie Williamson, our O-Line coach, and I went to work on designing the offense. Eddie, by the way, was offensive line coach at TCU and coached for thirty-five years. Wonderful guy, good coach. He and I sort of put the words together and invented the Duke terminology.

During practice against the defense, I would ask the wide receivers, "Can you see what coverage it is so we can call an option route?"

"Oh, yeah, Coach, I can tell what coverage that is."

So we started experimenting. We didn't name it anything fancy. Just the Duke offense. Later in 1987 when I came back to Duke as Head Ball

Coach they called it "Air Ball"—like in basketball, but in a positive way. When we hit a long pass the students started chanting, "Air-r-r-r Ball-l-l-l! Air-r-r-r Ball-l-l-l!

WE WERE NOT exactly an overnight success. We went 2-9 in 1980 but we did beat Clemson and Georgia Tech. We lost some close ones but we weren't very good. Young Ben Bennett threw for more than two thousand yards that season, however.

We were playing at North Carolina, which had two excellent running backs in Amos Lawrence and Kelvin Bryant. They both gained a thousand yards that year. Kelvin needed about 40 or 50 in the fourth quarter to get it, so they were feeding it to him, feeding it to him.

I said to myself, "Maybe one day I'll be in position to repay those Tar Heels for trying to run up their record on our Duke football guys." Sure enough, that chance would come years later, in 1989.

WE DID MAKE a little progress, so at least we all kept our jobs at Duke another year. But we started off the 1981 season by losing our first two games—both on the road—at Ohio State and South Carolina. We played only five home games every year I was at Duke. Back then the idea of getting a good paycheck from our opponents was most important to the administration at Duke.

In our third game of 1981 we played at Virginia. We were losing 24–15 in the fourth quarter. Ben Bennett was out—he had sprained his shoulder. The backup quarterback was Ron Sally, a good, smart quarterback from St. Louis who took us on two eighty-yard drives for touchdowns. We overcame a nine-point deficit in the fourth quarter and beat Virginia 29–24. This turned out to be one of the biggest wins for both me and Duke football—a truly divine appointment day.

That was a big turnaround for Duke and a validation for some of the things we had been trying to do. And you talk about some celebrating in the locker room! And it didn't stop there. Jerri had rented a bus for all the wives and children to go to the game in Charlottesville. So they're all out there waiting on us. My kids were ten, twelve, and fourteen. We're all hugging. When you're 2-11 over two seasons at Duke and you win one like that, it becomes a hugging game! This was truly one of the happiest moments in my life after a game and one of my favorite key victories, which led to our first winning season in a long time. Nobody could remember when Duke had come from nine points behind in the fourth quarter to win a game.

Virginia was also 0-2 and, like us, Coach Dick Bestwick was in the hot seat. While we were outside the stadium, here came the secondary coach for Virginia, who had a bunch of little kids, too, and they were all down in the dumps. Just heartbroken. At moments like that you realize what a difference winning and losing is to assistant coaches and their families. Especially those who are saying, "Where's my next job after this year, if I even have one?"

That's the downside of somebody winning and somebody losing. But it's all part of the game. And here I was in my fourth year as a coach, my third job, hoping to establish myself and hang on with a staff that could stay employed.

On our side, the win over Virginia was a bit of a milestone because we began to believe in ourselves. We began to find out how to win at Duke University.

About that same time, Duke's basketball program was undergoing a big change as a young coach arrived from Army. Coach Mike Krzyzewski, who had played for Bobby Knight at Army and then coached with Knight at Indiana before returning to West Point, was just starting his forty-plus-year reign that would lead to nearly one thousand wins at Duke, a dozen Final Fours, and a fifth national championship in 2015.

You could tell right off how competitive Coach K was, whether he was playing or coaching basketball. In those early days, sometimes at noon, the football and basketball coaches would play a friendly pickup game in Cameron Indoor Stadium. All of us were in our thirties then. And we were soon introduced to Coach K's rules. His team very seldom, if ever, lost these pickup games.

Coach K was a decent player and could shoot a little bit. He liked to post up, especially if he was guarded by a smaller guy. But there was a definite pecking order: He was already head coach and I was an assistant. And we could never win. Every time it was close he would drive to the basket and if he missed it was, "Foul! A foul!" Since we were assistant coaches and he was the head coach, we couldn't complain. I told him one time years later, "Man, your team was hard to beat, because you always called a foul!" He'd laugh. All of us coaches were so competitive—we didn't want to lose. Later, I'd say, "Boys, we don't have a chance against the Head Basketball Coach!"

Coach K is an amazing guy, terrific coach. Works hard at his trade. He doesn't play golf. Used to play a little tennis. I think he works out a little bit, but in those days he had that bad back and was forced to have surgery. He and his wife, Mickie, are also very good friends with my wife, Jerri, and me. He still sends us pictures of his grandkids, and we saw a couple of them on a TV commercial with him.

When I became head coach at Duke I played a lot of golf with Tom Butters. Mr. Butters would tell people, "An athletic director isn't supposed to play golf and hang out with his football coach. I played golf and had dinner with Steve and Jerri many times when he was our head coach."

Duke was where I learned to be whatever kind of coach that I became. Coach Wilson was a wonderful man and allowed me to create stuff in his laboratory. He also gave me something equally as valuable—something I had never seen before: In 1980 and '81, he handed out copies of "Guidelines for a Good Player-Coach Relationship" to his staff members. He had also given us a sheet called "Winners and Losers," pulled from the book by Sydney Harris. Later in this book, I'll expand on how I've adapted and used those items throughout my coaching career.

Coach Wilson's list of ways to become a successful ball coach, which I used the remainder of my career, contained such advice as:

- Your practice plans are important. Know what you're doing, all through practice.
- Fundamentals are the most important thing you can teach.
- Never argue with or criticize another coach in front of a player.

This was a blueprint on how to be a coach. I had never seen anything like it!

I modified it over the years, added a few ideas of my own, and mixed in some John Wooden stuff, but retained many of the same points. I call it "Guidelines for a Good Ball Coach." And every year I would go over them with our coaching staff.

Coach Red also gave me a list of excellent quotes from famous people.

In 1982 we got over the hump, led by our quarterback Ben Bennett. Having a chance to coach a quarterback like Ben was a real pleasure, and he put up unprecedented numbers at Duke. As a freshman in 1980 he was voted ACC Rookie of the Year. Although I was gone by his senior year, Ben became the top passer in the history of NCAA Division I-A football with the most passes attempted (1,375), most passes completed (820), and the most yardage (9,614). He set seven NCAA, fifteen ACC, and forty-two school records.

Some of the other major contributors were running backs Greg Boone, Mike Grayson, and Joel Blunk; and wide receivers Chris Castor, Ronnie Fredrick, Cedric Jones, and Marvin Brown.

We opened up in 1982 at Tennessee, who had Reggie White at defen-

Brother Graham, Dad, Mom, sister Sara, and me. Green Cove Springs, 1991.

The Spurrier Boys: Uncle Bob, brother Graham, Dad, and me.

With my Science Hill football coach, Kermit Tipton, who gave me a shot to call my own plays.

A happy day in Johnson City with Coach Ray Graves when I signed with Florida. Coach Elvin Little (standing left) and Coach Kermit Tipton are flanking Mom and Dad.

Our freshmen team beat Georgia 45–12 at Florida Field.

LEFT: With Tennessee governor Frank Clement and my high school receiver Jimmy Sanders on a Vanderbilt recruiting trip in 1962. Jimmy signed on to play for the Commodores and graduated from law school.

RIGHT: #11

BELOW: After kicking the winning field goal against Auburn, with my wife, Jerri, and my brother, Graham.

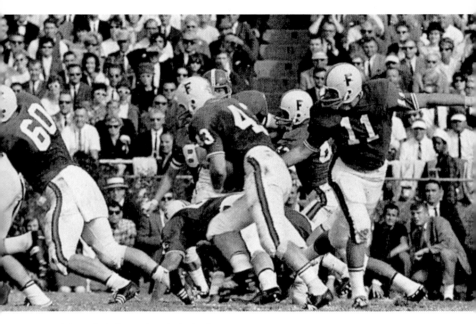

We did run the ball. Handing the ball off to my roommate and really good friend, Graham McKeel (#43).

College Football Hall of Fame, class of 1986. I'm top left. John Brodie is in the front row in the middle. John David Crow is in the front row, second from the left, and Mike Ditka is on the far right.

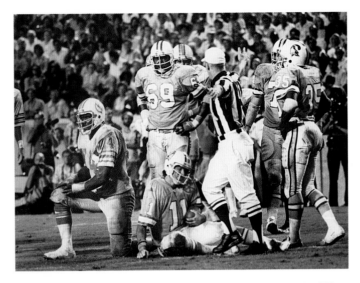

That's me on the ground in a Tampa Bay Bucs–Miami game in 1976. I should have gotten rid of the ball sooner!

Meeting up with Joe Willie Namath in 1967.

Proof that I actually wore the visor as HBC of the Bandits in 1985.

Honored to meet President
Ronald Reagan.

*To Steve Spurrier
With best wishes,* Ronald Reagan

With my youngest son, Scotty, in 1989.

With our outstanding offensive line twenty years after winning the ACC at Duke: Chip Nitowski,
Brett Tulacro, Bubba Metts, Pete Petroff, and Chris Port.

With Scotty, Lisa, and Amy tubing down the Itchetucknee River with coaches and families in 1990.

Shane Matthews, middle, with TEs Greg Keller and Kirk Kirkpatrick. That 1990 team will always be SEC champions to me.

Looking for a play on third and goal with quarterback Danny Wuerffel (#7), receiver Jack Jackson (#1), and backup quarterback Eric Kresser (behind Danny).

Our 1996 National Championship coaching staff. *Back row (left to right)*: Jamie Speronis, Steve Spurrier Jr., Carl Franks, Jimmy Ray Stephens, Rod Broadway, Bob Sanders, Lawson Holland, Aubrey Hill, and Jerry Schmidt. *Front row*: Bobby Stoops, Barry Wilson, The HBC, Dwayne Dixon, and Jim Collins.

sive end and Willie Gault at wide receiver. Greg Boone, our fullback, ran a kickoff back for a 104-yard touchdown. Ben Bennett connected an 88-yard touchdown pass to Chris Castor.

The key thing about that game was in the fourth quarter we had the ball on our own 1-yard line with 9:15 left in the game and we ran the ball mostly from there to their 1-yard line. We threw one pass on third and fifteen. Our backup tailback, Joel Blunk, rushed for more than one hundred yards alone in the final period. As they used their last time-out, I told Ben, "Don't you dare sneak that ball into the end zone," because they would've had forty or fifty seconds left to come back and try to tie us.

We beat Tennessee, 25–24—a huge win for the Duke football team and our program.

Our offense often cranked out over 500 yards per game in '82, including thirty-two first downs in the last game of that season, to beat North Carolina for the first time in ten years, 23–17. Carl Franks, who later coached with me, caught the winning touchdown pass. We went on to have a 6-5 record that year—Duke's first back-to-back winning seasons since 1971. The students tore down the goalpost and passed pieces of it through the stands. Ben Bennett threw for twenty touchdowns and more than three thousand yards that season.

After we had beaten Tennessee, South Carolina, and Virginia, I started hearing from the Tampa Bay Bandits, who wanted me to meet with their owner the night before our game against Virginia Tech.

Meanwhile, I was still learning and trying to refine our offense with hopes of being a head coach someday—itching to have my own team. We were fourth in the nation in total offense. And that's what gave me a chance to become a Head Ball Coach. Fate was working my way.

I had been at Dunwoody High School that day when Coach Red Wilson just happened to be there. I had just happened to call the plays for the first time ever against Duke. Coach Wilson liked what he saw. And he wound up letting me be the architect of the Duke offense.

I just happened to be at Duke the same day with the recruit who would become the all-time leading passer in college football by the end of his fourth year in 1983—Ben Bennett!

You talk about the right place at the right time! It's scary! Another divine appointment.

And if Jerri didn't say, "Do you have a job?" I might have still been sitting around there waiting for Bill Curry to call me back.

During that time someone had given me *Leadership Secrets of Attila the Hun,* and I read about how important it is for a leader to want to be in charge. And I certainly fit that profile, because I truly thought I was ready to become a Head Ball Coach.

Chapter 10

BECOMING THE HBC IN THE USFL

With Bandits player personnel director Bugsy Engelberg at a press
conference as I assumed my first Head Ball Coach job.

A guy named Bugsy Engelberg had been contacting me during my last
season at Duke. One day he called to say the Tampa Bay Bandits
managing general partner John F. Bassett wanted me to become the offensive coordinator for the team.

I wasn't unhappy at Duke or a pushy type guy trying to promote himself. However, I was beginning to gain confidence as an offensive coordi-

nator. Now that coaching was my full-time profession at age thirty-seven, I was hopeful that it was time for me to move on and move up.

I had heard through friends like Tom McEwen of the *Tampa Tribune* about the Tampa Bay Bandits of the new upstart United States Football League, scheduled to play in springtime—a league conceived in 1965 by New Orleans businessman David Dixon. The Bandits were looking for a coach and would field a team in just a few months.

Bassett was a media czar and advertising/marketing expert who started out working at his family-owned *Toronto Telegram* newspaper. He was also a sportsman who played for the Canadian Davis Cup tennis team. Later, his daughter Carling would become an international tennis star.

John was no stranger to football, having played a little in college, and his father once owned the Toronto Argonauts of the Canadian Football League. He was one of the founders of the World Football League, which began play in 1974, and was awarded the Toronto franchise, which he named the Northmen.

Before they even played a down, the Canadian Parliament threw the WFL out of Canada and Bassett moved the franchise to Memphis and renamed them the Southmen.

Bassett soon made a splash by signing three members of the Super Bowl champion Miami Dolphins—Larry Csonka, Jim Kiick, and Paul Warfield. At the time it was the biggest sports contract ever, a combined $3.5 million deal. The league folded halfway through the 1975 season and the trio of Dolphins returned to the NFL in 1976.

Bassett's original idea was to make John Rauch the Bandits head coach. Rauch, former head coach of the Oakland Raiders and Buffalo Bills, had been an offensive assistant with the Bucs while I was playing for them. Meanwhile, Bassett hired Engelberg, who had coached with him for the Raiders, Bills, and Toronto Argonauts.

Bugsy was one of the USFL's most colorful characters, a real talker who hailed from Waycross, Georgia. He'd been a student trainer at FSU under Bill Peterson, developed into a kicking coach, and was later hired as a special teams coach at age twenty-one—one of the youngest coaches in NFL history.

Bugsy called everybody Bubba. He had phoned me in mid-season and said, "Bubba, we want you to come down here and be offensive coordinator. We've got John Rauch ready to be the head coach. He and John Bassett think you could do a good job as offensive coordinator."

That's when I started to think about what Attila the Hun said: You must want to be in charge.

I said to Bugsy, "Bubba, do you know I'm already an offensive coordinator? My next step is going to be called head coach. So if Mr. Bassett is interested in me being head coach, then tell him I'd be interested in talking to him. But I'm not going to go down there as offensive coordinator."

Bugsy said, "Really?"

I said, "Yep."

Later, he called back and said, "He'll interview you for head coach."

So John Bassett visited me in Durham in the fall of 1982 for a face-to-face interview. Don Disney and Maston O'Neal, two minority owners, came with him. After dinner I suggested we go by my house so he could meet Jerri and my family. When we arrived, my dog came out barking.

John asked, "What's your dog's name?"

"Bandit," I replied.

He looked at me in disbelief and replied, "Nahhhh! Did you name him that just for today?"

I assured him I had not. In fact, Bandit was our family pet for many years. Maybe it was just meant to be. We all hit it off and agreed to a deal. I told him let's wait until after Duke's last game was over to announce it.

I was on my way to becoming a Head Ball Coach for the first time on November 21, 1982. Rauch was named director of scouting and offensive backfield coach. I accepted an offer in principle with the Bandits and then attended a press conference in Tampa without knowing my salary.

Everything seemed to be fitting together perfectly in Tampa.

When it came time for me to talk money, Bugsy said, "Bubba, Mr. Bassett wants to pay you fifty thousand dollars a year." Now, I was making thirty-three thousand dollars as an assistant at Duke. So I said, "Bubba, wouldn't that be an embarrassment to the team if they knew I was making far less than everybody else? Wouldn't that make the franchise look a little cheap?"

"Well, Bubba, we want to start you low and let you work your way up," Bugsy replied.

And I said, "That's what I want to do, too. But that low?" I thought they would offer me about $75,000. Some of those other coaches were making a lot more. George Allen came into the USFL the next year and was paid around $125,000. So we settled on $60,000. But by the time I got to my second year I was up to $125,000.

We were going back to Florida, where we had lots of friends. This was a wonderful new challenge to create my own system as a head coach. Although Tampa was a place where our last experience, with the Bucs, had been tough on Jerri and the family, this time there was a fresh new attitude and we were all happy to be back. The whole concept of the USFL was to have fun and win—which seemed well suited to my style and approach.

Meanwhile, it just so happened that the Tampa Bay Bucs, my old team, had hit a rough patch and were about to slide into a fifteen-year losing streak. From 1983 to 1985 they went 10-38. With no major league baseball team yet in the area and the NFL reeling due to the strike, it was a good time to launch a new league and new team with a fresh marketing strategy.

Jim McVay, then the director of marketing for the Bandits and later CEO and president of the Outback Bowl, came up with some fun and unusual promotions—everything from giving away new cars, to burning mortgages, to awarding some lucky fan a million-dollar deferred annuity. Sometimes things got a little out of hand, like the time seven new Dodges were driven on the field to give away and one of the drivers turned thief, driving off, never to be seen again. The joke was he stole a car in front of fifty thousand witnesses and was never caught.

The Bandits celebrated scores with a black stallion emerging from the stands and galloping down the field, ridden by a pistol-packing masked man. We called the horse "Smokey"—as in *Smokey and the Bandit*, a series of movies starring Burt Reynolds, one of our minority owners. The first "Bandit" movie, by the way, was only behind *Star Wars* as the highest-grossing film of 1977, and Reynolds was one of the biggest movie stars in the world at that time. Burt had played some college football at Florida State and was a teammate of Lee Corso.

The USFL made big headlines by signing star quarterbacks Jim Kelly to the Houston Gamblers and Steve Young to the Los Angeles Express. The biggest bombshell was the signing of Heisman Trophy winner Herschel Walker by the New Jersey Generals, who also would have Donald Trump as an owner (although Trump was not the one who signed him). Former Bucs quarterback Doug Williams went to the Oklahoma Outlaws. Some future NFL All-Pro linemen got their starts in the USFL, such as defensive tackle/end Reggie White of the Memphis Showboats and offensive lineman Gary Zimmerman of the Express.

In 1983, at age thirty-seven, I was suddenly a Head Ball Coach of a pro team and was coaching in a league that was supposedly "coach-driven," with people like George Allen, Jim Mora, Lee Corso, John Ralston, Chuck Fairbanks, Jack Pardee, Pepper Rodgers, Marv Levy, Lindy Infante, Mouse Davis, and Craig Morton. During that period, there were three other thirty-seven-year-old head coaches—Les Steckel of the NFL's Minnesota Vikings, Jim Bates of the San Antonio Gunslingers, and Joe Pendry of the Pittsburgh Maulers. None lasted more than one year as head coach.

All the pro football experts picked us to be at the bottom of the league. Of course! I was a college assistant coming in as head coach. We also had the lowest payroll and lowest-paid coaching staff by far in the USFL.

The Tampa Bay Bandits—energetic, brash, and exciting—adopted the

All decked out for a London trip
with the Bandits, 1984.

slogan "All the Fun the Law Allows." The media nicknamed our offense "Bandit Ball." Country music star Jerry Reed even wrote and sang a song called "Bandit Ball."

We were introduced to the public on March 6, 1983, and drew 42,437 for our opening home game. I made up my mind to pull out all the stops. We started with a no-huddle offense against Boston. With "Bandit Ball" in Tampa Bay, we showed them how to have fun and win. We started out like a house afire that first season, winning four straight to lead the USFL. That sent a message to the fans that we were going to go wide-open, full-throttle. "Bandit Ball" was the antidote to what critics in those days called the NFL—"The No Fun League."

We wound up with some very good players, including former Florida Gator quarterback John Reaves, who set the all-time USFL record for passing completions, with 766, and during the 1985 season threw for 4,193 yards and twenty-five touchdowns.

That first year, Reaves and Jimmy Jordan of Florida State split time at quarterback as John was injured. We had some excellent receivers in Danny Buggs from West Virginia and Eric Truvillion from Florida A&M. They both had 1,000-yard seasons receiving. Buggs was No. 2 in the league with seventy-six catches for 1,146 yards, and Truvillion caught sixty-six passes for 1,080 yards. On defense, tackle Fred Nordgren posted fifteen sacks, second best in the USFL. But we ran out of gas, losing three of our last four games to finish 11-7.

We were winning and having fun, so naturally people kept telling Bassett what a genius he was. He loved every minute of it. Bugsy said, "Steve, you don't realize—this is the first time he's ever won with a team. He had the Memphis Southmen. All of a sudden he's a winner. You don't know how happy he is!"

I said, "I understand now."

Our best year was 1984 when we went 14-4, one of those four losses being to Coach Pepper and the Memphis Showboats. But we were ready for them the next time we played, two weeks later. Right before the game against the Showboats, I told the guys, "If we don't win the toss, we're going to open up with an onside kick. If we don't get it, don't worry about it. Defense, just go in there and stop 'em. We'll be fine."

My son Steve Jr. was the ball boy then and he worked both sidelines. On the Memphis sideline, Steve Jr. ran into the Showboats quarterback, Mike Kelley, our quarterback at Georgia Tech. Stevie went over to speak to Mike and said, "Mike, you need to watch this opening kickoff."

Mike said, "Why? Y'all aren't going to onside kick it, are you?"

Stevie said: "I'm not saying. I'm not going to tell you that."

So Mike told Coach Pepper, "Stevie says they might onside kick it."

Coach Pepper said, "Really?" and the on-side kick occurred. And Pepper didn't adjust or react in any way.

We onside kicked, got it, and scored. We kicked off the second time, but they managed to run only three plays and punted. We scored another touchdown to go up 14–0. Then I called another onside kick. We got the ball again and scored another touchdown. We were up 21–0 and Memphis had had the ball for three plays. We beat the Memphis Showboats 42–24 that night.

Coach Pepper later claimed, "Stevie told us and we were expecting an onside kick." If he did, then Pepper must not have believed him.

During our 14-4 season in 1984, we were the second-most-prolific USFL offense. Gary Anderson was an outstanding all-purpose back. He and fellow 1,000-yard rusher Greg Boone of Duke, along with Reaves, helped us become the first team in football to have two 1,000-yard rushers and a quarterback throw for 4,000 yards in the same season. Anderson rolled up 1,008 yards and nineteen touchdowns, plus sixty-six receptions for 682 yards. Reaves threw for 4,092 yards and twenty-eight scores that year and Truvillion had seventy receptions for 1,044 yards. Tight end Marvin Harvey had almost a thousand yards receiving. Wide receiver Willie Gillespie was also a major contributor. But we lost in the first round of the playoffs to the Birmingham Stallions, 36–17.

Then, in 1985, I ran into my first major disciplinary problem as a Head Ball Coach, causing me to reflect back on one of the teachings of John

Jerri and me with one of our best Bandit players, Gary Anderson, 1984.

Wooden, which was number 17 on my "Guidelines for a Good Player-Coach Relationship": Be willing to suspend or remove a star player if he's disruptive to the team.

Eric Truvillion had made the team after trying out and developed into one of our best receivers. But he also developed an attitude, moping around because apparently he thought he deserved to be in the NFL. And that became a real problem. He did stuff like rolling instead of flipping the ball back to the official or the ball boy; or he would stand outside the huddle and not get in it; or he had a snarl on his face if something didn't go his way.

I brought him in, showed him my list of "Guidelines for a Good Player-Coach Relationship," and said, "Eric, do you see that number seventeen on the board right there? You're being disruptive right now and I'm going to kick you off the team if it continues. You understand? You do what everybody else does! You can go to the NFL when this is over—nobody's going to stop you from doing that. But you're not going to be disruptive."

Sure enough, Truvillion started pouting, kicking the ball around. I brought him in again and said, "You're finished." And he said, "No, Coach, I'll change." And I said, "You've had your chance." He was disruptive and I had to remove him from the team.

In 1993, at a ten-year reunion of the Bandits, we had a nice chat and he apologized. I said, "Okay, I'll accept it, but you know I had to remove you." He said, "Yeah, I know that."

The good news was that the Bandits probably had more longevity and financial stability than any USFL team. As it turned out, we were the only franchise that had the same coach and the same owner and stayed in the same city for the three seasons of the USFL's existence. In three seasons, the Bandits averaged 43,758 in attendance per game.

In what turned out to be our final year, 1985, we got the news that the cancer of owner John Bassett had returned and it was terminal. We were inspired to win it for John. Anderson continued to blossom with 1,207 yards and sixteen touchdowns, plus he was our leading receiver with seventy-two catches. Reaves threw for 4,193 yards and twenty-five TDs. Wide receiver Larry Brodsky caught sixty-nine passes for 1,071 yards and Spencer Jackson made important receptions. We fell short in the playoffs again, however, losing to the Oakland Invaders 30–27, after a 10-8 season.

Only one of our players made the all-time USFL team—offensive guard Nate Newton, who later went on to play for three Dallas Cowboy Super Bowl championship teams and made six Pro Bowls. Anderson, who ran for over a thousand yards twice, was fourth best all-time among rushers and named second team all-time USFL.

During the 1984 season, some USFL owners began talking among themselves about challenging the NFL head-to-head in the fall. Despite the recommendation of a consulting firm to remain a spring league, the USFL owners, on October 18, 1984, voted 12–2 to become a fall league in 1986, hoping to win an antitrust lawsuit against the NFL and leverage a new lucrative network deal. Bassett was one of two no votes and wanted to form a new spring league.

After the 1985 season, Bassett had to sell the team due to his failing health. Minority owner Lee Scarfone agreed to take over the franchise and keep the Bandits in the new USFL with Arizona, Baltimore, Birmingham, Jacksonville, Memphis, New Jersey, and Orlando, as a newly reorganized Tampa Bay team. John Bassett died in May 1986. We were scheduled to play an eighteen-game schedule that fall. But we never made it back to the field. A month before the season began the league folded. Soon after that, despite winning the antitrust suit, a nominal fee of $1 was awarded; it was tripled under antitrust law to $3. A check to the USFL for $3.76 (the 76 cents was for interest) was never cashed.

Among the league's game-changing legacies were the NFL's eventual adoption of the two-point conversion and the right of the head coach to challenge officials' rulings on the field with the use of instant replay.

I was out of football for the season of 1986. It was time for me to go job shopping again.

Meanwhile, former Alabama quarterback Steve Sloan from Cleveland, Tennessee, resigned after four seasons at Duke. He became athletic director at Alabama, his alma mater, in 1986. Despite some success at Vanderbilt and Texas Tech, he wasn't able to turn the program around at Duke, where he won just thirteen games in four seasons.

That meant there was a Head Ball Coach job in Durham.

TAMPA BAY BANDITS
1983–1885
Overall Regular Season Record: 35-19 (.648)

Annual Record and Average Home
Attendance of the Bandits
1983: 11-7 (39,896)
1984: 14-4 (46,158)
1985: 10-8 (45,220)

USFL Franchises
Arizona Outlaws (1985; result of Arizona/Oklahoma
  merger)
Arizona Wranglers (1983, 1984; Arizona and Chicago
  traded players)
Birmingham Stallions (1983–1985)
Boston Breakers (1983)
New Orleans Breakers (1984; moved from Boston)
Portland Breakers (1985; moved from New Orleans)
Chicago Blitz (1983, 1984; Arizona and Chicago traded
  players)
Denver Gold (1983–1985)

Houston Gamblers (1984–1985)

Jacksonville Bulls (1984–1985)

Los Angeles Express (1983–1985)

Memphis Showboats (1984–1985)

Michigan Panthers (1983–1984; merged with Oakland for 1985 season)

New Jersey Generals (1983–1985)

Oakland Invaders (1983–1985; merged with Michigan for 1985 season)

Oklahoma Outlaws (1984)

Philadelphia Stars (1983–1984)

Baltimore Stars (1985; moved from Philadelphia)

Pittsburgh Maulers (1984)

San Antonio Gunslingers (1984–1985)

Tampa Bay Bandits (1983–1985)

Washington Federals (1983–1984)

Orlando Renegades (1985; moved from Washington)

Chapter 11

THE RETURN TO DURHAM

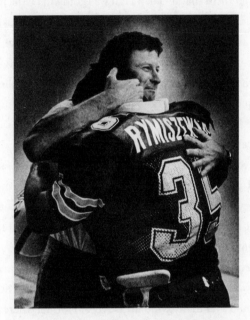

A big hug for John Rymiszewski after Duke's big win
over North Carolina, 35–29, in 1988.

With the USFL folding, while I was awaiting the outcome of the legal battle in 1986, I wound up interviewing or inquiring about four jobs. I had saved a little money, but it would have to last as I went job shopping again. Mr. Scarfone paid me from June 1985 to December 31, 1985.

I thought I'd have a good shot at a major college if the right position opened up. Basically, I wanted about any decent one I could get. Florida, at the time, was not an option.

While I was with the Bandits in 1984, two representatives from the University of Florida, AD Bill Carr and his associate AD, Richard Giannini, had visited me in Tampa. They said there was going to be a change and that I was about to be part of a "national search" after Charley Pell was fired. I told them that if Galen Hall was going to be the interim, then he would wind up being the head coach because Florida was loaded with good players and he would win there. Which is exactly what happened.

The Tampa Bay Bucs had fired Leeman Bennett, so I figured owner Hugh Culverhouse was in the market for a new coach. I called my friend Tom McEwen of the *Tampa Tribune* and asked him if he thought I had a shot with the Bucs. McEwen gave me the phone number of Mr. Culverhouse and I called him.

"Well, Steve, I appreciate you calling," the Bucs owner said. "But I've already hired a guy and I'm going to be announcing it in a day or so."

I was interviewed at Mississippi State and California but neither job was offered. I must admit that Jerri and I weren't really all that fired up about either job, so maybe I didn't interview well.

I also interviewed at LSU—one of the premier jobs in America and one that I really wanted. Coach Bill Arnsparger was stepping down as head coach and would eventually wind up as AD at Florida, where he would be among those interviewing me as coach for the Gators three years later.

I flew into Baton Rouge, talked to the committee, and felt I had a good shot at the LSU job. But I was never invited back for a second interview. Instead they chose Mike Archer, a former player and assistant coach at Miami, to replace Bill Arnsparger as head coach. Archer was Arnsparger's defensive coordinator in 1985 and 1986, and, it turned out, his hand-picked successor.

Alabama head coach/AD Ray Perkins turned out to be the new Bucs coach. He was replaced in Tuscaloosa by Coach Bill Curry, and since Steve Sloan was hired as AD at Alabama, the head job was open in Durham. In early January I was invited to Duke and interviewed by Tom Butters, who told people he had previously recommended me to several schools, including Stanford. Mr. Butters basically made an offer in principle but he said, "I want you to go home and talk to Jerri before you accept." I told him I'd call him back that night.

In the meantime, Coach Ray Graves had set up a meeting in Atlanta through Taylor Smith, son of Atlanta Falcons owner Rankin Smith. The Falcons were about to hire a coach. On my way back from Durham to Tampa, the Smiths met me at the Atlanta airport in one of those Delta Sky Club rooms. The first thing Taylor said was, "We want you to know we've already hired a coach."

I said, "Well, what are we doing here, then?"

He said, "We're just doing Coach Graves a favor to talk to you. We think we've got a real good one that everybody knows about. He's proven."

I said, "Thanks for coming. But I really didn't need a courtesy interview."

The Smiths thought they were getting Coach Dan Reeves, who was between Super Bowl seasons with the Denver Broncos. But something happened so they wound up hiring Coach Marion Campbell, a good guy but not their first choice.

I was most likely going to take the job at Duke, anyway, but I didn't want to miss any of those other opportunities that might come my way. I eagerly looked forward to getting back to college coaching, especially in a place familiar to my family. We all loved the people at Duke.

So off to North Carolina we went. It was a big recruiting weekend in Durham. We had the press conference, but still we had to work out the salaries for the coaching staff. Tom said, "Come by on Monday morning and I'll tell you what everybody is making." So the first two head-coaching jobs I got, I did not know my salary until after the press conference. I tell people that because of the coaches who make the mistake of demanding big money when they haven't had much of a track record. They should know that turns off owners and athletic directors.

Come Monday morning, Mr. Butters said, "The last coach made seventy-four thousand five hundred dollars. I'm going to bump you up all the way to seventy-five thousand dollars even. Five hundred more than the last guy."

I said, "That's fine. How much are my assistants making?"

The low man was about $24,000 and the high made about $35,000.

So we got all the numbers straight. And the deal was done very simply and quickly.

As I went through my coaching career, what really intrigued me and fired me up was to coach somewhere that offered me a chance to achieve breakthroughs—accomplish things at a place for the first time—or restore a winning tradition. Duke was a place where I could reach those goals. It was also a place where winning had become a huge challenge, which is exactly why I got the job.

When I first got into coaching, in the back of my mind I thought it would be wonderful to be the head coach at a medium-sized college and make $100,000 to $200,000 someday—enough to provide for my family. Maybe Duke could become that place.

Being out of football for a season, I realized how much I had missed it. I was ready and eager to get to work. I was reminded that coaching could be challenging and rewarding and I thoroughly loved doing it, which meant I had the right job at the right time in the right place. Returning to college football as a Head Ball Coach at forty-one was a wonderful opportunity.

Life was good for the Spurriers back in those days. With a 90 percent graduation rate, we didn't have to worry about kids at Duke flunking out. Our student athletes rarely got into trouble. There were no athletic dorms, and the players ate in the same cafeteria as the students.

In coaching you want to see your guys play well. You want to prepare them as best you can, teach them to play well and see the team win—help the players become successful in life.

By the time we kicked off against Colgate on September 5, 1987, it had been a long time between coaching games—the last one on June 30, 1985.

The first team I had at Duke in 1987 was maybe just as good as any of them. We could have had an excellent record, but we just couldn't finish games. We lost some really close ones—five of the six by seven points or less. You're talking about losing 47–45 to NC State, 30–27 at Wake Forest, 23–22 at Maryland, 17–10 at Clemson, and 7–0 at Rutgers.

Something always happened. It took a little while to get the program going, but we could see that our players were developing a fresh new attitude, even while we were struggling my first year. We'd just lost to North Carolina State and were playing the Tar Heels, whom we hadn't beaten in five years—1982, my last year as a Duke assistant.

It was time for us to get fired up. Gene Ellenson had been an outstanding leader and defensive coordinator at Florida. He left the field when Coach Graves resigned after ten seasons to become AD and became the executive director of Gators Boosters Inc., a fund-raising group for the school. He was a brilliant motivator who spoke to our team before the 1987 game and our 1988 game against NC State.

The night before that North Carolina game in 1987, Coach Ellenson came up to Durham and told the story of Horatius at the bridge, one of my favorites, written about a mythical Roman warrior from the late sixth century B.C.

As the story goes, Vandals from a neighboring state had come to conquer Rome. The Vandals were on the other side of the Tiber River, urging the Romans to "give up your wives and all your possessions—we're taking over Rome." There was a bridge over the Tiber between Rome and the invaders, and Horatius defended it with vigor.

The brave young Roman soldier was willing to die for Rome, so he stepped forward and basically said, "I'll fight those guys! I'm not afraid of them!" The leader of the Vandals told his best soldiers, "Go down there and kill that guy and we'll take Rome."

Horatius killed the first Vandal and their leader sent two more, saying: "Go down there and kill that guy and let's take Rome." But they couldn't kill Horatius, who was jabbing, ducking, fighting . . . and he killed the next two Vandals as his fellow soldiers watched in amazement. And they said, "We can't let Horatius die like this! Let's go help him!" The invaders were beaten back; the bridge was destroyed. Rome was saved.

The moral of the story, in football terms, is that one player can make a difference by displaying courage and guts, and the rest of the team could get behind him. Coach Ellenson had the players fascinated. He asked each one to sign the chalkboard underneath the oath "I will play my best for my team, teammates and school."

We took that board with us to Chapel Hill, where we played really well, especially on defense, and beat the Tar Heels 25–10. It was a terrific way for our guys to end a 5-6 season and gave us something to build on.

Part of Coach Ellenson's agreement for after the speech was that he promised to "dance a little jig in the locker room after we beat these guys." The players started saying, "Coach, when are you going to dance?" So he did his little dance for a happy bunch of Dukees.

Steve Slayden, my first quarterback as a head coach, had an excellent senior season with twenty touchdowns and 2,924 yards, capping off a four-year career. In addition to the record six-touchdown pass game against Tech in 1987, he threw for over 8,000 yards and forty-eight touchdowns in that span from 1984 to 1987.

When we laid an egg at Rutgers I benched him. The next week in a loss to Clemson I put him back in and Steve enjoyed the four best games of his college career, winding up as the MVP of our team. Later on Steve Slayden would always remember the day I started as coach at the University of Florida because I visited his parents at Shands Hospital that day right after Steve's brain surgery by Dr. Art Day, from which he would recover completely.

Once again, Mr. Butters and I talked salary at the end of the season.

I figured I'd make $75,000 again in 1988. He said, "You did pretty good—you guys were competitive in every game but one."

I said, "I know, but we didn't have a winning season. We went five and six."

Mr. Butters shook his head and said, "No, I'm going to give you a ten percent raise." So my salary went up to $82,500.

We came back in 1988 and won seven games—the most of any Duke team since Coach Bill Murray's 1962 squad that went 8-2. It had been a long time since Duke was a factor in championships and bowl games. After the Atlantic Coast Conference was formed in 1954, the Blue Devils became a powerhouse, winning or tying for the ACC title six times under Coach Murray, who had led Duke to its last bowl appearance and last ACC title, shared or outright. So we were chasing a little bit of Duke history.

Oddly enough, the 1962 ACC Champion Duke team turned down a bowl game and the Gators benefited from it. After being invited to the Gator Bowl to play Penn State, the Duke players went to Coach Murray and said, "Coach, are we going to clobber each other for the three weeks? If so then we don't want to go." Coach Murray said, "I'll tell you what, we'll just turn down the bowl and we won't go! How about that?" And that's how Florida got in and beat Penn State 17-7 in a December game that got me intrigued enough to find out more about the Gators. I'd had no contact from Florida to play for the Gators at that point, but after watching the Gator Bowl game, I said, "Man, those guys got some fire and energy!"

We began the 1988 season with two road wins—31–21 at Northwestern and 31–26 at Tennessee—and soon found ourselves 5-0. But we went into a slide and lost three of our next four, before tying NC State 43–43, during which a bad call by an official cost our team a bid to the Peach Bowl.

On fourth down and 10 with under a minute to play, we were playing a two-deep underneath man coverage. Our guy pushed somebody a little from the side at the line of scrimmage and all the players ran downfield. NC State lobbed the ball up and we intercepted to end the game. But an official said our guy pushed their guy in the back. NC State was allowed to keep possession of the football and kicked the tying field goal as time expired. That call by that official robbed us of an invitation to play in Duke's first bowl game since the 1961 Cotton Bowl, when Duke beat Arkansas 7–6 in front of 70,500 spectators.

Before our game against the Wolfpack, the Peach Bowl committee had told me they were going to take the winner of Duke–NC State.

Back then there was no sudden death, and with the tie the bid went to NC State. So that call and the subsequent tie were devastating.

I'd never seen that call before and I've never seen it since.

So I blasted the official and said somebody ought to investigate him for such a terrible call. I remember saying after the game that it was "the worst call in the history of Duke football." And it's still the worst call I've ever had, although I think most officials do an excellent job these days.

Well, the ACC didn't like it and Commissioner Gene Corrigan drove from Greensboro to Durham to suspend me for the game against North Carolina the following week. They told me the rules for a suspended coach were that I could talk to the team before the game and at halftime. No live wires or headsets were allowed. The game was on TV in my office and I could see a little on the field.

We won 35–29 with a winning drive in the final minute to finish a very respectable 7-3-1. But because of that call, Duke did not receive a bowl invitation for the twenty-seventh season in a row. Some of our players had excellent years. Among them was quarterback Anthony Dilweg, who passed for twenty-four touchdowns and 3,824 yards.

So I guess I was the first coach to win a "suspended coach" game.

Despite all that, we were 11-9-1 after two seasons and headed in the right direction toward what we felt would be a big year in 1989 and a chance to possibly have a winning season and a bowl game for the first time in twenty-nine years.

Prior to the '89 season, Mr. Butters offered me another 10 percent raise, this time up to around $92,000. That's when I went in and said,

"You know, Mack Brown at North Carolina is making two hundred fifty thousand dollars. Don't you think I ought to be making sort of close to him? We've beaten North Carolina twice."

He said, "They've got more money that we do. They're a state school."

And I said, "In other words, if I want to make as much money as Mack Brown, I need to get away from Duke? Is that what you're saying?"

"Oh, nah, I'm not saying that. Come back tomorrow and I'll see what I can do," he said.

I came back the next day. He said, "I've got you a thirty-thousand-dollar bonus for this coming year. You're going to make one hundred twenty thousand dollars, plus your TV show. And all you've got to do is agree not to leave after this coming season."

I said, "In other words, it's like a two-year deal and I can't leave?"

He said, "That's right."

I said, "I don't need thirty thousand dollars that badly. I'll be a free-agent coach next year."

I just figured it was time. If you give up all power to negotiate, you never know what's going to happen.

We returned some really good players for the 1989 season. Along with our coaches, those players sensed something special about this team.

That summer, I had read an article about goal-setting and I kept hearing that it was good to put them down on paper. So I decided we should do it for my first time as a head coach. This was a major breakthrough for me as a coach, as setting goals would lead to winning eight division titles, eight conference championships, and a national title over the next thirteen years.

AT DUKE THAT YEAR we assembled our thirty seniors and captain. I said, "Let's set our goals for the season. This is our team, you guys are the senior leaders. So I want you to put things on paper that we realistically can achieve. And we're going to write them down. And we'll see how we did at the end of the year. Don't say national champs or something like that. Just what we believe we can accomplish."

They started out with: "We won seven last year, so let's put 'Win Seven' on there."

I said, "How about eight? Y'all think we can win eight?"

"Yeah, yeah, eight!" they said.

I said, "Okay, that's enough, we're not going to put down nine. If we go eight and three that will be a wonderful year."

Someone said, "Top twenty?" And they said, "Yeah, we got a team that can do that!"

They kept throwing out stuff. One player said, "Win all of our home games?" I said, "You realize we got Clemson, Georgia Tech, NC State . . ."

Somebody shot back: "Yeah, Coach, but we're good at home."

Another goal was go to a bowl—we hadn't been to one at Duke in twenty-eight years.

Then one of our captains, Bubba Metts, said: "Coach, we've been talking. We think we can win the ACC championship."

And I said, "Come on, Bubba—do you guys believe that is realistic?" If that word got out to the fans and opponents, we would look foolish. But Bubba insisted, "Nah, Coach, we've got all of those teams at home and we think we can win. So we want to put that on the books." I said, "Okay, we can put it on there, but let's keep this within our team."

We all agreed that would be a goal.

Despite our strong motivation, we had a rocky start, losing to South Carolina, Tennessee, and Virginia on the road to begin 1-3. So we were upside down right away, with Clemson coming up next.

The week before, Virginia had beaten us, 49–28, and we never forced a punt. Clemson was 4-0 and No. 7 in the nation. We were about nineteen-point underdogs. I told the media, "Our chances of beating Clemson are about a million to one." After I was quoted as saying that, Coach Danny Ford of Clemson responded that if Duke felt that way, "Why are they bothering to play the game?"

What I didn't tell the media, of course, was that we changed our entire defense; went to using eight- and nine-man fronts.

I got with our co–defensive coordinators Jim Collins and Bob Sanders, and told them to "blitz, blitz, blitz."

I said, "Fellas, if they make an eighty-yard touchdown run then that's okay. But if we can stop 'em and force some punts we've got a chance to win."

Our leading tackler, Erwin Sampson, was the strong safety but basically became an extra linebacker. If we could stop Clemson, I felt we could do some things on offense because we had a big, strong offensive line and the best wide receiver in the ACC in Clarkston Hines.

Meanwhile, as the week rocked along, a big Gator booster, Frank Campisi of Tampa, called me and said: "Coach, they're going to fire Galen Hall after the LSU game this week. Us Gators in the know found out. We want them to hire you, but we can't hire you if you go three and eight, four and seven, or something like that. Is there any way you can have a winning record or maybe five and six or something like that?"

I always liked Galen—played some golf with him—and didn't wish him any bad luck. Besides, I was focused on the task at hand. I said, "Frank, I'm worried about my team I've got right here."

The Gators had won four straight games and Emmitt Smith was on his way to rushing and receiving for a combined total of 1,883 yards in 1989 when the NCAA came out with more charges against the Florida program. As Campisi said, interim president Dr. Bob Bryan forced Coach Hall to resign and the reins were turned over to his assistant, Gary Darnell. Ultimately, Florida was hit with a two-year probation that would eliminate any possibility of playing in a bowl until after the 1990 season.

My only thoughts were on our Duke team and trying to beat Clemson. This game was so crucial. We were either going to be 1-4 or 2-3. We were finally going to get to play Clemson on our home field. Talk about the emotion!

The first two years I was there, Tom Butters had sold the game to Clemson and it was moved to Memorial Stadium. And the year before I got there Duke had also traveled to Clemson. I asked him, "Why are you doing that?" He said, "Because we make a hundred and ten thousand more dollars playing there than we do here. And we're not going to beat them, anyway."

I said, "Doesn't that send a terrible message to the football team, that our AD doesn't believe we have a chance to beat Clemson?"

He said, "We didn't have a chance before, but now that you're here, we'll play them here."

Coach Danny Ford admitted playing in our Wallace Wade Stadium for the first time in four years was going to be something totally foreign to his Clemson team. "This is going to be a new experience because none of these guys have ever been up there to Durham," he said. "It's going to be weird. That place is small. It's not loud. Strange environment."

The night before, the team went to see the movie *In Country*, starring Bruce Willis. It was about a girl whose father was killed in Vietnam. It was her goal to find out who he was. At the end of the movie they were at the Vietnam Veterans Memorial in Washington, D.C., with the names of American servicemen who died or went missing in Vietnam.

As I watched that movie I realized how blessed I was that I never was drafted or had to go to the Army. Jerri and I got married in college and had three children between 1967 and 1971. Young fathers or expectant fathers were exempt from the draft. I honor and deeply appreciate those brave veterans who served our country—especially those who made such a huge sacrifice so that we could all remain free. I will always be grateful for their courage and commitment. So thanks to them, guys like me never had to worry about being drafted or getting shot up and having our legs blown off. But my heart goes out to those wounded warriors who did. I sort of had an emotional moment while watching that movie, something that a coach maybe does every three or four years, and the players sensed that it was real and natural. It just happened. That night I told the guys how thankful I was and how blessed I was.

"And here's what we want to do tomorrow, fellas," I said. "It's supposed to rain a little bit. Good for us! Because Clemson's team speed will be about like ours. So we'll have a good little rainy day. All I'm asking you to do is do your best."

We had a grease board and marker. So I said to the players, "Sign the board here that you will play as hard as you can, the best you can. Okay? But don't make a liar of yourself. If you're not going to play hard and fast and do the best you can . . ."

They all signed the board.

We came to the ballpark and kicked off, but nothing good was happening early. We were behind 14–0 at the half, but when we assembled in the locker room, no one panicked, no one said anything negative. I said, "You guys are playing hard. You're playing well. Come on! Something good's going to happen real soon! Let's keep giving it all we got."

At the start of the third quarter, we threw a swing pass down the sideline and our tailback Roger Boone, brother of former Blue Devil Greg Boone, got the wind knocked out of him. So backup Randy Cuthbert wound up rushing for almost seventy-five yards in the second half. Randy would turn out to be a key performer in the future as well and one of the key factors to us winning the ACC.

Then our starting outside linebacker, Randy Sally, the brother of the quarterback who had played for us, got his shoulder bonked out again. We put in redshirt freshman Derrick Jackson without knowing how good a player he really was. They couldn't block him! He was fantastic! He was all over the place, making thirteen tackles.

It was still 14–0 when we got the ball at about our thirty-yard line in the third quarter. We took a sack. Got a penalty. It was third and thirty. In those days, when it was third and thirty, I'd say, "Well, we gotta throw the ball thirty yards and see what happens." We sent in a play where we wanted four receivers to run vertical routes downfield. The week before, we had the outside guys running comeback routes on the same play, but we made a coaching mistake and didn't change it. The player on the left ran a comeback route. So our quarterback dropped back and threw it.

Clemson had a cornerback named Dexter Davis, who intercepted it about fifty yards down field. Davis ran to midfield, reversed his field and dropped the ball, and, lo and behold, our alert wide receiver Darryl Clements recovered it. I can still see him diving on the ball.

It was our ball on their 25 and we advanced it to the 5. Cuthbert ran off tackle and it looked like they had stopped him, but behind Chris Port, Bud Zuberer, Brett Tulacro, Bubba Metts, Chip Nitowski, and Pete Petroff, he carried about three guys with him in a scrum. A whole wad of players went over the goal line. When your running back starts running over people, that kind of spirit can be infectious. We probably only had about fifteen thousand of our fans there but they started yelling and screaming. Now we were down only 14–7.

Coach Ford was most likely over there at halftime thinking, *We've got this game in good shape,* and maybe he got a little conservative. We put another drive together and quarterback Billy Ray hit receiver Clarkston Hines on a corner route for a touchdown and it was 14–14 still in the third quarter.

Chris Gardocki, their left-footed kicker, made a fifty-yard field goal, so we trailed 17–14 in the fourth quarter. We drove down to their 8-yard line. On second down we tried a maximum-protection play with the receivers running corner routes. Clemson doubled-covered our outside receivers. Our fullback had nobody to block so he went up the middle and I noticed there wasn't anybody within five to seven yards of him.

So I immediately called a Back Option, where everybody clears out and we throw it to the back, hoping they would mess up again. And they messed up again! Billy Ray hit our fullback Chris Brown and he backed into the end zone. That put Duke up 21–17 with four minutes left.

We knew we had to somehow stop Clemson. Fortunately, they didn't have a strong passing attack and were forced to run. We made two or three shoestring tackles where there was no one behind them if the tackler had missed. With about a minute left, it was fourth and twelve and Clemson used its last time-out.

As a coach, you tell yourself you've got to protect the first-down line. George Edwards, our senior middle linebacker and captain, came over to the sideline during the time-out and I said, "George, what do you think we ought to do? Protect against the first down or what?" He said, "Coach, we've been blitzing every play of the game. Why stop now?" I said, "You're right! Blitz 'em!" We rushed eight guys on fourth and twelve. Hit the quarterback. The ball hit the ground. We were able to take a knee and end it. We beat the No. 7 team in the country, despite throwing five interceptions. But they fumbled two of them back to us. I had never seen that before in my playing or coaching career.

We won, 21–17, as a nineteen-point underdog. It was a huge moment for Duke football. It also ranks as the most impactful win of my football coaching career. If we'd have lost and gone 1-4, I don't know where that season or my coaching career wound have wound up.

The Clemson victory began a seven-game winning streak to close out the regular season. We could see what was coming, but we tried to divert attention away from it and stay focused on the task at hand—as the cliché goes, on that proverbial one game at a time.

At the Tuesday press conference before the game against Wake Forest, one of the sportswriters said: "Coach, do you realize that if you win the last three games you're going to win the ACC?"

I said, "Our team knows where we stand, but right now we're getting ready to play the very best we can against Wake Forest. They're a good team and they beat us the last two years."

Until then, none of the media boys—or girls—had even thought of it.

Of course, every week they asked about it and we kept trying to divert attention away from it.

From being only 1-1 in conference play, we beat ACC opponents Maryland, Georgia Tech, Wake Forest, NC State, and North Carolina—won all our home games. Twenty-eight years after Duke's last ACC championship, we thumped the Tar Heels at Chapel Hill 41–0 to win the conference.

A special moment in Durham as I receive the 1989 ACC championship trophy at a Duke basketball game from Bob Harris, the Voice of the Blue Devils.

We had met all our goals, knocked off Clemson, and even cracked the Associated Press Top 20, finishing up 8-3 and heading for a bowl game. For the first time in nearly three decades Duke won eight games. I was honored to be named ACC Coach of the Year for the second straight year.

Like Bubba Metts had said, we could—and did—win the conference. We were actually co-ACC champs with Virginia at 6-1. They don't use the word "co-champ" and neither do us Dukees.

Randy Cuthbert rushed for more than one thousand yards that season.

Clarkston Hines made All-America and was ACC Player of the Year. Dave Brown set new school and conference marks in the last three games of the season. Billy Ray and Dave Brown passed for more than thirty-five hundred yards and twenty-nine touchdowns, both with more than a 63 percent completion, thanks in part to receivers like Walter Jones and tight end Dave Colonna. We set an ACC record for total offense, with more than five hundred total yards a game.

Right after the win over North Carolina in the last game of the season, I was visited in Durham by Florida interim president Dr. Bryan, AD Bill Arnsparger, and Athletic Board member Dr. Nick Cassisi.

Arnsparger started talking numbers. "Galen made about two hundred twenty-five thousand dollars and I think we can get you up to two hundred fifty thousand or two hundred seventy-five thousand," he said. I said, "We'll talk about all that later." I wasn't going to negotiate with him at that time. "Let's wait until this bowl game is over and we'll talk about all that."

Soon the word got out to the players that I was being courted by Florida. I told them, "I'm going to be with you through the bowl game. Guarantee you that. We're gonna enjoy winning the first ACC championship since 1962."

The night before the All-American Bowl game at Legion Field in Birmingham, I announced to the players and coaches that I was leaving the team for Florida. Looking back now, I realize I should have waited until after the game because we didn't play worth a crap and lost. I'm not going to say that was the reason we lost to Texas Tech 49–21 and dropped out of the final Top 20 rankings, but there is no doubt that on a tight-knit team—after all we had been through together—it had an impact.

I will never forget a moment in that game when I looked out on the field and saw one of our guys not running hard on the kickoff. So naturally I hollered at him to hustle. He turned and looked at me as if to say, "You're not my coach anymore!"

There is never any easy way for a coach to leave on his own. I tried to remember over the next few years that when it came time to change jobs, it's best to make a decision and move on quickly.

Despite that loss in the bowl game, the 1989 season was a memorable conclusion to a three-year run in which our overall record was 20-13-1. We'll always be proud that we were able to prove that, despite what others had suggested, it was, indeed, possible to win at Duke.

Mr. Butters knew the Florida job was not only the one that I wanted and needed, but it was the right thing to do. For them. For me. For everybody. So he didn't try to stand in my way. He probably caught grief from some of the Dukees for not trying to keep me, but he knew a counter-offer would not be the right thing to do.

I will always be grateful for what Duke meant to me during my coaching career and have attempted to show that gratitude and respect any way I could. Later on I even used my 25th-place vote in the Coaches' Top 25 poll for Duke until they asked me to stop. Grant Teaff, the executive director of the American Football Coaches Association, asked me to not do that because it compromised their poll. So I stopped for a while, but when Duke started winning again I put them back in it.

We made lasting relationships at Duke and had some really good times.

Lynn Butters was brokenhearted the day Jerri had to tell her we were leaving. They were such close friends. We were fond of Mary Dinkins, our football secretary who went on to become an Iron Dukes director for the alumni. And I coached many interesting young men, such as Claude Moorman, son of Duke's famous "Lonesome End" Claude "T" Moorman from the 1960 Cotton Bowl champions. Young Claude, or "T" Jr., played guard for us in 1981 and 1982 and is now the director of sports medicine and team doctor at Duke. His daughter, Marianne Moorman, wanted to come to South Carolina in the worst way. She was on a wait list so we were happy when she was finally accepted.

Over the years I stayed in close contact with many former Duke players. The associate AD at Duke then, Joe Alleva, is now the AD at LSU. Sometimes we would talk every two or three weeks. He's a good friend.

Whatever kind of a coach I became it was because of Duke University.

I really think I learned how to coach there. People ask, "Why do you love Duke so much?" I say, "Listen, they hired me twice when I had no job." I'll always be indebted to Duke University, Coach Red Wilson, and especially Athletic Director Tom Butters, who devoted more than twenty years to the job.

We received the sad news in late March of 2016 that Mr. Butters had passed away at age seventy-seven. Jerri and I attended his memorial in Durham. Tom Butters was a big inspiration in my life. I don't know what I would have done without him hiring me twice. He's one of the guys I owe my coaching career to. Good friend—wonderful friend.

Upon the news of his death, Coach Mike Krzyzewski said, "There may not be a person who had a greater positive impact on my career than Tom."

IN DECEMBER 1989, I was invited to Florida president Bob Bryan's house. I flew to Jacksonville in mid-December, rented a car, and drove to Melrose to stay with my lawyer friend Uncle Willie O'Neill in his home on Long Pond to begin working on details for a contract. I already had a list of a few things I felt were fair when I arrived. And Uncle Willie had his list.

"I've done a little survey, checking around with Coach Doug Dickey and what some other guys are making," Uncle Willie said, "and I've got an idea of what we need to ask for."

I said, "I've done the same thing and let me go over with you what I think is a very fair deal."

I think I asked for about $400,000 a year, which at that time was a little high. Then I asked for a $50,000 loan. The deal on the loan was that if we didn't win the SEC in the first five years of my contract, we'd pay it back. I told Uncle Willie, "I've got a mortgage on a condo at the beach. And I haven't sold my house in Tampa."

Uncle Willie said, "They won't do that!" But I asked for it.

I remember President Bryan looking at his lawyer, Tom McDonald, and asking, "Can we do this?" Tom said, "Sure we can!" So they approved the loan. And Florida eventually took the Tampa house off my hands and sold it.

I didn't ask for anything unreasonable. They looked at my whole list and said, "That's fine." And I said, "As soon as our bowl game is over, I'm here and I'm ready for a press conference here the next day, or the day after."

As we were walking out of President Bryan's office, Uncle Willie, using my middle name and what some good friends call me, said, "Orr we didn't ask for enough." I said, "Yes we did, Uncle Willie!"

Both sides were trying to do what was right and fair.

For a change I was actually going to know my salary before the press conference.

At the press conference I said I wanted to do three things:

> Bring back the blue jerseys.
> Replace the artificial turf with real grass.
> Put Miami back on the schedule.

We were able to do two of the three. Well, two and a half. We did have Miami on the schedule for one year.

At the press conference I also told them I had been at Crescent Beach the night before and when I walked out at night to see the ocean, I started reflecting on the words of the University of Florida alma mater:

> *Where palm and pine are blowing*
> *Where Southern seas are flowing . . .*

This remains a fond memory for me, hopefully just like it is for all Gators.

Researching Florida's history, I began to realize the Gators had never been known as consistent winners and didn't have much in the trophy case to brag about. Now, instead of wondering if I could win at Duke, critics were probably beginning to wonder if Steve Spurrier was going to be able to win at Florida.

Chapter 12

THE JOB I NEVER THOUGHT WOULD BE OPEN

The Spurriers on December 31, 1989,
the day I was hired as HBC at Florida.

I'd pretty much given up on ever having the chance to return to my alma mater as Head Ball Coach because I didn't think the job would be open while I was coaching. So having that opportunity was a bit of a wonderful miracle.

I got to Gainesville at just the right time, even with Florida possibly facing NCAA penalties for 107 violations in football and basketball. We realized a punishment was coming down, but weren't sure when or what or how it would impact us. That wasn't our only hurdle: We inherited an 0-9 losing streak against Auburn, Georgia, and FSU, and Florida's history, going all the way back to the 1940s when the "Golden Era" teams went winless in 1946 during a six-year streak of losing seasons, wasn't much to brag about.

Despite all that, we felt we could reach our goal of winning the SEC championship. Our motivational talks began that spring to dispel the notion that Florida couldn't win championships.

On the flip side, the 1989 Gator defense, ranked No. 3 in the nation, returned eight starters.

Amazingly, when I got back to Gainesville twelve years after leaving as an assistant, Florida had a losing SEC record (148-166-15) and still had not won the conference title. Until the 1990s, the Gator football program had never won much of anything that could be kept in the trophy case. Never won more than five SEC games in a season. Never won more than nine games total in a season. Finished in the Top Ten rankings just once (No. 3). And never scored 350 points in a season.

Many times the Gators of old would drop a game or two here or there because they couldn't close the deal. It became an acceptable way of life and there was always a ready-made excuse for not winning The Big One.

"We should be playing Georgia home-and-home instead of a neutral site in Jacksonville."

"We shouldn't be playing Auburn and Georgia back to back."

"We have too many rivals."

Their favorite lament became "Wait 'Til Next Year"—just like the frustrated fans of the old Brooklyn Dodgers and the Chicago Cubs.

Under Coach Ray Graves, Florida posted three nine-win seasons (1960, 1966, and 1969). Galen Hall's teams won nine games three straight years (1983–1985) but the SEC presidents took away the conference title awarded to the Charley Pell/Hall team of '84. After Pell was fired, Hall coached the last eight games that year and went 8-0.

That was pretty much the extent of the Gators' postwar-era success. As Coach Doug Dickey reminded me in 2016 when we chatted, all of the sixteen seasons leading up to his senior year as a player at Florida were losing seasons until his 1952 team ended that drought with an 8-3 Gator Bowl–winning team—the first bowl in school history.

When I played for Florida we were usually underdogs in big games—especially against our main rival, Georgia. Back then, the Bulldogs beat us two out of three (1964, 1966), knocking us out of an SEC championship my senior year. Since my playing days, the Bulldogs had kept up that tradition, winning seventeen out of the last twenty-four games since my senior year. This was obviously a trend we wanted to reverse.

There was doubt even among the Gator family that we could overcome the Bulldogs' dominance. My old college roommate Bill Carr, former AD at Florida and Houston, came into my office one day and said, "You've got to play Georgia home and away. You'll never win the SEC playing Auburn and Georgia back to back." I said, "Bill, give me two or three years, and if that happens, I may have to think that over. I can't believe that they take a plane down and we take a bus eighty miles to Jacksonville to play in the Gator Bowl on Florida soil that it can't be advantageous to us."

We needed to get over this losing mentality and put an end to our excuses.

As soon as I got settled in Gainesville I felt we had the material to win. The cupboard was full of good players. All-American running back Emmitt Smith might have been one of them, but he was in a quandary about whether to stay for his senior year. So we met right away.

"Emmitt, you've got to do what's best for you," I told him. "I'd love to have you come back. But if going to the NFL right now is best for your future, you need to really consider that. I'll understand if you leave. Running backs have just so many years. If you get hurt your senior year . . . And you're a first round pick . . . ? So I understand it."

What Emmitt heard from most Gators was, "Please come back, Emmitt! Please come back! Everybody loves you!" So all of a sudden Emmitt probably thought he was hearing me say, "Maybe you ought to leave." He probably thought, "Man, this guy doesn't even want me." That wasn't the case at all. I wanted him to do what he wanted to do. I've always told players with one year left that it was their call and they should maximize their NFL earning potential. If a player gets hurt his last year and misses his chance to go pro, a coach and player have to live with that the rest of their lives.

Emmitt wound up as the NFL's all-time leading rusher, a Hall of Famer, and one of the so-called Triplets—quarterback Troy Aikman and wide receiver Michael Irvin were the others—who starred for the three-time Super Bowl champion Dallas Cowboys.

I think Emmitt understands it now and we are okay. In 1995, when we beat FSU to go 11-0, Emmitt was on the field with a sideline pass. Standing under the goalpost when Jacquez Green caught a touchdown pass on a post route from Danny Wuerffel, he jumped out of the way and then congratulated Quezzie.

Several years ago, Emmitt and I were out in Lake Tahoe playing in a golf tournament. And I said, "Emmitt, if you'd have stayed and played you might have gone to one of those cold Northern cities. So it worked out pretty well for you going pro, didn't it?" He smiled and said, "Yeah, it worked out pretty well."

Emmitt is a Super Gator and a wonderful guy. And he may have been the best running back in NFL history.

I was very fortunate to get to Florida at the time the junior and senior classes were as good as anybody's in the SEC—maybe better. Which would give us a chance for a conference championship the first two years.

Picking the right quarterback was going to be one of my first critical decisions. We were looking for a leader who had the football skills to get his passes out quickly and the football intelligence to get us in the right play. Those characteristics often didn't exist among most four-star or five-star players as rated by recruiting services. The media and fans kept wanting to know our starter before spring practice. I just kept responding, "I don't know, but whoever it is will lead the SEC in passing." I wasn't being arrogant. I just believed we had the talent to run an offense that would work in the current SEC.

The depth chart at quarterback was fuzzy, but probably looked something like this before spring practice:

1. Kyle Morris, the starter from 1989
2. Lex Smith, a holdover who had been heavily recruited
3. Donald Douglas, a runner with blazing 4.4 speed
4. Brian Fox, a transfer from Purdue

Somewhere behind them was Shane Matthews, who was happy to hear that I had opened the position up and eager for a shot. Shane, born in Cleveland, Mississippi, transferred to Pascagoula High School in his junior year to play for his dad. Bill Matthews had played football at the University of Mississippi. Shane's mom, Peggy, was an Ole Miss cheerleader and huge football fan. The family usually went to high school games on Friday and traveled to see the Rebels play on Saturday.

Shane was developing into a prospect while playing for Pascagoula and, despite his Ole Miss roots, had his eye on Alabama, but didn't get an offer. His mom didn't want him to go to Florida State for some reason. So he chose to go play for Galen Hall, where I found him after two seasons of inactivity at Florida.

Shane had remembered watching us on TV when I was coaching my last game at Duke in the All-American Bowl. After the game he told his dad, "I could run that offense." We were going to find out in the spring game if he could do what he said.

In 1990, after our first week, we had a scrimmage on the practice field. There were five quarterbacks, and four got into the scrimmage. They all did sort of okay. Shane wasn't one of the five. After the scrimmage, one for our administrative assistants came over with a gentleman and said, "Coach, this is Billy Matthews, Shane's dad." And I said, "My bad! Shane didn't even get a snap." He was fifth string and didn't even get in. I started apologizing to Coach Matthews. He said, "Don't worry about it, Coach. I'm a coach also. And I know sometimes you just can't get everybody in the scrimmage. I just wanted you to know that Shane told me he really likes this offense because it's not just one receiver, throw it to him or run—it features 3-4-5 receivers out in formation. And it allows the quarterback to make a decision. And he thinks he can make those decisions very well."

"He's definitely going to get his chance," I assured Coach Matthews. "Don't worry, he'll get in next week and more and more as we go."

As spring practice went on, two of the quarterbacks got hurt. Brian Fox sprained his ankle. One of the others got nicked up as well. Douglas transferred to Houston. Lex Smith, who had actually started a homecoming game before I got there, accepted a position change and contributed as a linebacker–defensive end–special teams player, which made me very proud of him. So all of a sudden Shane moved up a couple notches.

We held the spring game in the Gator Bowl over in Jacksonville because renovations were under way at Ben Hill Griffin Stadium. We were ripping out the Astroturf, so it wasn't playable. A pretty good crowd of about fifteen thousand showed up and Shane had a wonderful game as starter for the Orange. All of a sudden he looked quicker, hitting eight of eleven, three of them for touchdowns, and led his Orange team to the win. But we said nothing about who would start. I told the guys that a lot of times quarterbacks can really, really improve in three or four months over the summer and said: "In August, preseason practice, we'll let you guys compete again for the starter's job."

At the Jacksonville Gator Club that summer, I said that whoever our quarterback was would lead the SEC in passing and be the SEC Player of the Year. The media around the South laughed, but Shane Matthews was to fulfill that prophecy.

Shane worked very hard. After a couple weeks in preseason practice, I named him as the starter and we had our quarterback for the new offense that would eventually be dubbed the Fun 'N' Gun. And I said, "I think Shane will play very well in this offense because he's got a lot of outstanding players around him." Offensive line, receivers, running backs—and our defense was one of the best in the nation.

My thought was that if we were a better team than FSU and Miami, we would definitely be the best team in the SEC. At that time in 1990, Alabama, Tennessee, and Auburn were the top SEC teams, but weren't winning national championships like FSU and Miami had done in the late eighties/early nineties. If we could be the best in Florida, we could certainly be the best in the SEC.

For the opening game, we also wanted to send a message that things were going to be different around Gainesville.

The NCAA probation hurt our program at Florida and we were behind both Miami and Florida State. So we needed to rally the Gator Nation so the students would get back behind us.

I decided to use a direct appeal to the student body, as outlined in my letter printed in the student newspaper, *The Independent Florida Alligator*: "We trail FSU and Miami heading into the 1990s. We have the resources to catch and pass them and that is our target. When we start beating them on the football field and producing a higher percentage of graduates, that will become a reality."

In our final scrimmage on Wednesday, ten days before our first game, our defense got the best of our offense, which really struggled. We had trouble making first downs, maybe one drive and a couple field goals. The defense really shut down the offense convincingly.

Back in those days, I opened up scrimmages to both the media and the fans. Jack Hairston, columnist for *The Gainesville Sun*, wrote of our first game against Oklahoma State that "the Gators should win this game and are favored by 12 points but that might be a little too much."

After that scrimmage, I got the offensive guys together and said, "Don't worry about that last scrimmage. We've got really good defensive players. They've been watching us all spring and they've got a pretty good feel for us. We're going to be okay. We're going to start game-planning for Oklahoma State and we should be able to go up and down the field against these guys. Feel confident that we're good enough to do that."

Sure enough, Oklahoma State played on defense the way they had the prior year. We had watched a lot of their games where they used a certain coverage against each formation, so it was pretty easy for us to have a good play called just about all the time.

On September 8, 1990, the new-look Florida Gators received the opening kickoff in our debut at Ben Hill Griffin Stadium before a crowd of more than seventy-five thousand. We opened up the same way I had with Tampa Bay and Duke—the no-huddle. And sure enough, the Cowboys were in the defense we had hoped for.

Shane hit Ernie Mills on a crossing route for 26 yards—the first of three straight strikes. Next came a 17-yarder to wide receiver Tre Everett over the middle, followed by a 22-yard curl route to Mills again. We scored in under two minutes as Dexter McNabb ran it in a toss sweep to cap a 70-yard drive. Shane threw for 332 yards that day without an interception and we beat Oklahoma State 50–7.

The fans really liked that—it wasn't off tackle here or off tackle there or "establish the run game and play solid defense or field position." It was "Hey, let's go score as often as we can."

One thing I am sort of proud of is that in the first game I coached at Florida we scored fifty and in my last game in the Orange Bowl we would crack fifty again, beating Maryland 56–23.

The beginning of the Shane Matthews Era of 1990–1992 signaled the trend of wide-open offenses in the SEC, where the running game had once ruled. Some people said our pass-oriented attack would eventually impact and—maybe even transform—our conference in a significant way.

Our strong defense was good enough to win games as well and got the ball back for us frequently to give the offense more chances to score and set school records. Right away we started forcing punts—somewhere between eight and twelve a game. And we were going to need a strong defense at Bryant-Denny Stadium the next week, when we faced Alabama. Fortunately, we had a superb defense.

That first win against Oklahoma State had been special, but a victory against defending SEC champion Alabama in Tuscaloosa could earn the Florida program a new level of respect and give us an idea of what it was going to take to compete with the best.

At The Wynfrey Hotel in Birmingham the night before the game, I noticed several of our players were giddy, silly, and unfocused—reverting back to the old attitude of feeling a little too good about themselves. A little too much noise. After our blessing before dinner, I rapped on my glass with a knife and gave them a piece of my mind: "We're going to get our butts beat tomorrow if you continue to laugh and giggle and not understand how important this game is." I assured them the Alabama players, under first-year coach Gene Stallings, weren't laughing and giggling during their pregame meal. Suddenly the room got quieter.

The Crimson Tide jumped out to a 10–0 lead at halftime. Shane responded by taking us on a sixty-seven-yard drive and we closed the gap on his touchdown pass to Terence Barber. Our defense stepped up bigtime when defensive back Will White intercepted the first of three passes by Alabama quarterback Gary Hollingsworth at our 2. Shane hit Ernie Mills on first down for a seventy-yard gain on a post route. We got a field goal. And in the fourth quarter, Jimmy Spencer blocked a punt and Richard Fain fell on it for a touchdown.

Beating Alabama 17–13 on the road was our first crucial conference win. A writer for *The Gainesville Sun*, Bill King, said something that stuck with me: "Florida played like the Alabama teams used to play. And Alabama played like the Florida teams used to play."

And away we went, pitching and catching the ball around the SEC. We believed we could win the championship with our 1990 team.

We had not heard yet what the NCAA penalty was going to be. I was hoping we'd lose only a few scholarships but still be eligible to win the SEC and compete in the postseason. I felt it was unfair for these players to pay a stiff penalty for something they really had nothing to do with. The only penalty we pled guilty to was a coach sending a graduate assistant coach to Palatka in 1986 with $360.40 to pay a child-support payment for Jarvis Williams—but it never was proven. Coach Galen Hall vehemently denied sending any coach up there with that money. Later, I learned that the Ford dealer in Palatka was the person who paid it and he supposedly had a prior relationship with Jarvis. And if that's so, it wouldn't have even been a violation. So no coach or player had anything to do with it.

The next week the bad news broke: The NCAA ruled that our only punishment was no postseason play. No bowl game. In the SEC if you're ineligible to play in the bowl, they would not allow you to be called the champion. They had a deal with the Sugar Bowl that it would get the SEC champion. So therefore we became ineligible for the title—even if we won it.

Following the first two games, after the penalty was handed down, everybody of importance at UF gathered in a meeting room just outside the athletic director's office to sort it out. The question for the group was: "Do we accept the penalty of the bowl ban or do we appeal it, hope we win the SEC, go to the Sugar Bowl and win the conference?"

Among those attending the meeting in the stadium were the new UF president, John Lombardi, and UF attorney Tom McDonald, Associate AD Jeremy Foley, UF dean of students Bob Lanzilotti, and faculty rep Nick Cassisi.

President Lombardi said: "This is pretty simple to me. If we believe we are going to win the SEC, we should appeal this right now and see if we have a big season, as it appears we can do. Coach, what do you think?"

They all looked down at me. And I answered: "I think we have a very good shot at winning the SEC. Obviously, I can't guarantee it. We've still got to play Tennessee, Auburn, and Georgia. And Georgia's not as strong this year as past years. If we split and only have one loss, usually that will get you a share of the conference championship. We've got a chance to maybe only lose one SEC game—or maybe win them all."

Everyone looked around. And then Dean Lanzilotti said, "Wait a minute! We haven't won the SEC in the history of our school since it started in 1933. All of a sudden we've won one SEC game and we think we're going to win a conference championship? Let's be smart! Take the penalty, get it out of the way! And let's move forward!"

In a way he had a good point. We needed to move on. It wasn't a just and fair penalty, but they had already determined it. Life is not always fair.

In later years, as we began winning the SEC championships, whenever I saw Dean Lanzilotti I would say: "Ye of little faith!" But we probably would have been ineligible the second year also.

I told our 1990 team, "I'll always consider you SEC champions if we win it. You will be the first to win it—and we're going to win a bunch of them." And they all looked at me and sorta said, "Let's go win it anyway!" And that was our goal.

We beat Furman, Mississippi State, and LSU to go 5-0, but then had to travel to Knoxville, where we were going to get our comeuppance.

Our defensive coordinator, Coach Jim Bates, looked at the scouting report on Tennessee and warned us, "This is probably the best team you'll ever play against." He said their two offensive tackles, Charles McRae and Anthone Davis, were going to be first-round NFL draft picks. In Chris Mims and Chuckie Smith they had maybe the two best bookend defenders. Defensive back Dale Carter was an All-American. Carl Pickens and Alvin Harper were outstanding receivers. Andy Kelly was having an excellent season at quarterback.

Coach Bates would prove to be right on all fronts: They put together one of the best teams ever to play in the SEC. With more than ninety-five thousand looking on at Neyland Stadium, we fell behind 28-3. Shane took a beating. We couldn't block their pass rush and it was apparent we had no answer. Their players were doing a defiant Gator Chomp before every kickoff and their fans were jumping around, having a big time celebrating. So I made the decision to pull Shane in the third quarter. We lost 45–3. The critics came out, loudly criticizing my decision, claiming I was a quitter.

In the book *The Leadership Secrets of Attila the Hun*, one of Attila's most interesting tactical maneuvers was, "If defeat is inevitable, retreat and save your warriors to fight another day." We applied that to our game in Knoxville.

We licked our wounds and got out of there with nobody seriously hurt. Some of the Tennessee people said, "Spurrier took his quarterback out in the third quarter. He gave up." The media asked me why I took Shane out. And I said, "Because I thought our chances of winning were zero and I wanted to make sure he was ready to play next week."

We didn't quit, didn't give up—we just retreated and lived to fight another day. And that would set the tone for the weeks to come as Florida football was becoming relevant in the SEC again.

Tennessee had celebrated and celebrated and celebrated after beating us. Then Alabama came to Neyland Stadium the following week and beat them 9–6 with three field goals.

Johnny Majors, coach of the Vols that year and still a good friend of mine, likes to say, "We kicked your tail in Knoxville that year." I always liked to respond: "Well, you beat us, but Alabama came in the next week and kicked your tail nine to six. By the way, it's a full season."

Sure enough, the next week we crushed Akron 59–0. We had blown out Mississippi State 34–21, crushed LSU 34–8, and hammered Auburn 48–7.

By the time our big game with Georgia rolled around, we were playing at a high level. Not only were Shane Matthews, Ernie Mills, running back Errict Rhett, and tight end Kirk Kirkpatrick excelling on offense, but our defense was rock-solid, with players like linebacker Huey Richardson and Mark Murray, defensive linemen Brad Culpepper and Tony McCoy, and cornerback Will White performing at their best. Just in time for our most meaningful game of the year: Georgia.

When I took the Florida job in 1990, I said to former Georgia Bulldog player and our defensive/motivating Florida coach Gene Ellenson, "You've got the Georgia game!" We were a twenty-point favorite, and our guys were ready to play. The night before the game rolled around I said to him, "Coach, I don't know how much more [motivation] our guys need."

He said, "Coach, they don't need much at all. I can tell by their attitude, the way they're handling themselves the night before the game." In fact, he said, "They won't remember a word I said." They didn't need it, and he was smart enough to know that.

We whipped Ray Goff's team pretty good, 38–7, and it should have been by even more. We fumbled on the 1-yard line and didn't score three other times inside the 20. This began our twelve-year dominance over the Bulldogs, during which we won eleven games.

We finished 6-1 in the conference and No. 6 nationally.

And even with the lopsided loss to Tennessee, we won the SEC, despite not being able to claim the trophy.

Tennessee went 9-2-2 overall and 5-1-1 in the SEC, but they were crowned the league champions because we were disallowed.

In the next-to-last game we polished off Kentucky 47–15.

Once again, too much celebrating tends to make a team lose sight of the next important thing, especially when you are headed to Tallahassee the next week. While we had reached our goal of having the best record in the SEC, our unofficial league champions were tripped up by FSU 45–30. But our 9-2 season began our journey toward a bunch of trophies that established groundwork for future success.

When the school began honoring our teams who won the SEC championships in Ben Hill Griffin Stadium, I insisted we put the 1990 team on the façade as "Best Record in the SEC," along with the 1984 team.

That season, Shane passed for twenty-three touchdowns and more yards (2,952) than any Gator quarterback ever, leading the SEC, as I had predicted. First-team All-Americans Will White and Huey Richardson anchored one of our best defensive teams in history. In those first four or five years, the Gator defense was either No. 1 or No. 2 in the SEC as we started knocking down those barriers.

The table was set for a memorable twelve-year run by Florida. The Fun 'N' Gun was clicking in the first year. Shane would go on to be named SEC Player of the Year twice. Errict Rhett, who was also an excellent receiver, began with 845 yards rushing that season, on his way to more than 4,000 in his college career. Ernie Mills of Dunnellon, Florida, was on a path to stardom, catching about a dozen touchdown passes from Shane—probably eight of them off the deep post. We named the deep post the Mills Route. Ernie would go on to play nine years in the NFL and catch twenty touchdown passes.

The Mills Route lived on because we put it in as a signal: I'd cup my hands around my eyes like fake binoculars, because Ernie Mills wore glasses. Then the quarterback would do the same thing to the receiver. When our opponents figured it out, we would often change that signal, and also use it as a dummy signal.

Fans were beginning to sense that the 1991 team was about to become something special. All of a sudden there was a big demand for seats at Ben Hill Griffin Stadium, which already had an expansion program under way. On September 14, the newly refurbished arena was unveiled with ten thousand extra seats in the north end zone, eighteen luxury suites, and a lounge area called Touchdown Terrace. Alabama was coming to town.

The season had started nicely with a 59–21 victory over San Jose State. This time on our own turf, the No. 6 Gators clobbered the No. 17 Crimson Tide 35–0—one of the worst SEC defeats for Alabama in school history.

All the stars were out that night for the Gators: Shane passed for 251 yards and three touchdowns. Errict rushed for 170 yards and a score. Brad Culpepper led our defense, which allowed only 257 yards, and he was named SEC Defensive Player of the Week.

How would we handle success? Sometimes players get cocky and tend to turn a deaf ear to their coaches. And on occasion we coaches may be prone to listening too much to outside advice.

I'd always coached with a lot of passion, shown my emotions on the sideline, and asked our players to execute with detail. When they didn't, I got angry at myself and at them, occasionally slamming my visor to the ground.

A few friends had been telling me that maybe I needed to calm down on the sideline for fear I might eventually burn out. I even got some letters about it. So I took that advice and tried to be different when we flew up to Syracuse to play in the loud atmosphere of the Carrier Dome.

I had warned our team on several occasions to watch out for trick plays by Coach Paul Pasqualoni—especially a reverse on special teams. Sure enough, Kirby Dar Dar took the opening kickoff ninety-five yards for a touchdown. It was going to be a long day in Syracuse, where we stumbled out of the gate and lost 38–21. Our defense gave up more than two hundred yards rushing and our offense was also bad.

I was furious about our lack of effort, but I had tried to show a calmer demeanor on the sideline—and that was a mistake. No more of that! I told our coaches to have the players ready to run the stadium steps Monday morning. I was never going to take advice again from fans and friends about how to act on the sideline or the way to coach. I remember what Coach Graves would say: "When the coaches are ready to compete with all they've got, the players will be ready also."

Next up was No. 21 Mississippi State, which had moved its home game to the Citrus Bowl in Orlando. On the bus trip down, I was reading a book by former Michigan coach Bo Schembechler, who said, "Running teams are tougher teams." So I decided we needed more offensive balance. It was time for us to hand the ball off more to our talented running backs—Errict Rhett, Dexter McNabb, and Willie McClendon.

The Bulldogs came out with five defensive backs and even though we started out in the no-huddle, we ran the ball forty-seven times, more than

With coach Ray Graves, his wife Opal, and Jerri after Florida's
first-ever official SEC title in 1991. It took fifty-eight years!

twice as many as we passed it, and won 29–7. Errict Rhett, alone, rushed
for 142 of our 195 yards.

In 1991, Florida beat a lot of ranked teams and finally got a legitimate
SEC championship trophy that could never be taken away. We put together a string of seven straight victories, including LSU, 16–0; No. 4 Tennessee, 35–18; Auburn, 31–10; and Georgia, 45–13.

After beating Georgia, the worst we could do was to tie for the league
championship. To win it outright, we had to beat Kentucky in the final
game of the season in Gainesville. We were thirty-five-point favorites in
the game. But I did a poor job of getting the team prepared for the game
because it was a nail-biter.

We scored quickly. Shane and his guys rolled up a 28–7 halftime lead.
For some reason we had guys laughing and giggling, ready to start the
celebration of Florida's first official SEC championship. Kentucky put in
an outstanding running quarterback, Pookie Jones, who ran around us

and through us and over us—and completed passes. Our defense went completely flat in the second half. We started throwing interceptions, started fumbling—giving Kentucky a chance with our turnovers.

The score was 28–26, Florida, with seven minutes left. They kicked off to us and on first down our offensive lineman got a penalty for hands to the face mask, to give us a first and twenty-five at our own 10. We're beat if our offense can't stay on the field and make a drive because our defense couldn't stop 'em a lick.

Shane hit a couple passes and we were sitting on third and six. We had to make it. We called a play where Errict Rhett goes out and hooks up, or can take a left or a right—the Back Option play. Kentucky had a line stunt and the defensive lineman was running right at Shane. Errict still had his back to Shane, who had to hope he'd turn around or he was going to hit the Kentucky linebacker right in the numbers. Fortunately, Errict got his hands up, caught it, and put his shoulder pads down, carrying Kentucky's middle linebacker about three yards for the first down. We didn't pass again and Errict took a toss sweep to run it in for a touchdown with about a minute left. That put us up by nine. When the game ended Kentucky was on our 15 firing at the end zone when it was over.

After winning 35–26, we all celebrated the first and only SEC championship won on Florida Field. We brought out the PA system and thanked everybody. It was a special day, even if we did almost blow it. And it was a lesson learned. We did finally capture our very first SEC championship—and on our home field. The next year, the SEC ushered in its championship game, which was played in Birmingham for two years before being moved to Atlanta.

Only Florida State stood in our way of becoming the first Gator team to win ten games.

Once again we brought in coach Gene Ellenson to help the team reach "Another Level." We proudly wore those words on our lapels the night before the game.

Then we went out and won a game by one of the lowest scores ever, 14–9, over Bobby Bowden's Seminoles before one of the loudest Ben Hill Griffin crowds in history. We scored on a first-quarter run by Rhett. The difference was a seventy-two-yard bomb from Shane to wide receiver Harrison Houston in the third quarter. Our defense held on for the victory when Del Speer knocked down a Casey Weldon pass on fourth down late in the game.

That clinched a 10-1 record with a No. 3 ranking and a Sugar Bowl berth as SEC champs, since there was no title game yet.

In our first bowl appearance of my time as Gator Head Ball Coach, we ran into a Mack truck named Jerome Bettis and lost the Sugar Bowl 39–28 to Notre Dame. We still had the SEC title and wound up seventh in one poll, eighth in another, but our Sugar Bowl performance wasn't our best.

Ten Gators were named All-SEC first team in 1991, totaling nineteen over our first two seasons. Brad Culpepper was picked as the school's thirty-seventh All-American and won the Draddy Trophy as the nation's top scholar-athlete. Shane was an established star and the pieces of our offense were coming together.

We were building a new tradition, a new brand at Florida that we wanted to be unique. Even though it was called Ben Hill Griffin, our stadium needed a nickname.

After reading some school history, I found out Florida president John J. Tigert had been seeking a new site for our football stadium in 1930 when he chose a marshy swamp on the western edge of the campus. Perfect! "The Swamp" was born. Over the last several years some people had tried to call it the Swamp, but it never stuck.

I told our athletic director Bill Arnsparger, "I think we ought to start calling it the Swamp." To which he responded: "Let me talk to our marketing director." And when he bounced it off the marketing director, the reply was, "That'll never work! That's not a good name for our stadium." Soon after that the marketing director left and became an AD at some small school in Iowa. I loved the word *swamp,* so I just started calling it the Swamp. And we always liked to point out: "The Swamp, where only Gators get out alive!"

"Swamp" is something that college football players enjoyed saying. Almost every opponent that came in there loved to say, "We're going into the Swamp. We'll give the Gators all they can handle." Given our home record of 68-5 over twelve years, however, the Swamp was very good for the Gators.

In '92, when the SEC went to eight conference games, we figured that was the right time to drop Miami. AD Arnsparger came in and said, "Coach, you don't need to be playing Miami when you've already got FSU and eight SEC games on the schedule." I said, "You know, you're right." And he said, "I can get out of it by just saying we added a conference game." And so we gave Miami some money and got out of it. It was the right thing to do.

Our defense was improving and we had some good young players on offense, but we had lost a lot of seniors. Although 1992 didn't appear to be a season the Gators would be in contention, I was reminded how a big win over a rival can turn your season around.

Georgia had bragged about recruiting all those offensive players like quarterback Eric Zeier and running back Garrison Hearst. The publication *The Red & Black* had predicted Georgia would win the SEC because of being "No. 1" in recruiting the past four years, according to their rankings. Alabama, Auburn, and Tennessee were also ranked ahead of Florida.

Shane was coming back for his final season, but with true freshmen Jason Odom and Reggie Green starting at offensive tackle, we had to make offensive adjustments. We started off slow, losing at Tennessee badly, 31-14, and then at Mississippi State, 30-6, before righting the ship by beating LSU, 28-21, and Auburn, 24-9. So coming into the game against our rival, seventh-ranked Georgia, our SEC record was 3-2 and we were twentieth in the polls.

The Georgia coaches would always try to blow smoke and build us up. I was tired of hearing them BSing about how good Florida was and our people saying, "Isn't that nice of Georgia's coach, saying how good we are!" instead of saying, "I'm tired of him saying that every year and then kicking our butts!"

My first year, Ray Goff had said all that crap and we beat them 38–7. The second year he started saying it again. I told the coaches: "If we're fortunate enough to beat these guys, this will be the last year he talks about how 'big and strong and fast and talented' the Gators are. I'm going to put an end to that." We won that second game 41–13. After that game, I told the media: "We're sort of tired of the Georgia coach talking about how big, strong, fast, and talented we were and his poor guys were going to have to find a way to scratch and claw to beat us. They are supposed to be number one in recruiting. What happens when they get on campus? I don't understand it! You guys tell me."

In 1992 we beat Georgia for the third consecutive time, chewing up the clock with three straight first downs to win 26–24 and knocking them out of the SEC title picture. It remains my all-time favorite win over the Bulldogs, because that was the only time we were ever the underdogs to them while I was coaching at Florida.

Posting his thirteenth 300-yard career game, Shane threw for 301 yards, with second-quarter TD passes of nine yards to Jack Jackson and 14 yards to Willie Jackson. He hit Harrison Houston for a 14-yard score to seal the victory. That gave him 72 touchdowns passes for his career, at that point an SEC record.

In those three wins, Shane passed for 948 yards and nine touchdowns with no interceptions, which caused Coach Goff to say, "The greatest thing about Shane Matthews is he's a senior and we don't have to see him again."

There was some more good news that day: South Carolina upset Tennessee 24–23, which was the Vols' third SEC loss. That made us SEC East Division champs and qualified us for a chance to go play Alabama in the first SEC championship game.

As our young tackles began to mature, Rhett came on with a big year, scoring ten touchdowns with more than thirteen hundred yards of total offense. By the time we headed into Tallahassee, we had won seven straight. But we got beat by Florida State 45–24.

The next week we rebounded and played very well in the SEC title game—except for one play that could have been our winning drive against Alabama.

We had been down 21–7 but were able to tie the game on a four-yard touchdown pass from Shane to Willie Jackson in the third quarter and Rhett's twenty-one-yard run with eight minutes to play. Shane was taking us on what looked to be the winning drive when Alabama defensive back Antonio Langham bounced out of the shadows at Legion Field in Birmingham, intercepted Shane's pass, and ran twenty-seven yards for the winning touchdown with 3:16 left.

The receiver was supposed to run a five-yard hitch against Alabama's Cover Two defense and he drifted back about three yards too deep, so Antonio was back there watching the quarterback, came around and picked it off. Not Shane's fault.

Alabama beat us, 28–21, and then won the national championship with a 34–13 victory over Miami in the Sugar Bowl.

It was such a famous moment that there have been TV documentaries built around it on ESPNU—"The Play That Changed College Football"—emphasizing how Langham's interception allowed Alabama to win the national championship. It was a heckuva play by Langham. Lost in that, however, was the fact that these Gators were on a bit of a run themselves. Except for that interception, we might have won or finished first in the SEC seven straight seasons.

After we lost to Alabama, we were invited to the Gator Bowl, where we beat North Carolina State, 27–10, in my first bowl win and wound up 9-4 on the year. In the final poll we were No. 10. Over the summer I finally was beginning to realize how important bowl games were, because people talk about that game until the next season's opener.

Shane was our team captain and a brilliant performer. He led the league three straight years in passing overall, completing 722 of 1,202 passes for 74 TDs and 9,287 yards. But as Shane has said many times, if he could take back any of those 1,202 passes, it would have been the one that Langham intercepted. But really it wasn't his fault.

Although he never got a chance to play for a national championship, Shane was as much responsible for that "official" SEC trophy in 1991 as anybody and helped us establish a legacy of winning. As a three-year starter, his teams went 19-4 in the SEC. Rhett would finish with 4,163 yards and thirty-four touchdowns rushing and two receiving. That broke Emmitt Smith's career rushing record. Errict also led the Gators in rushing all four seasons—a record that most likely will never be equaled at Florida.

Bill Arnsparger resigned in mid-January of 1993 to become the defensive coordinator of the San Diego Chargers, and Jeremy Foley moved into the AD chair.

ALTHOUGH SHANE WAS GONE, we had some promising recruits coming in and our fortunes took an uptick in 1993. Quarterback Terry Dean of Naples had attended one of our camps at Duke and was one of our first recruits at Florida. He was redshirted, sat behind Shane two years, and waited his turn. As a redshirt junior, Terry stepped in to play a key role in securing another SEC title. But not without a few bumps in the road.

Our quarterbacks had a horrible night in our road opener at Lexington. Terry had a particularly bad game with four interceptions. Danny Wuerffel came in and threw three picks, but when it counted, he hit Chris Doering on the winning touchdown with three seconds left against Kentucky and we won 24–20. The now-famous call of our radio announcer Mick Hubert lives on today: "Doering got a touchdown! Doering got a touchdown!" Doering, who walked on from Gainesville P. K. Yonge, had recently been awarded a scholarship and would go on to become the all-time leader in touchdown receptions at Florida and in the SEC after the 1995 season.

After the game I admitted Kentucky should have probably beaten us. We were very fortunate—the touchdown pass from Danny to Doering was maybe the biggest play of the season. Without that one play we wouldn't have scored that touchdown, wouldn't have won the East Division, wouldn't have won the SEC, and wouldn't have gone to the Sugar Bowl.

We followed that win at Kentucky by beating Tennessee 41–34, then Mississippi State 38–24, and LSU 58–3. But then we lost at Auburn 38–35 the week before we went to Jacksonville to play Georgia, where Terry came off the bench and helped us beat the Bulldogs 33–26 to clinch the SEC East title.

For some reason, the SEC championship game was played in back-to-back years at Legion Field in Birmingham. It was like Alabama's second "home field," site of Iron Bowl games with Auburn as well as some other regular-season games. Alabama had been playing games there all the way back to 1892. Birmingham, incidentally, was also the birthplace of Terry Dean, who was picked MVP of the game after we beat Alabama 28–13. I was told, or read somewhere, it was the first time Alabama ever lost a game for the SEC title at one of its "home" parks. After that, the SEC championship game was moved to Atlanta.

We finished 7-1 in the SEC and 11-2 overall after we beat West Virginia in the Sugar Bowl 41–7, as Rhett scored three touchdowns and Judd Davis, winner of the Lou Groza Award, kicked two field goals.

We were ranked fifth in the nation after the 1993 campaign.

For the first time in history, however, we vaulted to No. 1 in the preseason rankings before the '94 campaign. We stayed at No. 1 for six of the first seven weeks, averaging just under fifty-one points a game while going 5-0, including a 31–0 win at Tennessee. Dean had a big night in Knoxville, moving into what some writers were saying was serious early contention for the Heisman. I never like talking about the Heisman during the season, especially not after only five games. But after his success against Tennessee, Terry began getting a lot of media hype—not conducive to good team chemistry. Terry didn't need that additional pressure on himself, which maybe was one of the reasons he didn't play particularly well in our 42–18 win over LSU. Our defense did play well, though, with three interceptions.

Still ranked No. 1 in the nation, we hosted No. 6 Auburn in one of the biggest games ever played at Ben Hill Griffin. Auburn had won seventeen straight but was ineligible for the postseason. It was not a good day for the Gators or our quarterbacks. After he threw three first-half interceptions, I pulled Terry in favor of Danny. However, Danny apparently got the wrong signal and threw an errant pass over the middle that was picked off by Brian Robinson with 1:20 left in the game—one of Robinson's three interceptions. Auburn played opportunist and Patrick Nix threw an eight-yard touchdown pass to Frank Sanders for the win. It was a tough loss, 36–33.

Danny would become our quarterback the rest of that season and the two years that followed. After winning four straight, our defense collapsed in Tallahassee and we let one get away from us after leading 31–3 starting the fourth quarter. FSU cut our lead to 31–30, but Bobby Bowden elected not to go for two. Back then there was no sudden death for ties and the game ended 31–31. Even though we'd already won the SEC, tying that game felt like a loss, but it was still a tie. We tried to put it behind us as we headed to Atlanta for the SEC championship game against No. 3 Alabama.

We always practiced what some might call "gimmick plays" for every game, even though most of them were a staple of our playbook. If we were ahead, we didn't use them—saved them mostly for a fourth quarter in case we were behind. Which was exactly the case in the Georgia Dome: We trailed Alabama 23–17 after Alabama's Cedric Samuel tipped a pass into the hands of teammate Dwayne Rudd, who ran twenty-three yards for a touchdown with 8:56 left in the game.

Now it was time for us to reach into our bag of tricks. First was the hobble play. The signal for Danny was if he looked over and saw that Eric Kresser had his helmet on. When Danny got hit hard, I sent the strong-armed Kresser into the game on a mission as Danny limped off the field convincingly. It was third and about twenty. The play called was for Eric to fire a twenty-five-yard pass down the left sideline to Ike Hilliard. Fortunately, it worked beautifully.

"How'd I look? Pretty good acting job, huh?" Danny joked later about his limping role. "You're hoping the defense will be thinking the substitute will be conservative."

Danny came back on the field after Eric's completion—this time not limping—and in four plays helped orchestrate a sequence that Gator fans still love to talk about, centered around the running of the Emory & Henry formation, named after the small school in Virginia. It features clusters of receivers and offensive linemen bunched in triangles wide on each side, with three linemen in the middle of the field and the quarterback and running back behind them. Off that formation, Danny hit Reidel Anthony, who almost broke it, gaining nine yards.

On the next play we executed a double-pass play: Wuerffel to Doering, who then connected with Aubrey Hill to the Alabama 2. Danny called an audible and hit Chris in the end zone on a slant pattern for the winning score. We beat Alabama 24–23 for our third official title. That put us in the Sugar Bowl, where we got beat in a rematch with Florida State 23–17. The 10-2-1 finish showed us we were on the right track but still had some obstacles to overcome. Soon enough, two of the best teams in Florida history would be unveiled, both of which would play for national championships.

Chapter 13

THE GATORS OF '95 AND '96

Talking with Danny Wuerffel.

All Gators remember the national championship team of 1996, but what people might not remember is how talented and successful our undefeated '95 team was—until we ran into a buzz saw called Nebraska. We were embarking on an unprecedented two-year run at Florida, even after getting clobbered in the Fiesta Bowl.

These Florida Gators were now viewed as winners. You could see it in the way they carried themselves. The players on the '95 squad felt they were going to win every time they took the field. They competed fiercely in practice, dreamed big and laughed hard. And they had fun.

"It isn't just being confident," middle linebacker James Bates said in an interview after leaving football. "It isn't just believing in yourself. It's an all-out 'there's no way I'm going to lose this game . . .' To me, that's swagger personified. It's just so contagious for a football team and so much fun! And then when you go out and back it up it's exhilarating."

Bates, a defensive captain from Sevierville, Tennessee, and son of a coach, was our team clown who once showed up at practice wearing a pumpkin for a helmet during Halloween week. If he'd had a nickname other than Batesy, it would have been Captain Fun.

As a coach, you give a little more leeway to team leaders when you're winning. Especially when they play with the kind of heart that Batesy did. In the mid-nineties, he was one of those who carry themselves with "swagger"—or call it what you will.

We always tried to make the game fun for the fans, the students, the coaches, and—most of all—the players. It's only fun if you win. We always emphasized this.

"You can't believe how much fun we had on the team bus ride before games," Batesy remembered. "I'm surprised Coach Spurrier even let us get away with it. But he was cool with it, because we were committed to winning."

THE LIFEBLOOD of a successful team, of course, is recruiting. And the best recruiting magnet you can have to attract other good players is the fun of winning games and championships.

There was this misguided notion that I didn't emphasize recruiting enough. That was simply not true. It was never my nature to try and to talk a player out of going to another school by offering promises I might not be able to keep.

At Florida as the head coach, I was actively involved with every player we recruited at all schools. As well as we did, it seemed FSU almost always out-recruited us.

An Orlando columnist wrote after national signing day in 1992, "This was a bleak day for the Gators." Back then there was no early enrollment and a lot of the kids would wait until signing day to tell you their choice of schools. We had six "undecided" recruits who kept telling us they liked Florida, along with FSU, Tennessee, Georgia, et cetera. And we didn't get any of them. I think five of them went to FSU. But we had enough good players to go play. And they proved to be the nucleus of a dedicated group that took us to "Another Level" that Coach Ellenson always talked about.

Sometimes things just didn't work out in recruiting as we expected, but maybe that was the way they were supposed to happen.

No matter what FSU did, or the critics said, after five years at Florida the pieces were falling into place. We had two No. 1 classes—1991 and 1999. The '91 group was the heart of the team that won four SEC titles. We had redshirted quite a few of them, including Danny Wuerffel.

I'll never forget how we wound up getting Danny Wuerffel. He was a gift—almost too good to be true: class valedictorian at Fort Walton Beach High School, basketball player, track and field athlete, and president of the Fellowship of Christian Athletes for three years. He was blessed with talent and was as sincere a young Christian man as I've ever met.

As a senior quarterback, he was considered the top high school recruit in the state and USA Today's high school player of the year in 1991 after leading the Vikings to the Class 4A Florida state high school football championship.

In those days coaches were allowed to go and watch the state championship games on Florida Field. Fort Walton Beach played St. Thomas Aquinas of Fort Lauderdale, which had eight players who would sign Division I scholarships. We signed a couple of them, including defensive end Cameron Davis.

I was up in the stands watching Danny warm up. And I said, "This kid drops the ball behind his neck almost and throws. How in the world is he going to play quarterback with that form?" Well, when the game started, he didn't drop the ball behind his neck—it came out with as quick a release as I've ever seen. So his warm-ups and his game were completely opposite.

Every pass Danny threw that day seemed to land perfectly. It was then that I began to learn about his divine assistance. I would say, "Danny's passes are guided by ten thousand angels." He threw a slant-and-go to receiver E. G. Green and the ball just dropped in beautifully. Touchdown! I was impressed. Then Danny hit little five-foot-seven receiver Scott Holz on a post route, he never broke stride all the way to the end zone. All of Danny's throws were very catchable and seemed to get there on time. I made a note to myself: "There's something about this kid that you can't explain!"

George Smith of Aquinas had coached sixteen years before reaching his first state championship game, only to be crushed in 1991 by Danny's Fort Walton Beach team 39–14. And he still talks about Danny's performance in that game—especially his eighty-yard scoring run.

Danny was a good runner but didn't have blazing speed. On an option play, he cut in front of the St. Thomas Aquinas bench, but hardly anybody expected what was about to happen: The safety couldn't catch him because of taking a bad angle and Danny was off to the races for a seventy-seven-yard touchdown.

"There is no way that Wuerffel kid can outrun our guys!" Coach Smith said. "But he did on that play that day! Something different was going on here. This kid's got something you can't explain."

Meanwhile, our recruiting was going full speed.

We already had a really good quarterback committed, Eric Kresser, from Palm Beach Gardens High School. We were recruiting one more quarterback—either Danny Wuerffel or Danny Kanell, who had played high school ball at a small Christian School in Fort Lauderdale, Westminster Academy. Both were highly recruited. Both visited Florida and Florida State. Wuerffel also visited Alabama.

After Fort Walton Beach beat St. Thomas Aquinas, I began paying more attention to Wuerffel and cut back my calls to Kanell. I had a good feeling about Wuerffel, but wasn't sure we'd get him. But I thought if Danny K. went ahead and committed to FSU that would maybe open up the door for Danny W. to come to Florida.

Sure enough, Danny Kanell committed first. And when I tell that story to Wuerffel, he always says: "Coach, his commitment to FSU had nothing to do with my commitment to Florida." Kanell had a good reason for going to FSU, where he started most of time and passed for fifty-seven touchdowns. He had a wonderful career at FSU and played six years in the NFL.

Everybody in the country also wanted Peyton Manning the next year. And we did, too.

Our recruiting coordinator Bob Sanders and I went to see Peyton in his New Orleans home. I had known Archie since before he played quarterback for the Saints. Peyton's parents, Archie and Olivia, are wonderful people. Peyton visited several schools and when decision time came, I remember Coach Sanders saying, "Coach, Peyton's going to Tennessee." And I said, "You know what—that's probably the best place for him."

Tennessee was a good situation for Peyton, and David Cutcliffe was a very good quarterback coach. I said, "Hey, I don't blame him." People said, "What?" I said, "Listen, we had to recruit him, but Danny Wuerffel's here. And we have complete confidence that he's going to really be a super player."

Years later I learned how close Peyton came to becoming a Gator. He once told a writer in Chattanooga, Ward Gossett: "Coach Spurrier was good to me and I liked the coaching staff when I visited there. I had to pick between them and I picked Tennessee."

After a spectacular pro career in which he led the Colts and Broncos to Super Bowl victories, Peyton established himself as one of the top quarterbacks to play the game—if not THE best. After his stirring retirement speech, Peyton rode off into the sunset with his second Super Bowl ring.

They retired his number in Indianapolis and are building a statue of him at the stadium. I am among those who think he should have also ridden off with that 1997 Heisman Trophy, but he didn't win it—all due respect to winner Charles Woodson of Michigan. Ironically, both Peyton and Charles played eighteen years in the NFL.

We immediately redshirted Danny and he began playing for us in 1993. His talent and heart and grit would be instrumental in our successful four-year SEC reign and first national title. Peyton began at Tennessee as a freshman in 1994. So the two of them would meet three times. It worked out best for us, because Danny never lost to the Vols. And Peyton's teams never beat us at Florida.

Beating Tennessee was always a big stepping-stone to the SEC title in those days. In 1995, we had one of our biggest games statistically. Danny enjoyed one of his biggest games, running for one score and passing for six touchdowns in his second head-to-head meeting with Peyton at the Swamp. He rolled up 381 yards throwing and would take us on a remarkable seven straight scoring drives.

Ike Hilliard made a record-tying four TD catches. Terry Jackson rushed for 119 yards. Ironically, we had trailed 30–14 late in the first half. Then the floodgates opened, our scoring burst happening over a two-and-a-half-quarter span. And although it didn't result in a score, the big hit Lawrence Wright put on Tennessee's Joey Kent, causing him to fumble, sent a strong message to the Vols.

The word was that *Sports Illustrated* had planned to put Peyton's picture on the cover the next week, but he really wasn't a factor in our 62–37 handling of Tennessee. Wuerffel, on the other hand, already had forty-nine career touchdown passes despite starting only seventeen games in his college career—on his way to setting school and SEC records for touchdown passes, passing yardage, and total offense per game and establishing himself as the most accurate passer in the nation. In the second half against Tennessee he completed thirteen of fifteen for 181 yards.

What better choice as a cover boy for *SI*'s cover than Danny? He got us off to a 6-0 start, including 5-0 in SEC play when we beat seventh-ranked Auburn 49–38 and moved up to the No. 3 ranking in the nation.

We were in the middle of a rare home-and-home series with the Georgia Bulldogs, due to the remodeling of Jacksonville Municipal Stadium to accommodate the Jaguar expansion team. Ray Goff's team had never beaten us and he was hanging on to his job by a thread. Although the game was in Gainesville, this seemed to be the perfect time for the Bulldogs to pull off an upset. And they certainly had bad intentions of spoiling our season. In 1994 at Ben Hill Griffin, our defense had rebounded from a 36–33 loss to Auburn two weeks before, which knocked us from No. 1, by getting four Georgia turnovers. We crushed the Bulldogs 52–14 and I gave away so many game balls we almost ran out. Our defense scored three times on touchdowns by Michael Gilmore, James Bates, and Darren Hambrick.

Bulldog fans were even more ticked off when the Gators traveled to Athens for the first time in 1995 and set what we believed was a record for most points scored in Sanford Stadium, winning 52–17. Danny threw for five touchdowns before coming out in the third quarter. Eric Kresser pitched two more.

The '95 team had a good group of seniors like Chris Doering, Mark Campbell, Henry McMillan, and Johnny Church. With their leadership we rolled through Northern Illinois 58–20, South Carolina 63–7, Vanderbilt 38–7, and sixth-ranked Florida State 35–24. We then beat Arkansas in Atlanta for our third straight SEC title. Linebacker Ben Hanks intercepted a lateral by Razorback quarterback Barry Lunney and returned it ninety-five yards for a touchdown in the third quarter of our 34–3 victory.

We were 12-0 and ranked No. 2. We'd just had the school's first unbeaten and untied regular season.

This was one of the top SEC teams of all time when you consider how difficult it was to go 12-0. That's happened only a handful of times in SEC history. Our offense was considered to be almost unstoppable, averaging 44.5 points a game. Our average margin of victory was 11 points. And we

Jerri, Amy, and Lisa after Florida's first-ever
unbeaten regular season (11-0) in 1995.

had beaten three Top Ten teams. We were on the cover of *SI*. So maybe
that's why we were a slight favorite of somewhere between 1.5 and 3.5
points over No. 1–ranked Nebraska in the Fiesta Bowl. The guys in Las
Vegas thought we were better. And so did we.

The Fiesta Bowl on January 2, 1996, was billed as a battle between the
undefeated Gators of the SEC and the undefeated Cornhuskers of the Big
Eight, a conference in its final days, about to become the Big Twelve with
the addition of Texas, Texas A&M, Texas Tech, and Baylor from the old
Southwest Conference.

Tom Osborne had built one of the all-time powerhouses in college
football history. And we were about to experience their wrath. Some say
that Nebraska team was the best team in history. I asked Coach Osborne
that question years later, but he wouldn't ever say one team was better
than the other. He did admit his '95 team was the only one that never had
a close game all season, with an average margin of victory of 38.6 points.

It was a bad night all the way around. Before the game started, a Gator
fan ten to twenty rows up in the Florida section had a heart attack and

died. On the opening kickoff, Kavin Walton tore up his knee. Nebraska scored and kicked off. Jacquez Green ran it back and did sort of a split—his hip was thrown out of joint on what looked like one of the worst injuries we'd ever seen. They stopped play for several minutes before Quezzie left in an ambulance. (Thankfully, he came back the next year and wound up making All-American.)

Nebraska had a good defensive plan and Danny felt the brunt of the Nebraska pass rush. They would fake the blitz or they'd come with the zone blitz—numerous guys on the line of scrimmage, some standing up.

"They had a [good] scheme and were really getting after us, coming at me," Danny remembered. "We weren't using the shotgun at that time, so the guys came clean off the ball. But even if we'd scored fifty points it wouldn't have been enough because their offense was so powerful."

Tommie Frazier, an option quarterback, was a one-man wrecking crew against us—he rushed for 199 yards, including a 75-yard touchdown run on which he broke eight tackles. Lawrence Phillips carried twenty-five times for 165 yards and two touchdowns. The Cornhusker defense held us to 269 yards of total offense, including minus 28 yards rushing, while registering three interceptions, a fumble recovery, seven quarterback sacks, and a safety when Danny was sacked during a 29–0 second-quarter run by Nebraska.

Some of our players took the loss to Nebraska harder than others. Danny just wiped it clean from his memory.

Offensive lineman Donnie Young of Venice, one of our captains, remembers the pain. "It was in none of our blood to lose a game—to be at the pinnacle of college football and taking a whippin' like that," he recalled. "It was pretty bad. I told *Sports Illustrated* I felt like my father had taken me out in the middle of the field and spanked my butt right in front of eighty-five thousand people!"

A few of our guys admitted they walked on the field expecting to beat Nebraska. Jacquez went on to say we were "full of ourselves," and he was correct.

So we learned a lot from the '95 season that really helped us in '96—like adopting the shotgun in the championship games to give our quarterback a better view of the blitz.

It stung, but we had to put that one behind us and shore up our weaknesses, because Gator football still had a bright future. We had to get bigger and stronger on defense, so we went out and got Jerry Schmidt as strength and conditioning coach. And it was time to make another staff change.

Our defensive coordinator, Bob Pruett, had resigned to become head coach of his alma mater, Marshall. Jeremy Foley brought me a stat sheet of the best defensive teams. Kansas State, coached in part by co-defensive coordinator Bob Stoops, was No. 1 in the country. I began calling out to Manhattan, Kansas, for Coach Bill Snyder in hopes of obtaining permission to talk to Bobby. After numerous attempts and no return call, I decided to try a different strategy.

One of the coaches on our staff, Lawson Holland, had come from Oklahoma State and had met Bobby at the Big Twelve coaches' meetings. So the next time I called Bobby and the secretary asked who was calling, I told her, "Tell him it's Lawson Holland," and finally got through. Bobby answered, "Hey, Lawson." I told Bobby who it was and then asked him if was interested in talking to us about our coordinator job—and he said yes. And Bobby turned out to be one of the best hires I ever made.

As for Coach Snyder, I called him back and told his secretary, "Please tell him I am trying to hire Bobby Stoops as our defensive coordinator." So he knew it. Coach Snyder and I are good friends today and we still joke about it.

What did I see in Bobby Stoops besides the stats sheet? I saw a very class individual who had an ability to relate to the players. We had never really gotten down to the X's and O's of his scheme, but once we hit spring practice I could tell he was an outstanding coach and our kind of guy.

When Coach Stoops arrived he jumped right in, with complete control of the defense, a key element in our championship chase.

We were loaded on offense and our squad had a bunch of fourth- and fifth-year players. Danny and his offensive guys loved to go up and down the field as fast as they could and score as many points as possible. And really Coach Stoops had not seen that type of offense in the Big Twelve—or the kind of speed that we had at Florida. So it was a bit different at first, maybe a bit frustrating, but an experience he would never forget. He recalled that first scrimmage:

"I looked out there and there's Danny Wuerffel, the [eventual] Heisman Trophy winner, at quarterback and Fred Taylor at tailback. You got Reidel Anthony and Ike Hilliard split wide. And Jacquez Green in the slot. They go about four plays, touchdown. Coach says, 'Okay, flip it around.' They go four or five plays, touchdown. 'All right, flip it around again.' Three more plays, touchdown. You talk about stressing out a defense! Coach [Spurrier] looks over at me and says, 'Stoopsie! We gonna be able to force a punt this year?'"

I was just kidding around with Bobby, of course. At K-State, their defense had been superb. He was accustomed to stopping people. But it was an awakening of sorts. The real wakeup call, however, came in Knoxville.

As a player at Iowa and a coach at K-State, Bobby was no stranger to big games at major venues like the Rose Bowl in Pasadena, California; the Big House (Michigan Stadium) in Ann Arbor; and Ohio State's Horseshoe in Columbus. But Bobby said he'd never seen anything like the hoopla surrounding his third game with the Gators on the night of September 21, 1996. He said, "The publicity and hype around that game . . . I had not been involved in such an important role in a game like that, so to me it was amazing."

The rain was falling hard in Neyland Stadium. The largest crowd ever to see a college football game to date (107,608) was about to witness a shootout between two of the all-time best college quarterbacks—Danny Wuerffel and Peyton Manning. We hoped Danny wasn't going to have an issue gripping a wet football, as he sometimes did.

We were ranked No. 4, going after our fourth straight win over the No. 2–ranked Vols. The outcome was also going to weigh heavily for

Danny and Peyton in the balloting for the Heisman Trophy, as well as deciding which team had a shot to win the SEC East Division conference championship—and maybe even more.

From the very start, we were in attack mode, converting a fourth and ten at the Vols' 35. Danny hit Reidel for a touchdown to start things off in what Coach Phillip Fulmer would later call "the darnedest first quarter I ever saw." On the Vols' first drive, Teako Brown intercepted Manning, followed by Terry Jackson hauling in a ten-yard TD pass. Early in the second period, in less than a sixty-second interval, Danny fired two more touchdown passes—first to Ike Hilliard and then, following an interception by James Bates, to Jacquez Green. That made four touchdown passes to four different receivers. Suddenly we were ahead 28–0. And then Anthone Lott returned a fumble for a touchdown to make it 35–0.

We intercepted Peyton four times that night, made eight pass deflections, recovered two fumbles, and threw their ball carriers for losses five times—impressive stats for Coach Stoops's SEC debut. The Vols would score just before the half. A bunch of their fans headed for the exits, giving up hope of their team staging a dramatic comeback.

Peyton was too good to be held down, however. With eight minutes left in the game, Tennessee cut our lead, 35–22. Although the Vols scored to make it 35–29 with ten seconds remaining, it was never really that close. We recovered the onside kick to kill the clock. But we had allowed them back in the game. And Danny had only 155 yards passing. "At least they can't accuse us of running up the score on them," I said to the media.

Because we were somewhat subdued in our locker room, one of the Tennessee writers wrote, "Big Crowd, Big Game, Big Stadium—No Big Deal to Gators." The article said it was "just another day at the ball park" for us. But that wasn't it. We didn't like the way we played after having a big lead.

Peyton threw for 492 yards, more than any Tennessee quarterback in history. He admitted he "picked a bad night" to throw four interceptions against a team like Florida." He simply saw it as a case of Tennessee falling behind and running out of time.

We went from No. 4 to No. 1 as Arizona State also beat Nebraska that night. A few weeks later Tennessee was upset by Memphis. In the coming weeks we turned it up a notch, thrashing our next four SEC opponents by a combined differential of 184 points: Kentucky 65–0, Arkansas 42–7, LSU 56–13, and Auburn 51–10. And that brought us to our annual game with Georgia, which was now back in Jacksonville.

The new-look Alltel Stadium was decked out mostly in Jaguar teal, except for the school colors and pageantry of Florida versus Georgia. That day, Wuerffel threw four touchdown passes and our defense held the Bulldogs to under three hundred yards total offense. Pretty soon there was more teal showing than red and black as Bulldog fans couldn't stand the sight of us handing Georgia one of its worst defeats ever, 47–7, and began departing early.

The next week we needed to beat Vanderbilt to clinch the SEC East, but it proved to be a tough game for us in Nashville. We led 28–7 when our starting offensive left tackle, Zach Piller, suffered a leg fracture. The pause of fifteen minutes for medical attention created a different momentum swing.

Danny checked to a quick pass and one of our guards didn't get the audible. Their blitzing linebacker knocked the ball out of Danny's hands; it took one hop and bounced right back to the linebacker as he ran for a touchdown. It was 28–14 just like that—bang, bang!—still in the third quarter. Then they scored to make it 28–21. On fourth and one, Danny sneaked for a first down and we ran out the clock. Vandy made us earn it. We survived to keep our No. 1 ranking.

Piller's injury turned out not to be as bad as we thought, although he wouldn't return for a month. In practice that week we also lost our offensive right tackle, Mo Collins, with a knee sprain. That left a big hole in a very good offensive line that included starting center Jeff Mitchell and starting guards Donnie Young and Ryan Kalich. And we were going up against one of the best front sevens in the country without either Collins or Piller in the battle of the undefeateds: No. 1 Florida versus No. 2 Florida State. It was believed to be only the fourth time in history that two unbeaten college teams had met in the final game of the regular season. Seems like we were always running up against one of the Seminoles' best teams in the final game. The problem was that the loser would drop a notch in the poll and leave a backdoor for Arizona State or Ohio State to jump over them. That's not something we were talking about or even thinking about, however, as we kicked it off against FSU.

Defensive end Peter Boulware from Spring Valley High School in Columbia, South Carolina, blocked a punt on us as the Seminoles took a 17–0 lead in the first quarter, but it was still a game we could win.

We had a touchdown pass nullified on a questionable holding call by an SEC official. Then those same SEC officials turned a blind eye to the numerous late hits by FSU on Danny, calling only three roughing penalties when they could have called twenty-three. Danny's father counted thirty-two times that he was knocked down—most all of them well after throwing the ball.

That was the year the FSU defensive players bragged about knocking out quarterbacks. Their coaching staff said they taught their players to hit "to the echo of the whistle." In other words, everybody else stopped on the whistle. But they got to keep hitting. It was not a team that I admired for the way they played.

Danny threw three interceptions in the first half, but he rallied in the second half to connect on three touchdown passes. I had great respect and admiration for the way he hung in there, despite taking a beating on those late hits. Some of his teammates felt they had let him down. Ike Hilliard felt so badly about the way he played that he apologized to some of his teammates. "Just to show you how bad I played," Ike recalled years later, "I didn't even start in the SEC championship game."

Warrick Dunn ran for a bunch of yards (185). Danny connected late with Reidel Anthony for a two-yard touchdown to make it 24–21, and we tried an onside kick that went out of bounds. So we had lost our first game, and maybe a lot more.

We were almost certainly out of any chance of winning a national championship at that point. Danny was one of the few who kept believing—he told the media he felt we still had a chance.

We needed to keep our focus on the SEC title game, but I also wanted to come to the defense of my player. As a coach, when your player takes a beating like that, you can't sit back and say, "That's just part of football— the referees have to control it." You have to speak out and defend your players in that situation. So I did. But it was only meant to support one of my players who was treated unfairly by FSU and the SEC referees.

On Monday after seeing the tape over and over, I called some of the media in to show them just how negligent the officials had been. It wasn't something I wanted to be forgotten. And what was about to transpire would bring the issue back front and center in the coming weeks.

Our starting tackles were back, but it was time to tweak our offense. I asked our center Wylie Ritch if he could snap the ball in the shotgun. He said he did it in high school and it would be no problem. Danny said he'd done a little of it in high school, too. They were both very comfortable with it. Looking back, we should probably have done a little bit more of it earlier. Although in the nineties at Florida we threw more touchdown passes than any school in America without using the shotgun.

We ran the new formation on about 60 percent of the plays against Alabama in the SEC championship game. Danny flourished, bouncing back from the bumps and bruises, passing for six touchdowns and 401 yards against the No. 1 pass defense in the nation as we beat Alabama, 45–30, for our fourth straight SEC title. Wylie said he remembered that he'd read before the game that "Alabama had only allowed six touch-down passes all year and Danny threw six against them."

Our SEC championship game victory eased a little of the pain from our FSU loss and so did Danny winning the Heisman Trophy a week later in New York City. It marked the first time a Heisman winner came from a school coached by another Heisman winner.

Once the news came that we were playing a rematch with FSU in the Sugar Bowl, we didn't even talk about the national championship in practice.

After losing in Tallahassee, we needed five things to happen for us to win the national championship. The odds on those five things happening, if each game was fifty-fifty, were 32–1.

1. Michigan had to beat Ohio State in the last game of the season.
2. Texas had to beat Nebraska in the very first Big Twelve championship game.
3. We had to beat Alabama in the SEC championship game.
4. Ohio State had to recover from a loss to Michigan to defeat unbeaten No. 2–ranked Arizona State in the Rose Bowl on January 1.
5. We had to beat Florida State in the Sugar Bowl rematch.

We had a month to prepare for the game in New Orleans on January 2, 1997. FSU and Arizona State were still undefeated and were ranked 1-2. Nebraska and Ohio State, each with a regular-season loss, were ranked 3-4. We had one loss and were ranked No. 5.

The first three happened. Underdog Michigan overcame its archrival Ohio State 13–9. We took care of number 3 by beating Alabama on December 7 after the Longhorns did their part on number 2 with a 37–27 victory over the Cornhuskers in St. Louis. Then, on the evening before the Nokia Sugar Bowl, we had just pulled into our hotel in Gonzalez, Louisiana, and turned on the TV with about two minutes left in the Rose Bowl.

With Scotty and Jerri celebrating the 1996 SEC championship.

Ohio State quarterback Joe Germaine hit David Boston for a touchdown to beat Jake Plummer's Arizona State team 20–17.

Our players came out of the Holiday Inn, jumping around, yelling and screaming. "There was no way we were going to lose another national championship game," said Donnie Young, who remembered all too well what happened the year before in the loss to Nebraska.

Quezzie Green said his teammates had been talking about it all week, "but we never thought it would happen." Defensive lineman Reggie McGrew said the confidence was reflected in the face of his roommate Ed Chester that "we had a chance!"

I told them: "Some way or another the Lord has put it in our hands. God helps those who help themselves. The opportunity is here. Now we have to take advantage of it. It's time for us to all come together."

I was going to do my best to see that the officials were aware of FSU's style of dirty play, which was widely known to a lot of coaches, and not like everybody else played. You want to beat a team like that.

I remember Joe Paterno said one time: "I want to beat your guys with my guys and nobody gets hurt. I want all your best players to play and my best players to play. And we'll have a heck of a game. And when it's over we'll shake hands and go on about our business."

FSU played Penn State in the 2006 Orange Bowl and the referees came to Coach Paterno and said, "Now, we're going to referee pregame warm-ups because we don't want any fights out there." Coach Paterno looked at them and said: "Fights? We're not here to fight! We're here to play football."

Why can't we all adopt that philosophy? That's what it's all about. We're here to play football, clean, fair, and hopefully nobody gets hurt. And the team that plays the best wins the game.

In that 2006 Orange Bowl, Penn State won over FSU 26–23 in the third overtime on Kevin Kelly's twenty-nine-yard field goal.

In thirty years I've never had anybody accuse our teams of playing dirty. And the only team I've criticized was the 1996 FSU defensive unit. So maybe people will believe I really had a point.

I've been to only one referees' meeting before a bowl game: the 1996 national championship game. Usually, we would send an assistant coach to talk about general rules. But this time I also went. And FSU sent AD Dave Hart, who had already called me a crybaby. "Give him a pacifier, put him to bed, and tell him to quit crying," Hart had said.

I asked Randy Christal, the head ref from the Big Twelve, to give me his interpretation on the roughing-the-passer rule. He looked at me sort of funny. And he said, "Common sense. After he's thrown the ball and the guy rushing knows he's thrown the ball, he has to get out of the way. He can't hit him."

I said, "You know what? I thought that was the rule. But we don't call it like that in the SEC. The SEC allows one step and you can knock the crap out of the guy. And that's okay? That's what the SEC guy told me in Tallahassee. He said he was 'within one step.' And I said, 'The ball's clearly thrown and the guy can still clobber him?'"

That was the SEC rule back then. Not anymore. They protect quarter-backs now.

So Hart said he wanted to know how they called holding because "those Florida linemen really hold a lot." And the head ref said, "I'm going to let these guys push and shove and if the hand gets in there, okay, but you can't tackle them and you can't bear-hug them." And I said, "You know what, I thought that's what holding was."

The one holding call they had made against us in the loss at Tallahassee was when our center snapped the ball and their guy hooked under his arm. And they called the touchdown back that Danny Wuerffel had thrown to Reidel Anthony. It was a bad call. Refereeing is much better now. They get trained better and they get rid of the ones that blow a bunch of calls.

So Dave Hart was wanting to know about the holding penalties. And Randy Christal finally said to him, "Let me tell you something. This ain't my first rodeo, as we say in Texas. We're going to have a good, clean, fair ball game here."

FSU got a couple roughing calls early in the game. And after that they quit hitting him late. But Danny also got the ball out of the shotgun quicker.

Clearly we needed somebody to make some big plays. We were leading 17–10 in the second quarter when it happened: Ike Hilliard was on a mission to redeem himself and about to execute one of the most famous plays in Florida football history to complete a four-play, sixty-five-yard scoring drive. At FSU's 31, from the right side, he ran a slant and leaped up in the air to catch the pass.

Ike could change directions as well as any receiver I've ever had so he was able to run that slant, get a foot down, put the brakes on, and dive into the end zone as the two FSU defensive backs collided.

"James Colzie was covering me," Ike recalled. "Danny got the ball out to me rather quickly. I was trying to protect myself because I thought Colzie was going to hit me from behind. I happened to see a linebacker coming out from the hash . . . and I just kind of leaned back. They ran into each other and I scored. I didn't spin out of it, but I did cut back. I was going left, planted my foot, and ended up going right."

Later Danny wrote in his book *Danny Wuerffel's Tales from the Gator Swamp* that Ike's move had "defied the laws of physics."

Reidel said later in an interview, "Ike's play was like a video game. I've never seen anything like it—the catch, stopping on a dime, reversing out, and going for the touchdown. It was one of the best plays I've ever seen. I've done similar stuff to it, but nothing like that."

Hilliard's touchdown was the first of his three in the game.

It was a close game at half and we led only 24–17. FSU's field goal cut our lead to 24–20 as the second half got under way. Then we put a drive together that reached their 1-yard line and I called an off-tackle play with zone blocking. But we allowed a blitzing linebacker to split our guys and they threw Fred Taylor for about a five-yard loss. Now it was second and goal at the 5. Then third and goal at the 7.

I couldn't find a play and we had to call time-out. Obviously we wanted a touchdown and not a field goal. I knew they were going to zone up a bit. So I made up the play.

We were going to get in our four-wide-receiver set. I told Ike and Reidel, "You be on the right here. They're going to play a soft Cover Two. You just sort of occupy that linebacker—sort of 'hug him up'—and clear through."

Reidel was supposed to be the target. Ike had caught a couple touchdowns in the first half. He was jukin' and jivin' and he was hot that day. And Reidel volunteered, "Coach, Ike's hot. Let him have it. I'll clear it through." Now, how's that for a teammate?

Under center, Danny dropped back, got hit as our left guard whiffed the tackle, and barely got the pass off. I thought their middle linebacker was going to intercept the ball or knock down the pass. The defensive back was all over Ike, but Ike hauled in a five-yard slant pass from Wuerffel and dove in the end zone for the touchdown to make it 31–20.

Also in the third quarter, Danny scrambled sixteen yards for the pylon and got hit at the goal line, but the ball broke the plane to make it 38–20.

Our defense dominated the second half, and except for that field goal, FSU didn't score again in the second. We threw only one pass in the fourth quarter and ran the ball very well to kill the clock. Terry Jackson scored on a pair of touchdown runs, forty-two yards and one yard, to finish off our fifty-two-point night.

The winner of the Miller-Digby Trophy as MVP of the game was Danny, who had kept on believing after the loss to FSU when many others didn't.

There was a lot of hugging and celebrating among our team as well as celebrating around the Gator Nation on the night of January 2, 1997. We had beaten our rival FSU, won the bowl game and maybe the national championship. But I still didn't know for sure. Norm Carlson came up and said, "We're the national champs!" And I said, "How do you know? They haven't voted yet." And he said, "Well, I think they're going to vote for us."

There were four teams with one loss. So we had to wait on the voting. What really helped us was being 12-1 and winners of the SEC championship game. I said, "We've only got one loss. But also our twelve wins really helped."

I think most everybody in the nation would say we had the best team in the country. After all, we lost one game by three points, at FSU, and they were No. 1 at that time. And in the game designated for the Bowl Alliance's championship, we beat them by thirty-two. But it was still subject to a vote.

That night we were back at the hotel celebrating when Norm said, "They voted and we won the AP poll." Without a playoff you are at the mercy of the voters. All we needed was confirmation of us finishing No. 1 in the Bowl Alliance, which was forthcoming in a matter of hours.

I guess the voters thought we were the best because they voted us No. 1. We finally accomplished that goal and won a national championship. Against all those odds, after losing the last regular game of the season at FSU.

College football is not fair. We know all that. We beat the No. 1 team by thirty-two points on a neutral field. But without the other teams losing it would have never been possible.

I see Coach Bowden now and then and we say hello but we don't get into all that late-hits stuff. He knows how I feel about the way they played back in that era—trying to hurt players, hitting quarterbacks late, hitting on the sidelines, etc. That was uncalled for and coaches can control that.

I've heard that somewhere in Coach Bowden's book, he mentioned that two nights before that Sugar Bowl game that I said to my team FSU was playing dirty—only to fire my boys up. I said it because I don't feel football should be played with the intent to hurt the opponent.

Today, Jimbo Fisher and the Seminoles play by the rules as well as anybody. I really have tremendous admiration for FSU, what they've done lately, including the national championship. Jimbo was 49-6 from 2012 through 2015. You've got to give them credit. I have no animosity toward FSU at all anymore. But I'll admit we did in 1996.

With the tough schedule Florida plays, what's fair about Florida playing FSU in the last game of the season? Nothing! We were in separate conferences. And in eleven of the twelve years I was at Florida, FSU was in the Top Five in the nation. We knocked them out some and they knocked us out a little bit more. We were 5-8-1 and we played them twice in bowl games. Most of the time they were Top Ten.

We like to tell everybody they beat us more than we beat them, but we won the one that really counted.

Final score: Florida 52, FSU 20. As someone once said, "Payback is hell!"

AFTER 1996, despite winning forty-nine games and another SEC championship the past five years, it just seemed like we'd lose that close one that hurt us in the SEC race.

Even though Danny graduated, we had some outstanding quarterbacks on excellent teams.

Eric Kresser transferred to Marshall in 1996. There his favorite target was Randy Moss, and the Thundering Herd won the Division 1-AA championship.

Doug Johnson (1997–1999) had an outstanding arm and led us to some big wins, as did Jesse Palmer (1997–2000).

Jesse and Rex Grossman (2000–2002) played extremely well in leading us to our sixth official SEC championship in 2000. Rex was consensus All-American, the 2001 Heisman Trophy runner-up, and Associated Press College Football Player of the Year.

Doug, Jesse, Noah Brindise, and Rex also benefited from some outstanding receivers during that period, like Travis McGriff (1994–99), Nafis Karim (1995–98), Reche Caldwell (1999–2001), Taylor Jacobs (1999–2002), and Jabar Gaffney (2000–2001).

After beating Peyton's Tennessee team 33–20 in september 1997 we went back to being ranked No. 1. It started to look like we were back on track.

We played three quarterbacks that year—Johnson, Brindise, and Palmer. Quezzie returned for an All-American season with sixty-one catches for ten touchdowns and over a thousand yards. Travis McGriff set school receiving records.

Fortune, however, took a turn. For the first and only time in my career at Florida, we lost to Georgia, 37–17, and for the first time we also lost to LSU, 28–21. We were out of the SEC race, and Tennessee, with one loss, won the Eastern Division. We had two losses, but we had a chance to knock out FSU and right the ship in the final regular-season game when they came in undefeated and were the nation's No. 1 team.

I really didn't know which quarterback to start or which one should play most of the game. So we decided to play two and rotate them every other play. I'm not a huge fan of doing that for a whole season, but I think once about every four or five years you can get away with it. So we rotated Noah Brindise and Doug Johnson the whole game. One of the positives about doing that is you don't have to worry about people stealing your signals—you just tell the quarterback and send in the play.

I didn't know which guy to put out there first—Doug or Noah. As I was driving my ten-year-old son, Scotty, to school, I said, "Which one of the quarterbacks do you run out there first to be the starter?"

He said, "Pops, Noah Brindise has never lost as a starter, has he?"

I said, "You're right! Let's run him out there first!"

Actually, looking back, maybe that's what we should have done every game.

So Noah was the starter and played well. Doug, who was the better passer, came in on the second snap.

It was a close game all the way. FSU was ahead 26–25, with a little over five minutes to play, and threatened to score after Warrick Dunn's punt return. Our defense made a tremendous stand and held them to a Sebastian Janikowski field goal, which gave the Seminoles a 29–25 lead with 2:28 left to play and FSU's No. 1 ranking on the line. I remember Janikowski doing the Gator Chomp as he was running off the field.

We were hustling to get a play in and so Doug had ten seconds on the play clock when he looked at Quezzie and signaled a curl-and-go. Doug loved to give him the curl-and-go signal, but most of the time it didn't work.

We needed a big play. We caught corner Samari Rolle biting on Quezzie's move and Doug threw a beautiful strike to him, a sixty-three-yard reception to the FSU 17. Fred Taylor ran it to the 1 and then carried the last yard for the score—his fourth rushing TD of the game. We had gone eighty yards in three plays, which caused CBS announcer Sean McDonough to say: "Perhaps too quickly!" There was 1:50 left.

Our defense stopped the Seminoles when linebacker Dwayne Thomas intercepted a third-down pass from Thad Busby at FSU's 31. Noah took a knee for the final snap. This time the quarterback rotation worked. As CBS color analyst Terry Donahue commented: "The quarterback play, between Brindise and Johnson, has been beyond expectations."

We won 32–29 in what some people called the greatest game ever played in the Swamp. One reason was that our win knocked FSU out of a chance to play in a national championship. But I've always said maybe it wasn't, since we didn't win a championship that night.

Robbie Andreu of *The Gainesville Sun* wrote: "It was a night to remember. This is a game that had all the elements. A near-brawl during warm-ups. Alternating quarterbacks and trick plays. Big scoring plays and big defensive plays. A dramatic winning drive late in the fourth quarter. A dramatic turnover to seal the win for the Gators in the closing seconds . . ."

That game put us in the Citrus Bowl against Coach Joe Paterno, one of my favorite people, and his Penn State Nittany Lions for a really fun week. We had a bet that if we won the game he'd have to wear my visor off the field. Or I'd wear a Penn State hat off the field. We beat them 21–6, but when I gave him the visor he wouldn't put in on—but I hear he kept it in his office for several years. I got a kick out of that and got a thrill out of competing against one of the all-time best coaches.

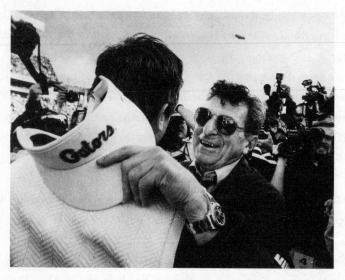

Coach Joe Paterno and I had a bet, but he didn't want to put on the visor after we beat Penn State 21–6 in the Citrus Bowl on New Year's Day 1998.

THE DEFENSES for the 1997–'98–'99 teams were just as good as '95–'96 when we posted back-to-back 12-1 seasons. Through 2001 we were blessed with All-American defenders such as: defensive linemen Ed Chester, Alex Brown, Jevon Kearse, and Gerard Warren; cornerbacks Fred Weary and Lito Sheppard; and linebackers Mike Peterson and Andra Davis.

We lost to Alabama in overtime during the 1999 regular season 40–39. After missing his first try, Alabama's kicker, Chris Kemp, got a second try at the winning extra point because we jumped offsides.

In that game our defense failed to stop Alabama's Shaun Alexander, who rushed twenty-eight times for 106 yards and three touchdowns. Doug Johnson and our offense got more yardage than Alabama, 449 to 447, and Doug threw four touchdown passes—with receiver Darrell Jackson grabbing three of those, including a seventy-three-yard touchdown catch.

We would wind up playing Alabama again with a chance for redemption—but couldn't get it done, losing the 1999 SEC championship to the Tide 34 –7. And with the 37–34 Citrus Bowl loss to Michigan State, we finished 9-4 with an SEC record of 7-1. Unfortunately, that meant we lost our last three at the end of the season. So we needed to get things turned around and back on track.

We went three seasons before capturing an SEC title again in 2000. One of our biggest wins was over LSU. I had closed practice Thursday and told the team about the message in country singer Lee Ann Womack's award-winning song "I Hope You Dance" and the lyrics "Promise me that you'll give faith a fighting chance."

WE BEAT Nick Saban's LSU team, 41–9, and then went on to defeat Auburn 28–6 to win our sixth official SEC championship. But in the Sugar Bowl that January we got knocked off by Miami 37–20.

We were in a position to win it all in 2001. We had a very good team and needed only to beat Tennessee at home in the final game of the regular season to win the SEC East.

We would have played Tennessee in our third game like we always did, but, in 2001, the third game of the season happened to fall on the Saturday after the 9/11 tragedy, when our nation's minds and hearts were on things bigger than college football.

But we had one of our best teams by the time we got to the final game. Rex Grossman was an outstanding passer with a strong and accurate arm, as evidenced by his 3,896 yards and thirty-four touchdown passes.

We had won six SEC games by an average of thirty-seven points. There were three excellent receivers in Reche Caldwell, Taylor Jacobs, and Jabar Gaffney.

Tennessee's offense struggled at times. The Vols came into the Swamp ranked No. 5 in the nation. We were No. 2.

Vols running back Travis Stephens had a big day against our defense, rushing for 228 yards on nineteen carries, most ever by an opponent in the Swamp and second most in history against the Gators to Herschel Walker's 238 in 1980, which took place in Jacksonville.

We trailed late in the game and Rex brought us back with a two-yard touchdown pass to Carlos Perez with 1:10 remaining. We went for two, but the Vols got pressure on Rex and his pass went over the head of Gaffney. We lost 34–32 in our final game of the year—and my final game on Florida Field.

Our schedule that year was ranked toughest in the country. For a record tenth time we went to a bowl after the 2001 regular season in what would turn out to be my twelfth and final season at Florida. We beat Maryland 56–23 to finish 10-2 and No. 3 in the nation.

Rex was Heisman Trophy runner-up, and receiver Gaffney and defensive end Alex Brown were consensus All-Americans. Alex was one of our all-time best pass rushers with a school record thirty-three sacks.

Ironically, as a player and a coach, I wound up losing both of my last games on Florida Field—to Miami as a player in 1966 and to Tennessee as coach in 2001. But as a player and coach I also won both of my last games in the Orange Bowl, beating Georgia Tech and Maryland.

After that, I felt like it might be getting time to move on.

Talking with Rex Grossman.

Chapter 14

GRIDLOCK IN WASHINGTON: WALKING AWAY FROM BIG MONEY

After beating Maryland 56–23 in the Orange Bowl on January 2, 2002, Jerri and I returned to Gainesville and then drove over to Crescent Beach. When we arrived, I said to her, "Let's take a ride down the beach." I wanted to discuss something important about our future.

"I think now is as good a time as any to go coach in the NFL," I said. At that point I had not talked to any pro teams yet, but it was clear in my mind that that's what was going to be next.

My last Florida team was probably as strong as any I ever had. We set all kinds of offensive records with Rex Grossman. During the 2001 season we'd had only two close games: a 23–20 loss at Auburn on October 13 and that 34–32 upset by Tennessee on December 1. And we clobbered everybody else. But we didn't win the SEC East Division—or titles of any kind. We really had nothing to show for it, except for finishing No. 3 in the final national polls.

Although I loved my time at Florida as both a player and a coach, it had hit me before the Orange Bowl game that it was time to go. However,

I really didn't get too emotional about it. At age fifty-six, I wanted time to pursue my dream of coaching in the NFL for five or six years, then resign or retire and head to Crescent Beach.

Ten years would have been long enough—twelve was pushing the envelope. I had read books and heard a lot of people say if you are a head of an organization, a decade is about long enough. Especially in coaching—unless you're ultrasuccessful like Bill Belichick or Bobby Stoops. They say that if you stay too long, sooner or later they'll get tired of you.

The longest my late father stayed in one job was eight years in Johnson City. He used to say they had probably heard all of his sermons. Maybe that was the case for me then—maybe they had heard all my sermons at Florida.

So I was about to resign as coach at the University of Florida after the 2001 season with that plan in mind.

I called Jeremy Foley and told him we needed to talk and he said he'd meet me at the beach. I told him about always wanting to coach in the NFL. He was pretty good about it. He said, "Well, you've been here twelve years—longer than anybody else—and we appreciate everything you've done here." Back then, to coach in one place ten or twelve years was considered to be a long time.

Despite rumors and suggestions to the contrary, there was never any rift between Jeremy and myself. All those rumors about me resigning over some issue are simply not accurate. There were no major issues that caused me to leave Florida. Over the years Jeremy and I had many discussions, and we ended all of them thinking alike and were always good friends. We remain friends and still get together every now and then. It was just a time in my life that I thought it was best for me to try something else.

I began to pursue the NFL job market, checking out three openings: the Washington Redskins, the Carolina Panthers, and the Tampa Bay Buccaneers. I didn't have an agent, but we had some advice from a financial adviser close to the family who also went with me to the Holiday Inn in Ocala to meet with Bucs GM Rich McKay and player personnel director Tim Ruskell. Since I had played for the Bucs, it seemed a logical fit for me as coach. Jon Gruden wound up getting the job in Tampa and won the Super Bowl the first year. He did a heck of a job. And I don't know if I would have had that team or not.

My talk with the Carolina Panthers was brief and didn't go anywhere.

Redskins owner Dan Snyder and my old coach and boss at Georgia Tech, Pepper Rodgers, flew into St. Augustine. I picked them up and we went to our house on the Intracoastal Waterway, which we call Wits' End.

Basically, Snyder made an offer I couldn't refuse. It was the most money any coach had made at that time. And when somebody is waving a couple million under your nose as a signing bonus, it's kind of tough to say "No" or "I'll wait."

I made up my mind to take the Redskins job about a week after the meeting with Snyder at the beach.

During our negotiations I told Snyder that in order for me to be successful we needed a general manager who knew the NFL inside and out—somebody I could really rely on and trust and work well with. "I'm not a general manager and head coach. I just want to be head coach," I said. After all, I didn't have any experience making trades, scouting for draft picks, or negotiating contracts. He told me that Bobby Beathard, the highly regarded former GM of the Redskins, was going to be hired in the next several days.

The way he described Bobby Beathard, it sounded like he was finalizing his contract. And I just assumed that he was on board and happy.

Beathard was a well traveled and astute front-office executive who worked for teams in Kansas City, Miami, Washington, and San Diego that competed in a total of seven Super Bowls, winning four of them: the Miami Dolphins after the 1972 and 1973 seasons and Washington after the 1982 and 1987 seasons. From 1978 to 1989, Beathard's Redskins teams played in three Super Bowls and won twice: XVII and XXII. So he sounded like the perfect choice.

I knew Beathard. He came to Gainesville when he was assessing our players for the draft. He is a quality guy and I thought he was an excellent choice. But I never talked to him about coming to Washington. I probably should have called him and made sure he was coming, but I didn't. Two or three days later Dan Snyder called me and said, "Beathard's out. He wanted too much money." I thought, *Well, we'll find somebody else.*

I think Snyder also interviewed Rich McKay and his protégé, Tim Ruskell, who had been in the Bucs' front office when I was coach of the Bandits. But Snyder decided he didn't want to hire either of them—he was going to be owner and general manager. Vinny Cerrato, who had previously served with the Redskins, was rehired as executive vice president of football operations and would be sort of the personnel director. The two of them pretty much had the final say.

You hear a lot about Dan Snyder—hard to work for, this, that, and the other. He was fine the first year. He let me bring in the coaches. We did the final cuts. For the draft, we leaned on their draft guys, since I didn't know much about it. We all worked together. We were lucky to hire Marvin Lewis, the Baltimore Ravens' defensive coordinator, current head coach of the Bengals. Marvin and his guys did an excellent job with our defense that first season. Preseason we were 4-1 and it got our hopes up.

But when the real teams showed up it was a little bit different.

For a while it even looked like we had a chance to win the division. The NFL is a tough league to win in with a lot of good teams all throughout the league. Every game you have about a fifty-fifty chance of winning. Obviously it is a bit different from college, where a lot of teams in the big conferences would schedule three or four opponents that they were a virtual lock to beat. If you split the other eight games and won the four games you should win, you could easily go 8-4.

It is much tougher coaching in the NFL, starting with finding and signing the right quarterback, which is not only essential, but critical.

We played three quarterbacks my first year in Washington—two of them I knew very well. We got Shane Matthews from the Bears and he opened the season as the starter. In 2002 with the Redskins, Shane completed 124 of 237 passes for 1,251 yards and eleven TDs in his eight games, seven of them starts. We went 3-4 with Shane starting.

We got Danny Wuerffel in a trade with the Houston Texans for defensive lineman Jerry DeLoach. Danny had been in the league five years—the first three with the New Orleans Saints, who drafted him in the fourth round. In 2002 he played in seven games and we were 2-2 in his four starts, during which he completed fifty-eight of ninety-two passes for 719 yards and three touchdowns.

And, finally, we went with Patrick Ramsey, the former Tulane quarterback, who'd been drafted thirty-second overall in 2002, as our starter. He played in nine games total, five as a starter. Ramsey completed 117 of 227 passes for 1,539 yards with nine touchdown passes. We were 2-3 in his five starts.

Stephen Davis was our workhorse running back, with 820 yards rushing in eight games. Our defense ranked fifth in total yards allowed, with competitive players like linebackers LaVar Arrington, Jessie Armstead, and Jeremiah Trotter; cornerbacks Champ Bailey and Fred Smoot; plus veterans like defensive lineman Bruce Smith and cornerback Darrell Green.

Through the first eight games we were 4-4 after beating Seattle, with hopes of settling on our quarterback and rising above .500 to make the playoffs. But we lost five of the next six, including one to the Jaguars. We wound up third in the NFC East with an overall record of 7-9. Just to show you how tight it was, nine of the sixteen teams in the NFC had the same record or worse. There is really no margin for error in the NFL.

By the second year, the coaching staff was not allowed to make the last cuts. Snyder and his staff made those. I wasn't even allowed to keep the quarterbacks that I wanted.

On the day we put the final roster together for 2003, I knew the end was near. I went home and told Jerri, "This has got to be my last year. This has no chance of working. I'm not in charge here. The Head Ball Coach has got to be in charge. The players look at me like I'm just another guy out there. We'll just have to do the best we can this year." And we did the best we could.

We started out 2003 beating three of our first four opponents, including New England. But we could never settle on a quarterback or keep our starter healthy, so we lost some close ones, dropping ten of the last twelve—five of those losses by four or fewer points.

Snyder pretty much decided we had to go with Patrick Ramsey as the quarterback. I was fine with that. But then Snyder and Cerrato brought in Rob Johnson from Southern Cal, who'd played at Buffalo as backup quarterback, but he never saw the field except in a limited role for two games. Ramsey couldn't finish the season because of a foot injury and we had to bring in another quarterback, Tim Hasselbeck.

I had wanted to keep Danny Wuerffel. But they said, "Nah, we're going to go with Johnson." I wasn't even the one to tell Danny he was cut. Dan Snyder's people told him first. And then I talked to him about it and said, "It wasn't my idea." So I knew my influence was diminished.

When the season was over I had a talk with Snyder. We finished 5-11 and he wanted me to resign, but he said he wasn't going to fire me. I knew he wanted me to resign and I knew I also needed to leave, because it was not the job I had signed up for. I walked out with a small "parting fee." Some people say I walked away from more money than any coach ever, since I had $15 million remaining on my contract.

I resigned and I could still say I've never been fired, although in retrospect that doesn't seem so important now. Maybe about two percent of all coaches can say they quit on their own terms—people like Barry Alvarez and Tom Osborne. I've always admired people like that.

I could have stayed on and probably got fired and collected a huge amount of money. But I'm not one to hang around just for a check.

I hadn't announced it to the media, although Snyder halfway announced it himself. He wanted to make sure I was finished. People started calling me. I said, "I haven't announced anything. I haven't signed any papers that I was leaving."

There were no regrets. I've been blessed to have made a lot of money. Besides, I like to be the first to do a lot of things. I'm told I was the first to make a million dollars a year coaching in college. Then I was the first to make $5 million in the NFL.

I've chosen really not to talk much about the experience in Washington, but in late 2015, when I was on David Feherty's golf show *Feherty*, he asked me what happened with the Redskins, and I told him: "I probably didn't do a very good job . . . And the situation wasn't what I was looking for, so it was time to move on."

The day I left the office in Washington I didn't even have to pack my stuff. They packed it up for me. I had already taken nearly everything else that I needed and wanted—all the books on the shelf and so forth. I came back from Florida and got the rest.

When I drove home from the Redskins office for the final time, I really wasn't feeling any particular emotion like relief, anger, melancholy, joy, et cetera. People ask me if I'm angry about what happened in Washington. No, I'm not, but I'm disappointed because I had asked for a good GM and was led to believe we were going to try and hire Beathard.

For me it was more about what I was going to do next. I just wasn't sure if I wanted to coach or not. But after a month or so it started hitting me that I needed to go back to coaching again.

As I have reflected on it over the years, I am still not sure what else I could have done in Washington, except maybe to have investigated details closer before taking the job and getting some stuff in writing.

Meanwhile, after leaving the Redskins, we stayed in Leesburg, Virginia, through 2004 so my son Scotty could finish at Loudoun County High School. I also discovered the importance of other things, like going to see Scotty practice and play football and lacrosse in high school. Leesburg was where he met his future wife, Jennifer Fairfax. They've since married and had a beautiful young daughter, Charlotte, with a boy on the way in the summer of 2016. Later Scotty came to Columbia and played for the Gamecocks before finally joining our coaching staff. He stayed on to work as an offensive analyst for Will Muschamp.

So a lot of good things did come to me because I took the Washington job. But I also found out that the lifestyle of the NFL coaches was not made for me.

I think taking a year off is good for coaches to recharge their batteries, if they can do it. It was good for me to step back. Suddenly I had plenty of time to work on my golf swing while I was sorting things out. I've always had great affection for golf. One of the things that attracted me to Florida as a recruit was the university course, where we played a lot in the summer and I learned how to make and win 50-cent bets.

I started messing around with golf as a teenager while living in Johnson City. I would head over to the Little League field at Kiwanis Park and hit an old 6-iron. I finally got a chance to play for free with the caddies at Johnson City Country Club on Thursday mornings. They had a set of clubs I could use and I'd bring some old balls.

I was fortunate enough to play the Augusta National course a few times and attend the Masters, which was memorable. I believe my best score was a 78. I've played in tournaments all over the country, made a lot of friends, and won a few trophies. So when I decided to get out of coaching again I turned back to working on and improving my golf game and played quite a few rounds. One of my more enjoyable days was when David Feherty of the Golf Channel came over and videotaped a hole with me at Marsh Creek Country Club in St. Augustine.

As I said to Feherty in that appearance on his show, at my best I was about a 3 handicap, but in later years my game hasn't been what I'd like it to be. In fact, during the hole we played with David he gave me a couple good pointers, including how to narrow my stance in order to gain a better follow-through.

I'd say David gained some pretty good insight about me as well. After taping the show, he told our local paper, "Football is certainly a big part of his life, but there are a lot more important things than football to Steve Spurrier."

Obviously the decision to coach in the NFL five or six years with the team I chose to coach didn't work out. So after two years of that and having a year off, I was hoping to go back into coaching, hopefully in the SEC somewhere. In 2004, I had pretty much gotten the word out that I wanted to return to coaching. I was a little over fifty-nine and still in good health. Friends and relatives had encouraged me, "Don't go out like this—go out a winner! Go out being successful!" And I said, "You're right. I don't want to go out the way I finished up with the Washington Redskins, resigning and all."

The Florida job actually opened up right about the same time when Ron Zook was fired in mid-season. For a brief moment, I flirted with the idea of returning to Gainesville. I thought, "Hey, great—right back in the same old slot and away we go."

I had three conversations with Jeremy—very brief. President Bernie Machen was obviously very much involved in it. They were doing a so-called national search, but Urban Meyer was even money to become the Gator coach.

The feeling on their end—and my end, now that I look back at it—is that a lot of times when coaches return to where they were so successful, they find it is very difficult to duplicate that success. For me it was a number of things: 68-5 at home in the Swamp. Those SEC championships, a national championship. And if you don't achieve what you did before, you may not measure up to your own track record.

Understanding that this president had been with Urban at Utah and he wanted him at Florida—he was a younger coach and ready to go—they made the right choice. And Urban did a super job there.

What's also interesting is that in 2004 the North Carolina head job was about to open up. Their coach, John Bunting, had gone 3-4 and was in the hot seat. But their kicker made a fifty-five-yard field goal on the final play

At American Football Coaches Association Golf Championship in Dallas, 1995.

Tossing the ball around with Heisman Trophy–winning quarterback Danny Wuerffel.

Ironically, it took beating South Carolina in 1996 to become the all-time winningest Gator football coach. With Jim Collins, Carl Franks, Bob Sanders, and Dwayne Dixon. All of them were on our staff for the 71 wins.

Our "Dookies" on the Gator staff celebrate four straight SEC titles: Bob Sanders, me, Jim Collins, and Carl Franks.

So who's that guy with Danny Wuerffel? Oh yeah, President Bill Clinton. The 1996 national champions visit the White House.

Me and 49er teammate John Brodie catching up years later in 1996.

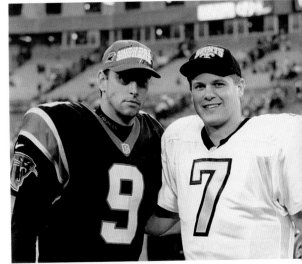

Two of the best in Gator football history before a Panthers-Saints game: Shane Matthews and Danny Wuerffel.

Riding the Daytona Beach waves with Steve Jr., summer '97.

Hiking with Jerri in the Lake Tahoe area before a golf tournament.

Getting a Gatorade bath from Kenyatta Walker in Atlanta after we beat Auburn, 28–6, to win the 2000 SEC championship game.

The Spurrier family in 2001.

In formal attire: Amy Moody, Steve Jr., Scotty, and Lisa Spurrier King in 2008.

With Jerri on our fortieth anniversary. "And when you get the choice to sit it out or dance, I hope you dance," as Lee Ann Womack sang.

Challenge golf match for charity at the Champions Tour pro-am in Birmingham vs. Tommy Tuberville. I was fortunate to play well and win. Lee Trevino was our pro.

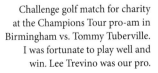

Kenny Chesney invited me onstage for my sixty-second birthday, April 20, 2007.

My hole in one at number seven on the Augusta National Par 3 course. Steve Jr. and Chip Presiozo attest.

Connor Shaw, the winningest South Carolina QB ever, who never lost a home game, celebrates our Top 10 year, state championship, Capital One Bowl, and Battle of Columbia.

Florida's Heisman winners at the Davey O'Brien Awards Dinner. Tim won the foundation's National Quarterback Award in 2007. Danny won it in 1995 and 1996. I was the Legends Award recipient in 2007.

These are the happiest times: Our family celebrates our third straight eleven-win season at South Carolina.

With South Carolina athletic director Ray Tanner and Governor Nikki Haley.

The Spurrier family celebrates my and Jerri's fiftieth wedding anniversary.

of the Miami game to beat them 31–28 and save his job, and the Tar Heels wound up 6-6. So North Carolina did not fire their coach that year. But I had one or two of their most prominent boosters call and ask if I was interested. I assured them I was. Even though they were our big rival at Duke. Everybody in the state knows the potential that the University of North Carolina has in all its sports programs.

But it wasn't to be, and soon the stars would align at the University of South Carolina.

Chapter 15

THE SOUTH CAROLINA YEARS

Both Steve Spurriers celebrate our first eleven-win
season at South Carolina.

A few people close to me probably thought I was naïve when they found out I had taken the South Carolina job. They wondered why I would want to coach in a program that had a losing record overall—maybe without much of a chance of winning an SEC title in my lifetime.

My old teammate Tommy Shannon said, "Steve, you don't want to do that! You can't win there. Nobody wins there! You'll be three or four years and then out."

I remember Jerri saying, "If you take the South Carolina job you've got to coach against Florida, Georgia, Tennessee, and all those guys."

And I said, "That's why we're going."

If I'd told them South Carolina, in the past ten years, had a record of 5-35 against Florida, Georgia, Tennessee, and Clemson, they definitely would have thought I'd become delusional. But I truly believed if we recruited well, given proper support, we could compete and maybe win an SEC championship. And I was willing to give it my best because this was an opportunity to go nowhere but up.

A negative attitude had crept into years of losing at South Carolina and hovered over the program for an extended period. The all-time win-loss record (501-512-44) was under .500. Since joining the SEC, the Gamecocks had won only about 30 percent of their conference games. Only three bowl wins—Lou Holtz's teams won two Outback Bowls and Brad Scott's team won the Carquest Bowl.

South Carolina's shining moments prior to that consisted of Paul Dietzel's 1969 team winning the ACC championship, George Rogers winning the Heisman Trophy in 1980, and Joe Morrison's ten-win season in 1984.

This was another welcome challenge: accomplishing something nobody had ever done at a school. Turning an average program into a winner—as my dad and others had said so often—requires the determination to change the mind-set. Winning coaches must get players believing they are good enough. And then it's "Let's go do it! Let's earn the victory!"

Our program would be built on better recruiting, a steady diet of good fundamentals, and a solid foundation of no-nonsense, no-excuse accountability. Then we wanted our players to exude the confidence that we could change things—that fate quite often would go our way. And we wanted them to have fun in the process of winning.

You try to prepare them every week to compete at a high level until the final whistle. To make that happen, a Head Ball Coach needs a like-minded staff. From the beginning I placed a big emphasis on hiring quality assistants. We needed more money to pay our staff better. When Mike McGee offered me $1.5 million a year, I asked him if I could take only $1.25 million and divide the $250,000 among the assistant coaches. And he said that was fine. So I might have been the first coach ever to take less than I was offered.

How were we going to change the mind-set at South Carolina? How had college football evolved since I'd left Florida? And what would the correct approach be upon returning to college football after a three-year absence?

The game had changed some, offering bigger challenges with far more decisions for quarterbacks. Most people think, *Just call a wide-open game, that's the way to do it.* Not necessarily. Sometimes that's not the best way to try and win. So quarterbacks shouldn't be given the total burden of calling audibles all the time at the line of scrimmage.

I remember in the early eighties at Duke, when we had our spring game, I told Ben Bennett, "You call the plays—I'm going to sit up there and watch and see how you do." After about the first three series, he said, "Coach, I don't want to call the plays. Because every time I call a play one of those linemen says, 'Let's run the ball . . . Let's run the ball!' And one of the receivers is saying, 'Throw it to me, I can get open on THIS!' So if you could just call them, it takes it all off me."

I said, "You know what, that makes sense!" He knew that I would generally call a wide-open game and use everything that was in the game plan. If it's in the game plan, let's give it a chance. But you can also be stupid as a play-caller.

Consuming the clock is part of winning the game. Sometimes being conservative is the best way to do that. You have to be "flexible"—that's the word I like to use. And throwing every time is not part of consuming the clock.

Some of these offensive coaches brag about running ninety-five plays and gaining six hundred yards. A lot of times they throw three straight passes and they're all incomplete. And then the other team throws three times and they're all incomplete. Thirty-five seconds has gone off the clock. That's how you get in those four-and-a-half-hour ball games that the fans don't like.

We already had a large base of passionate fans that showed up at Williams-Brice Stadium, the twenty-third-largest college football stadium in America with a capacity of 80,250. For a long time, it was one of the loudest places in the SEC. They screamed and yelled. Even that 0-11 season in 1999 they had a bunch of sellouts. They love their football in South Carolina, win or lose. There are no professional sports in the entire state. It's all about college sports. South Carolina. Clemson. Coastal Carolina. Wofford. Furman. Citadel. South Carolina State.

Still, it wasn't going to be easy at South Carolina. We won as many as eight games only once in our first five years. By 2010, in my sixth season, we finally launched the most successful run in Gamecock history.

We began turning the corner when we were able to start keeping some of the blue-chip talent at home, away from other rivals—especially Marcus Lattimore and Jadeveon Clowney, our two most notable recruits. Marcus was just a superb player and person. We were going 7-5 and 7-6 every year until he came along. Against Georgia in his second game he rushed for 182 yards and two touchdowns, breaking forty-two tackles on thirty-seven carries. I had an opportunity to introduce him at one of his speaking engagements years later and said, "Marcus Lattimore changed the face of South Carolina football." He really upgraded our team.

As we progressed, we also established more consistency at the quarterback position. Stephen Garcia got us started, but along came Connor Shaw and then Dylan Thompson at the peak of our ascent.

We won some big games, especially at Williams-Brice Stadium, probably none bigger than when we knocked off No. 1 Alabama in 2010. The week before, we'd just lost a tough one, 35–27, to Auburn and were 3-1 with an open date before Nick Saban brought his defending national champions to Columbia. South Carolina had never beaten a No. 1.

During the week we put together what we thought was a pretty good game plan. I had gone to Crescent Beach over the open date like I always did. So we had a little time to think about it some. And then we parlayed it into what some say is one of the best wins in Gamecock history.

As Lee Ann Womack sang in "I Hope You Dance," "Give faith a fighting chance." About once every couple years I tried to convince our guys if we did that, just maybe it would kick in for us. And so I said: "Fellas, if we give faith the best chance, prepare mentally and emotionally, get plenty of rest, eat correctly all this week . . . we're going to come to the ballpark with everybody committed to play the very best we can. And that's going to give us the best chance to beat Alabama. And then let faith take over." I told them even though we were underdogs, if we played well and the other team didn't, we could pull off a huge upset. This does happen.

I remembered what Ben Crenshaw said when he was captain of the 1999 Ryder Cup at the Country Club in Brookline, Massachusetts. The Europeans held what looked like an insurmountable 10–6 lead going into the final day. Crenshaw was one of the few people who thought the Americans could come back and win. "I'm going to leave y'all with one thought. I'm a big believer in fate. I have a good feeling about this," said Crenshaw. Justin Leonard's miraculous putt at the seventeenth hole sealed a half with Spain's José María Olazábal and capped what was then the biggest final-day comeback in Ryder Cup history.

We jumped on Alabama for a 21–3 lead with only a little over a minute gone in the second quarter. Quarterback Stephen Garcia had by far his best game ever as a Gamecock, completing seventeen of twenty passes for 201 yards and three touchdowns. Alshon Jeffery caught seven of his passes for 127 yards with touchdowns of twenty-six and fifteen yards that put us ahead of Alabama by eighteen.

We maximized every scoring opportunity. We punted only twice that day. Scored five touchdowns. Didn't have to kick field goals. Each team only had eight or nine possessions. And that's how underdogs pull off an upset: Play extremely well on offense and keep your opponent off the field.

Lattimore scored on a two-yard touchdown run with seven minutes to play and that clinched the win. Marcus had an excellent day with ninety-three yards rushing on twenty-three carries. Our defense played very well, sacking Greg McElroy seven times. Melvin Ingram and Stephon Gilmore had two sacks each. And we beat Alabama 35–21.

From there we went on to win our first SEC East Division title at South Carolina after beating the Gators in the Swamp 36–14 on November 13. Lattimore carried forty times for a career-high 212 yards and three touchdowns. Garcia played turnover-free football, completing fifteen of twenty-two passes for 156 yards. It was only our second win over the Gators in the last twenty games, breaking a twelve-game drought in the Swamp, where South Carolina had never won. This was Urban Meyer's last home game as Gators coach after winning two national championships at Florida. I couldn't help but make the comment: "Sometimes the Gamecocks get out alive!"

So we gave faith a chance and it worked out for us, all the way to Atlanta, where Auburn rocked us in the SEC championship game 56–17. We played and coached very poorly. The Tigers proved to be the real deal and they went on to win the national championship.

We lost to FSU in the Chick-fil-A Bowl, 26–17, and ended the season 9-5. Despite those losses, it was a major step in the right direction. I was fortunate to be named SEC Coach of the Year for the second time since taking the South Carolina job and our team finished ranked No. 22. With Marcus and the addition of Jadeveon Clowney, we upgraded and launched into a four-season run of forty-two wins, four bowls, and three straight Top Ten finishes (No. 8 in 2011, No. 7 in 2012, and No. 4 in 2013). When we all look back at those four seasons, I think Gamecock fans will cherish them even more as the high-water mark of our ten-plus seasons there.

We were very blessed with talent at South Carolina. Somebody recently told me that between Florida and South Carolina I've had more than one hundred players drafted by the NFL, the most of any coach. That's a tribute to our staff for recruiting them and coaching them up. I'll always be thankful and appreciative to the University of South Carolina and to our players and teams from 2005 to 2015, who hold just about every winning record there is.

It really started in the first year, when Sidney Rice developed into an All-SEC/All-America wide receiver. He played two years, '05 and '06, went to the NFL, and had an excellent pro career. His roommate Syvelle Newton was a very versatile all-purpose receiver/wildcat quarterback/defensive back for us during that time. Syvelle was one of four players in college football history with more than six hundred yards rushing, passing, and receiving. After that we continued to attract some high-quality receivers, including Kenny McKinley, who played for the Broncos until his untimely death in 2010.

I could write down a long list of players, but because of space I'm going to single out just a few others: running back Mike Davis; defensive end Devin Taylor; defensive tackles Kelcy Quarles and Melvin Ingram; defensive backs D. J. Swearinger, Johnathan Joseph, Victor Hampton, and Stephon Gilmore; wide receivers Pharoh Cooper and Bruce Ellington; punt returner/receiver Ace Sanders; linebacker Skai Moore; kickers Elliott Fry, Spencer Lanning, Josh Brown, and Ryan Succop.

Connor Shaw was special—our winningest quarterback in school history and one of my favorite players of all time. After we lost to Auburn 16–13 in 2011, I benched Garcia for his lack of consistent play. Connor came in and completed twenty-six of thirty-nine passes for 311 yards and four touchdowns as we hammered Kentucky 54–3. For that performance Connor was named SEC Offensive Player of the Week. We had found our next quarterback.

There was plenty of buzz about Jadeveon Clowney from South Pointe High School in Rock Hill, South Carolina, before he played a down because he was the No. 1 recruit in America and was such a force at six-foot-six and 240 pounds. Just think of a guy that large who was fast enough to be a sprinter on his high school track team. Players like Jadeveon don't come along in your state very often and coaching them is a wonderful opportunity.

In his time at South Carolina, Jadeveon made a huge impact right away. He went on to set school records in quarterback sacks (13.0) and

Jadeveon Clowney, No. 1 high school recruit and No. 1 NFL pick,
after we beat Michigan in the Outback Bowl. He made the
"hit heard 'round the world."

tackles for loss (23.5) per season. After his sophomore season he was unanimous All-America and SEC Defensive Player of the Year.

Of all his brilliant plays, there are two that will stand out forever in the minds of Gamecock fans:

1. As a true freshman, sacking Georgia quarterback Aaron Murray at the 10-yard line, creating a fumble that defensive lineman Melvin Ingram returned for a touchdown to put us ahead by ten in an eventual 45–42 win over Georgia in Athens.

2. That bone-jarring tackle he laid on Michigan running back Vincent Smith with eight minutes to play in the Outback Bowl after the 2012 regular season that went viral on the

Internet. Not only did Jadeveon stone Smith but he forced a fumble that he recovered and that set up the winning touchdown in our 33–28 victory. Jadeveon's hit won a 2013 ESPY Award for college football's best play of the season.

At the end of 2011 we set the table for the future with a 30–13 victory over Nebraska in the Capital One Bowl for our eleventh win, the most in school history. We finished No. 8 in the final polls, also our first Top Ten finish in school history.

The second leg of our "Hat Trick" of eleven-win seasons came in 2012. After we won our first five games, fifth-ranked Georgia was coming to Williams-Brice for a night game. ESPN's *College GameDay* was there and our guys were jacked up about it—especially Connor, who hails from Flowery Branch, Georgia. The way we came out of the gate caught the attention of the pollsters and we zoomed up to No. 6 in the AP poll.

There was a record crowd of 85,199 in our stadium. "I can remember how loud it was," Connor recalled. And it got louder, thanks to him, after he threw touchdown passes to Bruce Ellington and Rory Anderson and running for another score. Lattimore rushed for 109 yards and a TD and we added a 70-yard punt return by Ace Sanders. Along with Jadeveon and Brison Williams, who had seven solo tackles, our stout defense held Georgia running backs Todd Gurley and Keith Marshall together to just 76 yards rushing. We thumped Georgia 35–7 in one of those "statement games." Our guys were feeling it.

"We definitely sent a message out to the whole country," Lattimore said. "It's not the old South Carolina. We can play with y'all. We can play with anybody."

And that's how we felt after winning a school-record tenth straight game. I knew it was a special moment and I said as much. "If we play like this, maybe we have a chance for a real big year," I told the media. "Maybe." But I also was cautious because we had LSU and Florida, both on the road, the next two weeks.

We were 6-0, 4-0 in the SEC, and we soared to No. 3 in the Coaches Poll. Then we lost to LSU 23–21 in Baton Rouge. But when the first BCS polls came out after that game, we were still No. 7. Then we pretty much laid an egg in the Swamp, losing to Florida 44–11.

Connor was injured late in the year and we had to bring in Dylan Thompson to start against Clemson. He connected with Bruce Ellington on a six-yard touchdown pass with 4:17 to play at Clemson and we won 27–17. So with Dylan's help we were able to win our last five, capping off the 11-2 season with a bowl win. We were trailing Michigan 28–27 in the fourth quarter of the Outback Bowl when Dylan found Ellington on thirty-two-yard scoring pass to win the game, 33–28, with eleven seconds left. We wound up ranked eighth in the Associated Press poll and seventh in the Coaches Poll.

We were beginning to draw attention nationally as we headed into 2013 as the polls ranked us No. 6. Starting off with a 27–10 win over North Carolina, we slipped up the next week and lost to Georgia 41–30, for the first time in four years. We picked it up the next four games with wins over Vandy, Central Florida, Kentucky, and Arkansas. Then in our 23–21 loss at Knoxville, Connor came down with a knee injury and once again we called on Dylan as a starter at Missouri. But Connor came off the bench when we were trailing 17–0 and led us to a historic double-overtime comeback win, 27–24. His courage helped fuel our six-game winning streak that included beating Clemson for a record fifth straight year, 31–17.

Connor went out in style in the Capital One Bowl, where he accounted for five touchdowns and was named MVP. Connor passed for three touchdown passes, ran for one, and caught a nine-yard TD pass from Bruce Ellington as we beat No. 19 Wisconsin 34–24 and finished with our highest ranking in school history—fourth in the Associated Press Poll. He was the winningest quarterback in school history, with a 27–5 record as a starter, including that perfect 17–0 at Williams-Brice.

Unfortunately, Lattimore had suffered a major injury during the game

All the Spurriers were happy to celebrate the 34–24 Capital Bowl
victory over Wisconsin that marked yet another 11-win season.

against Tennessee, dislocating his right knee, tearing every ligament, and
damaging the nerve. Even though he had surgery on it performed by Dr.
James Andrews, Lattimore's knee was never the same. He was drafted in
the fifth round by the San Francisco 49ers but never played a down.

When it became evident he was never going to play in the NFL, Marcus released a statement: "I have given my heart and soul to the game that I love, and it's time for me to move on to the next chapter of my life and help others. I have given every ounce of my energy toward making a full recovery from my knee injury, and I have made a lot of progress. Unfortunately, getting my knee fully back to the level the NFL demands has proven to be insurmountable."

We all felt badly that Marcus never got the chance to show off his enormous talents at the highest level. He returned to Columbia as one of the most revered and loved Gamecocks. At one point he was going to be retained by Coach Will Muschamp as sort of an adviser/life coach, but in April the NCAA said because he was a former player and would be paid out of his own foundation, it wouldn't be allowed because of what the

NCAA considered to be a "recruiting advantage." But he remained on as a voluntary helper.

After Jadeveon's unanimous All-American sophomore year, his numbers were substantially lower. He made All-SEC and one All-American team in his junior season, but seemed to get nicked and dinged quite a bit. When the season ended, to nobody's surprise, he came out for the NFL draft and was the No. 1 overall pick by the Houston Texans.

Defensively, we began to struggle in 2014. In every game we won, our offense was on the field at the end of the game. And in games we lost—to Texas A&M, Missouri, Kentucky, Auburn, and Tennessee—we couldn't stop the other team. In 2014, we couldn't hold two-touchdown leads in the fourth period against four teams.

WE ALWAYS MADE it a point to celebrate our success and enjoy the game of football. That's why we went out of our way to lighten things up for our players—like our off-the-bench play in the spring game where somebody unexpectedly comes off the sidelines to catch a pass. We had been doing that off-the-bench play since I was at Florida with mostly walk-on receivers. One time, my son Scotty even caught one. Jerri was there watching and didn't know. And when he caught it, she screamed: "Scotty! Scotty caught a touchdown!" She didn't know that we snuck him off the bench.

It's a way to inject a little fun into spring games, because we don't play our regulars much, if at all. Jadeveon Clowney caught one. He was still on the team, but we didn't suit him up. He was wearing flip-flops and in his jersey. Connor Mitch underthrew him and Jadeveon was slipping and sliding everywhere.

In 2014 our women's basketball team had a big year, so I called Coach Dawn Staley. I said, "Dawn, we're going to introduce your team at halftime, so you're already going to be there. How would you like to catch the off-the-bench play back in the end zone—we throw this every spring game . . . if you can catch it." She said, "I can catch the damn ball! That will not be a problem!" I said, "Okay!" Turns out we were on about the 30 and it was getting late in the game, and it was going to be about a fifty-yard throw. I said to Dylan Thompson, "You've got to throw it, Dylan." It was in the air quite a while, but Dawn nestled it in and hung on.

Then we decided to go with celebrities. Darius Rucker is a big Gamecock fan, and has become a friend. My first year at South Carolina he did a concert and drew about forty thousand. And at our spring game in 2015, he caught the off-the-bench play. Conner Mitch almost led him out of the end zone and Darius barely got a foot in bounds!

Over the years I've become friends with fans who happened to be celebrities, including country star Kenny Chesney. I met him before the Tennessee game in '05. He's a big sports fan. Kenny knows Nick Saban and Sean Payton of the Saints—he's good friends with a lot of coaches. We're both from East Tennessee. I'd go to his concerts, go by his bus, sit around and talk a little bit. In 2014 he came by the office in Columbia. I talk to him about twice a year. He produced the ESPN movie about me, *The Believer*. I thought Kenny did a super job on the video—as most people have said.

Back in 1992 when I played in the Doral golf tournament in Miami, I got to meet Dolly Parton, who is also from East Tennessee. And I was really fired up that night when I met Jack Nicklaus, got to shake hands with him and took a picture with him. He was sitting with Dennis Erickson, then the Miami coach. We were playing in the pro-am. Dennis got the table with Jack Nicklaus and I went over and took a picture with him. But I also got one taken with Dolly Parton.

When people ask me how we were able to be so successful for three or four seasons and what happened the last two seasons at South Carolina, I tell them maybe we didn't recruit as well. Plus we lost some of our star players, like Jadeveon Clowney, Kelcy Quarles, Connor Shaw, and Marcus Lattimore. Defensively, we really struggled in 2014 and 2015, as we were at the bottom of the SEC in most defensive statistics.

How did we have those back-to-back-to-back banner seasons? We had better talent overall and quarterback Connor Shaw, I think. That's how you go 11-2. You don't do it by just winning every close game, but we did win a few. And in the last few years we often won our last game of the year and that gave us a head start on the next season. Winning the last four postseason games gave me personally an 11-10 bowl record. More and more I began to appreciate the winning records in bowls because that's what fans recall all summer. I'll never forget that 1991 season at Florida when we won our first ever SEC championship and our first ever ten-win season, but my good friend and big Gator fan Jim Kimbrough of Brooksville said: "Yeah, but you lost to Notre Dame in the Sugar Bowl." So fans value bowl games.

After my next-to-last win against North Carolina, at the start of the 2015 season, I was flipping around the TV and one of the TV guys—it might have been Dari Nowkhah on the SEC Network—said, "One thing I noticed about the South Carolina–North Carolina game last week was the stress on both coaches. Here was Steve Spurrier throwing his play sheet down. His quarterback threw a pass somewhere he shouldn't have. And then look at Larry Fedora over there. His guy threw an interception. Stress on these coaches is really getting greater than it used to be."

Well, Dari might have been on to something there about the stress. You can't sleep. You just lie there and your mind keeps going over and over things—"should have called this . . . should have called that . . ." All coaches do that. One reason the stress is there is that the money's so much bigger now, but we all accept that. But because it IS bigger than it was thirty or forty years ago, the stress on the coaches is bigger.

I was asked whether any coach would be around long enough—over a decade at each job—to become the winningest coach at two schools. He could, but it certainly wouldn't be easy.

Coach Saban moved around a little bit, but I don't think he'll leave Alabama. I think he's got five to seven more years, easily. His sixty-fifth birthday is October 31, 2016. LSU coach Les Miles is going to be sixty-three in November. Age is just a number. Mentally and physically you feel the same. When I was sixty-eight we went 11-2 and finished No. 4. However, your opponents start using your age against you and some of your own players start believing you will leave soon.

"I'm not looking to get out. I'm really not, even though I know that's going to start being talked about more now," Saban told ESPN a few months after winning his fifth national championship and going into his tenth season at Alabama. "What I have noticed is that it's the first time people are starting to say to recruits, 'He won't be there the whole time you're there,' because of my age."

You last thirty years as a head coach in my business and you see a lot of things and meet a lot of people. I think one reason I lasted as long as I did is that we did not have that many close games at Florida. We beat people by three, four, five touchdowns. When you win big, everybody on the bench gets to play. All the parents in the stands are saying, "My kid got to play." Next week in practice everybody is upbeat and happy. The walk-on kids are saying, "'I got in last week—maybe I'll get to play next week!'" Everybody's happy.

Then all of a sudden every game is going down to the wire. Backup players don't get in. I remember going over to our defense at South Carolina and asking the guys, "How much did you get to play?" And often they would say, "I didn't get in on defense, Coach." So I'm thinking, *His parents are up there in the stands and they'd kind of like to see him play.* But as coaches, you play your best players when you have to try and win it. When you have a lot of close games, which goes on all over the country, you don't get to play as many players, and the parents are unhappy. But aside from Alabama, Oklahoma, and Ohio State, not many teams win big all the time. When every game goes down to the wire, you second-guess yourself. You call a play that doesn't work and you say, "Gosh, I wish I had called something else. If I had called that play we would have had a minute and a half less in the game and we'd have won the game."

Then one day that expiration date arrives.

STEVE SPURRIER'S SOUTH CAROLINA TEAM RECORDS

- Home winning streak: 18
- Bowl wins: 5 total—4 in a row
- SEC wins in season—6 (3 times)
- Highest final rankings in AP and Coaches polls: No. 4 after 2013
- Beat Clemson 5 years in a row—2009–2013
- Beat Florida 4 of 5 years—2010–2014
- Beat Georgia 4 of 5 years—2010–2014
- Beat Tennessee for the first time ever in Knoxville
- Beat Florida for the first time ever in the Swamp
- Won 11 games in a season—3 times: 2011, 2012, 2013
- Finished Top Ten—3 times: 2011, 2012, 2013

Chapter 16

HOW AND WHY
I COACH
THE WAY I DO

You can't always appreciate it when you're in the middle of a uniquely successful run because you're usually so focused on the task at hand. We are all products of our environment, parents, schoolteachers, and coaches. As I have said, my dad instilled in his three children that if you competed in a game and kept score, you tried your best to win. And with that came a certain expectation that you would be successful. After being out of coaching for six months, I began to reflect back on some of the things I'd learned and done, realizing just how blessed I was to become a coach. Only then was I able to put some things in perspective. I'm going to sum up some of the ideas and thoughts I've touched on throughout the book, so I'm going to repeat myself a little, but every good coach knows the power of repetition.

Everything begins with having goals and an attitude to attain those goals without using excuses. You should also never settle for mediocrity. Decide on your goals and dreams and put them down in writing. Assemble the people and the team to achieve those goals. This practice began in 1987 when I started at Duke. And it set us on a path at Florida for a string of championships from 1990 to 2000—basically seven conference titles in eight straight years—and kept us at a high level of competition through three straight eleven-win seasons at South Carolina.

I encourage all coaches to do it. Pick some goals you feel you can make, but pick some that will be a reach, as well. It's okay if you don't hit them all. But it provides inspiration for better teamwork. I once read that "teamwork is the fuel that allows common people to attain uncommon results."

And that carried over from Duke to my next two head-coaching jobs in college.

I didn't get to Florida until I was forty-five, and I was sixty when I started at South Carolina. Head coaches at Power Five schools generally start in their thirties. So how does a guy begin as a head coach in the SEC at forty-five and become the winningest coach at two schools? No way that's supposed to happen! Besides, coaches usually don't last a long time at the same school anymore. It's just hard to do.

Despite the ups and downs of coaching, there are some things that give you great joy: winning—especially winning as an underdog; watching your players grow, achieve, and learn; accomplishing those goals together through the development of tremendous teamwork.

Some of the things I'm proud of:

- Our home records at Duke (12-3), Florida (68-5), and South Carolina (53-19). I always made it a point to show my appreciation of our home fans by clapping and pointing to the stands after those home victories, as my way of saying, "Thanks! You did your part. Now let's celebrate together until tomorrow and do this again next home game."
- Our record against all non–Power Five teams: 53-0.
- Rivalry games: Beating Clemson five times in a row at South Carolina (2009–2013). Beating Georgia seven years in a row at Florida (1990–1996). Beating North Carolina three years in a row (1987–1989) at Duke.

For me, it was also about calling ball plays. I don't know why some guys are pretty good play-callers and some are not. I think a little of it is that you're born with the instinct, or probably played quarterback during your career.

I called plays in high school—Coach Kermit Tipton let me do it. At Florida, Coach Ray Graves allowed his quarterbacks to call the plays. In the NFL, I called the plays occasionally, but mostly they were sent in.

We were pretty good at offense and I think play-calling is a big reason. When I became offensive coordinator at Duke in 1982, we were fourth in the nation in total offense. Calling plays came hand-in-hand with putting the offense together. This enabled me to become a head coach in the USFL at age thirty-seven after only five years as an assistant.

I kept adding to our playbook, and after formulating a philosophy, I wanted to take charge. Calling plays and being successful was what got me hired as Head Ball Coach of the Bandits in 1983. And I've done almost all of it during my coaching career since then.

Play-calling is something you have to practice because there needs to be a rhythm to it. So you need to call plays in practice if you're going to stay sharp for the games. I seldom used a script in practice, so it became more reflexive and made me think quicker, as if in game conditions.

Starting with Duke, I've carried a few of my favorite plays with me. And while many of them are based around passing, my ratio as a play-caller has been right around fifty-fifty running and passing.

There are certain elements of a coach's playbook that always remain, even if the ball plays evolve and change.

At Duke we ran two wide receivers, a tight end, and two running backs. In 1982, we put in two tight ends and one running back against Georgia Tech. We always called it our Tech formation,

The first time I ever ran the three-wide-receiver formation was at Tampa Bay. We called it the Bandit formation. Bandit Right, Bandit Left. Then we have a Bandit Left Over, Bandit Trips Right. We continued to call it that right through my time at Florida and South Carolina.

Signaling in the Bandit formation in 1992.

The Ernie Mills route—we called it Mills—was named after the post route Ernie Mills ran against Alabama in 1990. Shane Matthews threw out of our own end zone and Ernie nearly broke it for a touchdown. They had an angle on him and ran him down at about the 15. We scored, tied the game 10–10, and went on to post one of our biggest wins in school history, 17–13, in Tuscaloosa.

Trick plays are fun for everybody—but only when you win the game. Running trick plays and losing is no fun. You gotta win. That all goes together. Any fool can call a bunch of trick plays—hit some, miss some. But if you can win, that's what the fans love. Some people will remember the trick plays we pulled off from time to time, like the Hobble Play with Danny Wuerffel and Eric Kresser at the 1994 SEC championship. Or maybe the Emory & Henry formation. Looking back on it now, some observers say that drive changed the face of SEC football. Or springing the no-huddle offense on a team by surprise or perhaps an onside kick at just the right time. The important aspect of those strategies, plays, or formations is timing. Like when we went to the shotgun in the SEC championship game at Florida in '96.

We seemed to always come up with a nickname for our offense, although we didn't at South Carolina. At Duke we called it Air Ball. Being a basketball school, when we hit a long pass at Duke the students and fans would say, "Air-r-r-r Ball-l-l-l! Air-r-r-r Ball-l-l-l!" I didn't name our Florida offense the Fun 'N' Gun. Somebody else did, but it seemed to stick.

Our offense changed a little bit at South Carolina in about 2010. I hired Appalachian State offensive line coach Shawn Elliott. They'd had a lot of success with the quarterback read and the quarterback running the ball. We signed Marcus Lattimore that year, and he was very familiar with the zone read. And he was very good at it—maybe one of the best running backs in the history of college ball.

Unfortunately, because Marcus suffered several bad injuries that cut his career short, we'll never know just how good he would have become. But Marcus was a big boost for our running game and our team's success. We could use play action and also throw out of it with no problem.

Football has different trends as you go. In recent years, everyone has been more into the spread offense. While Mark Richt was at Georgia, he ran a fullback in the I formation—did it very well. Alabama also uses a fullback some. But now the latest style is a one-back scheme with a shotgun quarterback.

I just think you have to see what your players can do best and use that style of offense the most. I think there's still a lot of merit in putting the quarterback under center, handing off or dropping back to pass. But there's also merit in being in the shotgun, where you can get the ball out a little quicker and avoid the rush. I don't know where offensive trends are going to lead. I always took it year by year, talent by talent. Lately, running quarterbacks have been the new way to go. But there are two schools of thought.

There is also merit in having the quarterback tell the team what to do in the huddle as opposed to each player getting the signal. I'm a big believer in that, because the quarterback is your leader. However, for some reason, we chose to signal in to the wide receivers like everybody else. The assistant coaches thought that was the best way. We didn't ever huddle. We didn't get underneath center much. And when we did we fumbled a lot. It was just different.

As far as calling the plays and being the quarterback coach . . . we just stopped doing that because the game has changed.

Also, the kids come out of high school and they've been playing in the shotgun, so they'd rather be in the shotgun. So it's hard to tell them to get up there and drop back and throw. But I think there's a place for both underneath center and the shotgun.

I allowed a lot of delegation. Looking back, I wouldn't have delegated the play-calling as much. It was nobody's fault but mine. I acted like most other coaches the last couple years, which isn't my style. And we could have done a better job of hiding our signals. Everybody steals them now. It's common. You can't have just one guy standing there signaling them in so sometimes we had two.

Coaches have to be aware of teams stealing signals. It happens all the time. I watched how Nebraska tried to prevent it when I visited Lincoln in 2015. Coach Mike Riley has two guys with a towel or a big blanket shielding the signals. And the signal goes right to the quarterback. And the quarterback tells the team.

Skill sets were always critical, especially for our quarterbacks. Fundamentals went a long way toward developing them. We always believed success came by paying attention to detail and being repetitive in practice. Small things. For example, I used to line up basketballs for our quarterbacks when they were on their way out to practice so they could stop and snap off one hundred two-hand chest passes into the wall to improve their hand strength. Strong hands are crucial to really good passers.

The basic fundamentals of throwing the football are often overlooked by coaches. I know it came late for me, and I was on my way out of football as a player when I finally found a way to properly set up and pass the ball. But the best passing technique I learned as a player—and later came to teach as a coach—came in my last week with Tampa Bay. In 1977, before I was released by the Buccaneers, we had a new quarterback coach, Billy Nelsen, who had played for John McKay at Southern Cal. Billy was an NFL quarterback for eight years, mostly with the Cleveland Browns—made the Pro Bowl one year. Anyway, my last summer mini-camp with the Bucs he worked with me. And I found Billy Nelsen to be the best coach of quarterback fundamentals I ever had.

Coach Nelsen taught us the proper mechanics: Use two hands on ball position setup, right near the numbers, chest level. And he taught us that when setting up to throw, get the ball a little bit back to the right chest area—some people are higher, some a little lower—sort of like a batter with the bat in your hands. Stay up to throw. Get your head cocked to the left as much as possible.

I started doing that. And I really believe I was a better passer after my NFL career was over when I became a coach of quarterbacks than I ever was as a college or NFL player.

For many years as coach, I would throw with my quarterbacks in practice. But I stopped at about age sixty-four. And I always asked the receivers, "Who's throwing the best ball?" Of course the receivers always sided with the Head Ball Coach.

Billy Nelsen had three drills:

1. Hold the ball with two hands and run naturally downfield, turning your head back as far as you can and twisting your body slightly.
2. Keep those two hands together as you turn your shoulders so you will be in a better position to throw.
3. Turn the ball across your chest with your short karaoke steps, as quickly as you can. That helps with your footwork.

Billy was brilliant. I really enjoyed those three days right before I was cut. He lasted six years with the Bucs. I used those Billy Nelsen fundamentals and drills with every college quarterback I coached. So that's one positive takeaway from that one mini-camp with the Bucs. Thanks to Billy Nelsen I definitely became a decent quarterback coach.

Working regularly on fundamentals prepares you for that moment when your time comes to deliver. It also helps build confidence, so that you're ready. And no matter how much success you've had in the past, you cannot afford to take for granted that you'll continue to succeed.

Maintain flexibility in your thinking. Don't allow yourself or your team to become overconfident. One of the characteristics of a very successful person is the ability to transcend previous accomplishments. Put it away. That's one of the motivational keys I talk about all the time.

Often we hear stories of other teams in other sports that can inspire us as well. Like the one that came in the 1999 Women's World Cup soccer championship match when the United States beat China 5–4 in a shootout following a 0–0 draw.

With more than ninety thousand fans in the Rose Bowl and billions more watching around the world, the shootout was tied 4–4 with American Brandi, Chastain prepared to shoot. USA Coach Tony DiCicco said, "Brandi, you take it. But take it with your left foot." And Brandi, who normally practiced with her right foot, said, "Okay." She left-footed it across and curved it in. Then she took her shirt off because it was the winning kick, and away we went. It was historic for women's sports—for all sports—and a famous moment. It was her time and she stepped up.

Of course, everybody in the world knows it was Brandi Chastain's kick that won the game, 5–4, because she took the final kick. But the other four girls who made their kicks need to start a club called "I also made my kick!"

Brandi's story was about being ready at the "right time." You have to be as prepared as possible. And when the moment arises for your team, they're ready for you to go make the play. Brandi's was also a story about being flexible and the players' will. "It came down to them not allowing themselves to lose," DiCicco said.

BECAUSE I NEVER studied under one mentor, I tell people most of what I learned about coaching came out of books. So I am hoping there will be some things in my book—and especially this chapter—that can help coaches for years to come. But you also have to add your own touch when it comes to motivation.

Some people have this misconception that coaches can fire up their team with words alone, that by giving powerful pregame and halftime speeches they can elevate them to a championship level. As coaches, we try to get them ready for every week, to compete until the game is over. And that requires more than just motivational speeches. But a well-placed motivational speech can be effective a few times each year.

When I was in high school, at halftime about once a year in a big game against maybe Kingsport or Bristol, Coach Tipton would say, "Grab a partner." I remember when I was a sophomore and I didn't know what "Grab a partner" meant. It meant you got a teammate, hopefully somebody your own size, and you slapped each other in the face—Pow! Pow! Pow! That was supposed to get you fired up. During my time at Science Hill High School, I could never find a teammate to slap around. But our linemen and defensive guys sort of enjoyed that—a good slap in the face to get them going. I never taught that and certainly don't think that's a good way to get your team motivated, but it worked for the Hilltoppers of Johnson City.

I also believe that a good motivational talk is needed only once or twice a year. Personally, I tried to pick a big game for which maybe our team needed a little extra motivation. I also believe that if you give a big pep talk every week your players get tired of it. They turn deaf ears. I always told our team I wouldn't talk long, but demanded they listen closely.

There's a bunch of coaches out there who like to talk fifteen to twenty minutes after every practice. I don't do that. I tell them, "Listen up and we'll be out of here quickly and on our way."

From time to time you come upon something special that can become a tool for motivation, as I said about the Lee Ann Womack song "I Hope You Dance," which I used at both Florida and South Carolina. And of course I always remember Coach Ellenson's stories and the way he fired up players by asking them to sign the board committing to do their best.

On the other side of the spectrum, when things started going south at South Carolina in 2014, and we lost four out of five, I had to dig deep for something. We were reeling and I was starting to have deep concern. I heard Taylor Swift's "Shake It Off," and it occurred to me to tell the team and coaches to do just that.

After that we sort of adopted that theme. We shook it off and wound up winning three of the last four games, beating Miami for our fourth straight bowl victory and having a winning season. So in case I forgot to say it, thanks, Taylor, for reminding us to "Shake It Off."

As a coach, I was always searching for new goals, challenges, and different ways of doing things: some new wrinkles in our offense, maybe some different types of players and some new ways to accomplish more firsts, always with an emphasis on something that would fire up the players.

From the beginning I always tried to make the offense original. Before practice I printed up a schedule. One day in my first head coaching job at Tampa Bay, I handed one of them to John Rauch, former head coach of the Oakland Raiders and the Buffalo Bills. And he said, "Where'd you come up with all this?"

I said, "Little bit here, little bit there, along the way . . . does it look okay?"

He said, "Yeah, it looks pretty good."

Still he wanted to know where I got it.

I said, "Most of it I just sort of made up. And I guess some of it came from our 49er playbook."

And away we went.

Along the way you learn from experiencing new things. From being successful. And some things you can learn from failing.

Another one of Attila the Hun's best statements—and sometimes as coaches we forget this one—was "No chieftain will win every encounter. Sometimes you lose, regardless of how well you have prepared."

Sometimes in coaching we take tough losses very hard. We wish we'd done something differently. But that little quote right there—"No chieftain will win every encounter"—means you just have to keep trying to learn from the losses. Do your best every time out. Keep your focus.

That's why I would write something on the board every game: "Compete with Good Fundamentals," "Have Fun Competing," "Play Smart. Every Play. Every Snap," "Tremendous effort."

So in some cases, the pain of losing a game as a player can help you win later as a coach. We had that unbelievable 38–35 victory over Georgia at Williams-Brice Stadium. We beat Georgia a lot and overall I wound up 16-7 against the Bulldogs, but I never really got the chance to get even with Georgia. Because no matter how many times we beat them we can never take back that bitter loss I had as a player in 1966 that cost the Gators an SEC championship. If I count our win over Georgia my first year at Florida—freshmen could play only on the freshman squad—then I wound up 2-2 as a player against the Bulldogs. But they won the one that really counted my senior year, clobbering us in the second half. They ran the ball. They blitzed us. We didn't have pass protection for the blitz they were using, and I was trying to throw off my back foot and got one picked off for a score. We were not as prepared as we could have been. Blowing our chance to win an SEC title was a huge disappointment. But those memories of getting our butts beat last a lifetime. When I left coaching, the sixteen wins over Georgia were the most of any coach, of which I am proud. I will admit that my failure as a player certainly motivated me as a coach.

On the flip side, as old coaches used to say, you can't "sit on your laurels." One of the first things I did at Florida when I became the coach was tell the guys, "We may be four and zero, five and zero in the middle of the year, but we can't get full of ourselves because that's what, historically, the Gators have done." I told them we must "transcend previous accomplishments" if we were to win a championship. When you learn from past experience what you're facing, then maybe you can keep your players' attention and finish the job.

I'm convinced that our determination to "transcend previous accomplishments" helped me teach my players how to maintain momentum and factored in our successful record against the 'Dogs.

I HAVE MADE a collection of lists from the writings of my favorite philosophers, warriors, and coaches. As I acknowledged earlier, in chapter four, my list includes stuff from, among others, John Wooden, Attila the Hun, Sydney J. Harris, and Dr. James Garfield.

Dr. Garfield studied human behavior for sixteen years. He talks about characteristics and traits of peak performers—highly successful people. Maybe the most interesting thing Dr. Garfield said was: "Almost anyone can acquire these traits." So I wrote them down and I tried to acquire them. I tried to get our coaches to acquire them. And I tried to get our players to acquire them.

None were more important than his first one:

1. Attitude. We all know what a good attitude is and what a sorry attitude is. Always be positive.

Coach Red Wilson was the first coach I ever knew who handed out guidelines for becoming a successful coach. In 1980 the first one I saw was "Guidelines for a Good Player-Coach Relationship." I thought it was awesome and I had never seen anything like it. Over the years I added some of my own stuff and called it "Guidelines for a Good Ball Coach." I went over these with my staff every year and demanded that we follow these guidelines.

2. Treat all players fairly, the way they deserve to be treated. That was one of John Wooden's principles. Don't treat all players equally, because some of them haven't earned the right yet to be treated in any special way. Somebody asked one of Coach Wooden's former players, twenty years after he had retired as UCLA coach, "How did Coach Wooden treat his players?" He said, "It depended on how good a player you were." Star players? Yeah, they got a little extra special treatment.

3. After criticizing a player, say something positive to bring him back. If you must criticize, do it to a player's face. Not behind his back. Not to the media. Not downtown.

4. Try to make all players feel important—your walk-on players as well as your scholarship players. There was a kid named Trey Killingsworth, a walk-on at Florida, and after his playing days were over, he said: "Coach, us walk-ons always loved you because you made us feel important. We weren't just a bunch of guys out there—you talked to us all the time, got us in the game when we got far enough ahead." So, try to make all your players feel important.

5. Don't lose your temper or your emotions. Coach, coach, coach before you criticize.

6. Enthusiasm is contagious. Practice enthusiasm every day.

7. Your practice plans are important. Know what you're doing all through practice.

8. Fundamentals are the most important thing you can teach.

9. Never argue with or criticize another coach in front of a player.

10. Never allow a player to be disloyal to a coach.

11. Be concerned about injuries to all players. My first year at Florida, we were scrimmaging in the Swamp and Errict Rhett sort of got dinged on his neck. He lay there and lay there. I still remember, it was on about the 20-yard line at the south end. I ran out there and asked, "Errict, are you okay?" He said, "Yeah, Coach." So they came out and put the brace on him. We all stood there. Stopped the scrimmage. Everybody was standing around talking to Errict. Our trainer Chris Patrick came up to me and said, "Coach, I've been watching football here for thirty years. I've been a trainer since 1970. You're the first coach who ever stopped practice for an injury." He said, "Most of the time they say, 'Put the ball up there and let's go!' And everybody would walk off and leave the trainer with the player." So we cared about the players getting injured. But we got rid of the Astroturf on Florida Field before my first season in 1990. The players really were very appreciative.

12. Never allow a player to loaf.

13. Don't threaten a player unless you plan to back it up. If you make idle threats they won't believe anything you say.

14. Make the game fun for your players.

15. Do not berate the referees.

16. Don't use foul language.

17. Be willing to suspend or remove a star player if he's disruptive to the team. That one I applied in 1985, when I released the star receiver from the Bandits after warning him about his poor attitude.

18. Be open to new ideas and new techniques that can make your team better. Our passing game was new and different to the SEC in 1990.

19. Be sure to listen to your players. Don't do all the talking—let them talk some.

20. Honesty is the centerpiece of your coach-player relationship.

21. The priorities have got to be God, family, and then your team.

22. If you're a good coach, your players will play very close to how you teach them to play. This is one I tell our assistant coaches. Don't come in here and say, "He made a mistake, he made a mistake!" Well, you're a sorry coach if he keeps making mistakes all over the place. Teach him how to play and demand he does that.

23. When things are going good, you gotta stay on their butts to improve every day. When things are going bad, lighten up on them. That's a Vince Lombardi one. I think we did a good job in 2014 when we were 4-5. It would have been easy to chew their butts out. We took Taylor Swift's advice to "Shake It Off" and somehow won three out of four at the end of the season.

EARLIER IN MY COACHING CAREER, while I was attending the Senior Bowl in Mobile, Alabama, I was sitting around after practice with some old 49ers teammates, four or five of them, including linebacker Ed Beard. And Ed said, "Who'd have thunk that Spur would have become a football coach—and would have been a damn good one?"

That was a nice compliment, because I was not a very ambitious player and hadn't exactly been soaking up everything I needed to in order to become a coach.

What turned me around, I think, was a competitive fire that got me back to what I was missing as an NFL player. The 49ers drafted me and told me I was going to be groomed for four or five years as John Brodie's replacement. So I geared down. My "Give a Dang" was gone. I started playing a bunch of golf and enjoying life. So I didn't totally prepare myself as an NFL quarterback. Basically I lasted ten years, six of those playing behind Brodie.

That fire I lost? I eventually got it back as a coach. I think it was just a matter of having a wife and three kids and needing a job. And wanting to be successful in life. In coaching you want to see the guys you coach play well. You want to prepare them as best you can. Teach your players to play well. See the team winning. That's what it's all about.

That's the second part. The first part is establishing your own personal ground rules and a core philosophy. And that means sometimes having to take a stand for what you believe is the right thing to do when the majority doesn't agree with you. Doing your thing your way and never being afraid to be different.

One reward for having a decent season is getting to coach in All-Star games.

My first chance to be a head coach in an All-Star game was after the 1987 season at Duke. The director of the Blue-Gray game in Montgomery, Alabama, Fats Jones, called and invited me to be the Head Ball Coach of the Gray team. Our quarterback from Duke, Steve Slayden, was there, so we had good communication. Frank Howard, the legendary Clemson coach, was honorary coach of the Gray and former Missouri coach Don Faurot was honorary coach of the Blue. Frank Howard was a fun guy to be around.

We won 12–10, kicking a field goal with about ten seconds left in the game. I've still got the game ball.

In 1999 I was coaching in the East-West game in Palo Alto, California, at Stanford Stadium. I coached the East and Tom Brady was quarterback for the West. We shared the locker rooms and tried to avoid watching each other practice. Before practice one day, Tom came to see me and said, "Coach, would you watch me throw and tell me what you think?" I said, "Sure." We went outside the locker room and he threw to one of his teammates. I told Tom, "You have a natural, excellent throwing motion.

I've always believed you should hold the ball up near the numbers of your jersey, not down near your waist." So Tom raised the ball slightly in his pre-set throwing position. He is the only quarterback from either All-Star team who asked me about his throwing motion.

For whatever reason, I can only remember losing one All-Star game, and I must have coached in twelve to fourteen of these games. We simply tell our players that we will remember who won the game for the rest of our lives. Since we are keeping score, we might as well go out and "win this thing."

After an All-Star game played in Maui, Hawaii, I caught a ride on the LSU jet with Coach Nick Saban from Los Angeles to Baton Rouge. From there, the Florida plane picked me up and we headed to Gainesville. I've been known to bum a ride with other coaches: The Florida jet stops in Columbia, as every year all SEC coaches do the "ESPN Car Wash" interviews in Bristol, Connecticut. I've caught a ride on the Florida plane with Will Muschamp and Jim McElwain the last several years.

I have asked the Mississippi coaches and the Alabama/Auburn coaches why they don't ride up together. All of them say, "Ain't no way that's going to happen!"

After the 1992 season, I coached in the Japan Bowl. Barry Alvarez, Paul Pasqualoni, Spike Dykes, and I coached our team to victory. My quarterback at Florida, Shane Matthews, played in it and his dad, Billy, also made the trip. Billy was a former high school coach so I made him the defensive line coach. George Teague of Alabama picked off a pass from Mark Brunell to seal our victory.

At another All-Star game, my son Steve Jr. made the trip to Hawaii. He was a wide receivers' coach at Oklahoma so he got to be the wide receivers' coach in the game. My quarterback from Florida, Doug Johnson, called an audible with about ten seconds left in the game. We were up 28–21. He checked to a fade route and completed it for a touchdown and a 35–21 win. The West coaches were thinking I had run up the score in an All-Star game. Hopefully I convinced them later that Doug did that on his own, and I had no part in it.

As far as I know there are no limits on the number of voluntary coaches in All-Star games. Any person with coaching experience, I'd try to put them to good use. All-Star games are one place you can have fun in coaching, but I always tried to convince my team it was a lot more fun when you won.

Chapter 17

DOING THINGS THE RIGHT WAY

Growing up, I played whatever game was in season. I always loved competition. Although I always wanted to win, there was another important lesson to be learned in those early days: winning the right way.

First it was baseball, starting at age seven. My dad coached a team of twelve-year-olds. I was the batboy, so I got my first uniform. My brother, Graham, was on that team. Even though I was underage, I got into one game with the Giants. Dad put me in right field. The batter hit a drive down the line. I hustled over as fast as I could to make a diving shoe-string attempt for the ball, but it hit my glove and barely came out. I immediately rolled over and fired it back into the infield. The guy rounded the bases and the umpire didn't know what to do. He didn't know if I'd caught it or not. He walked halfway out to me and asked, "Son, did you catch that ball?" And I said, "Nossir, I didn't catch it." And he said, "Thank you."

Mom and Dad both always stressed honesty, and in everything that we did, truth was always the most important thing. That included playing by the rules. If you dropped a pass or you didn't catch a baseball, you'd tell the ref or umpire, "I didn't catch it." Don't try to get away with something that didn't happen! If you got hit by a pitch, you'd tell the guy you got hit by a pitch; if you didn't get hit, you'd tell him you didn't get hit.

Of course I wasn't going to lie and tell him that I'd caught it. The truth was always more important than trying to win a game the wrong way. You have to live the rest of your life with whatever you say.

AS A COACH, I was known as somewhat of a stickler for rules. Most athletes and coaches want to play by the rules and make the game as fair as possible. And I truly believe that most competitors today want an honorable game. Of course there are some who think that it's okay if you can get away with bending some of the rules. To me, that's just wrong.

What happens when an umpire or referee gets it wrong? Some people may think because I was so animated on the sidelines that I was too tough on the officials. I decided a long time ago I wasn't going to argue with officials, even though they missed calls. They're going to get some wrong, so you just live with it. I found that out the hard way at Duke when I had to sit out a game for what I said about the officials making a wrong call, which deprived us of a bowl game. You just hope that if they get it wrong it doesn't cost one team or another a big price.

You yell at an official one time and people think you're a jerk or that you're trying to gain an unfair competitive advantage. But you also earn your reputation with officials and they come to appreciate being shown respect. I'd tell them, "I think you missed that one," but that's about all.

In my younger days I maybe yelled a little bit. But screaming at the refs is something I just didn't want to do—especially in the last twenty or so years of my coaching career. They were very appreciative that I rarely said anything to them.

In the 2014 Duck Commander Independence Bowl they called roughing the punter on us. I don't know if our guy touched the guy's foot or not, but the punter did a good acting job. The official came over and said, "Coach Spurrier, you'd better tell those assistant coaches to keep their mouths shut! I ain't taking that from them. If you want to yell at me, that's okay." And I said, "I know what you mean, my man."

I will admit sometimes I got exasperated when I felt strongly that my team or players were treated unfairly. But officials are not the only ones who get it wrong. Coaches miss a few, too. And a few guys in the media do as well.

MOST MEMBERS of the media try to take accountability for what they write or say as being true. But occasionally some don't. Those are the only times I've had problems—when something was just not true. I've never worried about a writer saying I coached a lousy game or I made a bad call. Hey, maybe I did! But when they write something that's just not true that's upsetting. Especially when they write it knowing it's not true.

In more than fifty years as a player and coach, I've enjoyed an extremely good relationship with 98 percent of the media. They have written and broadcast many wonderful stories about our success, with only a

With my good friend Tom McEwen of *The Tampa Tribune* in 1990. One of my favorite media guys ever. Hard to believe both Tom and his old newspaper are gone.

couple exceptions. I've had some really good friends in the media—none better than the late Tom McEwen of *The Tampa Tribune*.

I've had only two sportswriters write untruthful things. When Larry Guest of the *Orlando Sentinel* and Ron Morris of *The State* in Columbia wrote lies about me, however, I just couldn't help but defend my reputation. So I went back to the advice of Attila the Hun on how to handle it. He said: "You are your reputation. If people speak evil of you, and erroneously attribute misdeeds to you, you must do away with them or you must behave in a manner that urges them to amend their judgment."

In other words, change their opinion. You've either got to do away with them or encourage them to alter their judgment.

Neither Morris nor Guest were willing to admit they got it wrong and neither would write a retraction. So I said, "Just let me say, if you're not going to write that you were wrong and correct it, and you keep writing it, you're going to get somebody fired. And it might be you."

Larry Guest wrote that I told the Jacksonville Quarterback Club that I backed the mayor of Jacksonville on not supporting the NFL franchise coming to their city. I called Guest and told him I never said that and that he ought to correct it. He refused. That was the end for me with Larry Guest.

Ron Morris wrote that I hurt the South Carolina basketball program because, when Bruce Ellington came to Columbia, I talked him into just playing football. That's not true. Bruce was a two-sport athlete and I would never do anything to hurt the basketball program.

Then, the next fall, Morris wrote that I played Connor Shaw against UAB after he was hurt, risking further injury. He also wrote that after I had my number 11 un-retired and assigned to a player while I was there, Florida re-retired it after I left in 2002. He said a sports information person at Florida told him this. All were complete lies.

I called Morris and said, "What you have written isn't true. And you need to go back and correct it." He said he had his "sources" and wouldn't back down. And he kept writing that. So I decided I wasn't going to do any press conferences as long as he was in the room. I told the media: "In twenty-six years as a head coach, I've had two guys that didn't write the truth, that I had to disassociate with. He's one of them over here. [I pointed to Morris]. Another one was a guy at Florida in '94, so in twenty-six years I've had two guys. And then I've learned that since he sits in on all these meetings I'm basically helping him to contribute writing negative stuff about our football program—simple as that. So I'm not gonna talk when he's in here. That's my right as a head coach. I don't have to talk to him, and I don't have to talk to him when he's in here. So here's what we're going to do. All you TV guys, I'm gonna do a personal interview with you in this other room, and the writers that are still left in here I'll come back and talk to you right after that."

And I did just that.

I don't get into fights with the media personally, but some of the Gators and Gamecocks fans do. I just declined to answer any questions from Guest. I've heard some of the Gators in Orlando called the *Sentinel* and said they weren't going to advertise in the paper. Eventually Guest retired from the *Sentinel*. But I never talked to him again.

On the matter of Morris, I said, "I'm not going to get into a fight with this guy. So that's a fight you can pick. I'm not going to have anything to do with it. Sometimes in press conferences I may not answer any of the questions as long as he is there."

So the newspaper took Morris off the beat. But he eventually came back and after that he was fine.

The lesson learned here by the media is that if you are going to pick a fight with a coach, you probably ought not to do it when he's winning. Who knows? Maybe if I'd been a losing coach that might have cost me my job.

As far as my overall relationship with the media, I try to avoid "coach-speak" and be honest. I've never been one to use the phrase "off the record," which writers used to use a lot. That's one of the no-nos I have learned. Because nothing is ever "off the record." I hope I'm smart enough to not say anything stupid and then have to hope the guy won't repeat it. But I think all coaches need to understand that.

We all have to be careful and know that what we say will be repeated. Maybe twenty years ago a lot of things that coaches would say were not repeated. Social media has changed all that.

CHANGE HAS COME in many forms over the last fifty years, as we have become more enlightened individuals and gained new perspectives. In the South that hasn't always been easy. People of my generation had to come to grips with the reality of fairness when it comes to race.

That thought came to mind when I saw the movie *Selma*. The movie showed Dr. Martin Luther King Jr. and members of the NAACP crossing the Edmund Pettus Bridge outside Selma and being approached by Alabama state troopers wearing gas masks. They ordered the marchers to turn back, and when the marchers refused, troopers attacked them with clubs, horses, tear gas, and other weapons. Several marchers were badly injured. This attack was shown on national television. Dr. King prayed and then turned around and led the group away, for which he was sharply criticized by some of his own activists. That evening, one of his followers was beaten to death by white racists on a street in Selma.

It struck me as I watched that movie that I had been very close to the Edmund Pettus Bridge just a few months before that all happened in March of 1966. On the way to the Sugar Bowl, I had traveled with Allen Trammel to his family home outside Eufaula, Alabama, in a little community called Spring Hill. They lived up on top of a hill, with almost a hundred-yard field down below.

Trammel had become a good close friend, which he remains today. Before the Sugar Bowl in January, we were practicing in Gainesville and had a week off. And then we were to meet the team at the hotel in New Orleans before the game with Missouri. My parents were in High Springs. Allen said, "Steve, do you want to go home with me for Christmas?" I said, "What we gonna do?" He said, "Well, we'll go huntin'. You ever shot a duck, or birds?" I said, "Not really." He said, "Well, come on!" While we were there we went out and shot a duck, or something.

What struck me was that Mr. and Mrs. Trammel probably had about twenty black employees, mostly in the kitchen. Or doing yard work. It was reminiscent of the Old South. Of course, this was 1965. We pulled in and an elderly black gentleman started picking up our bags and taking them in. And I said, "Wait a minute . . ." And Allen said, "He'll get it, he'll get it—that's what he gets paid to do. That's his job." I said, "Nah, I'm not comfortable with that—he doesn't have to carry my bag in."

On Christmas morning we drove to New Orleans. Allen said, "We're going to drive through Montgomery—Governor George Wallace wants to say hi to you." So we went by the mansion. Governor Wallace came out and said, "Hey, how you boys doin'?" Trammel worked for him in the summer. He had an Alabama auto tag that said GOVERNOR'S STAFF.

Then we went by and saw Allen's uncle, Seymore Trammel, the state's attorney in the judicial district where Governor Wallace lived. Uncle Seymore said hello to us, gave us each a twenty-dollar bill, and said, "You boys have fun in New Orleans!" Nobody had ever given me twenty dollars in my life! I said, "Man, this guy's wealthy!" So we went to New Orleans and Trammel taught me how to eat raw oysters. I learned to put it on the cracker with hot sauce. We walked around Bourbon Street a little.

I tell people all the time that Florida—unlike parts of the South in Mississippi, Louisiana, and Georgia—wasn't as racially challenged. Maybe even South Carolina. I guess we had our issues in Tennessee. After all, we were not integrated in Johnson City. There was never any racial tension in Johnson City. But I never went to school with a black kid. White kids were at Kiwanis Park and black kids went to Carver Park. But we'd go down to Carver Park and play basketball with the black kids. Never any problems. Chose up teams. It wasn't the blacks against the whites—sometimes three blacks and two whites. Played full court. Never any problems. Just go play.

And when it was over, it was "Well, he's going to his neighborhood and we're going to ours."

It was just accepted. We never stopped and asked, "Why is it like this?" Most of us were raised to believe that that's just the way it was. And we didn't realize how difficult it was for the black kids to get an education and have a chance to go to the same colleges we were going to. We just didn't even think about it. And now you look back and you think, *Man, it shouldn't have been that way!* But at that time the blacks in Johnson City weren't complaining. Everybody was just sort of happy doing their thing. To me it appeared that way.

Today there are some challenges between law enforcement and some African American communities, as we saw in Ferguson, Missouri. I can see merit on both sides of the struggle. While it's wrong to racially profile, I have a great amount of respect for the many good people in law enforcement. We had a situation that popped up at South Carolina with our star player when he first arrived on campus.

In his freshman year, Jadeveon Clowney went down to one of the bars near campus in an area called Five Points. He doesn't even drink. There was a robbery in the area and the suspect was a tall African American guy with long dreadlocks. When the police went to the bar and saw a tall black man with long dreads, they didn't know his identity. So they actually handcuffed Jadeveon and asked him questions. Then they let him go once he proved he wasn't the suspect, which is normal procedure.

There was a big stink about Clowney "getting in trouble and getting arrested." I tried to minimize that story and explain how "this could happen to anybody." So I decided to use it as a teaching moment.

After spring practice one day I asked Chief of Police Randy Scott to come out, pull me off the side as I was talking to the media, and handcuff me, which he did. He asked me a couple questions and then unhandcuffed me and I went back to talk to the media. The media were all watching. The players were watching, too, and I had tipped off a few of the guys.

But I didn't even tell Steve Fink, our director of media relations, who probably was saying, "I wonder what Coach did?"

Like I said, it could happen to anybody. Jadeveon handled it with class. And nothing came of it.

When I was in school at Florida I think there were only four or five black students. I had a PE class with one of them and he went on to become a principal at Edgewater in Orlando. And when I got the job at Florida in 1990 he sent me a letter and it was one of the nicest letters I ever got. He said, "Steve, when I was in college, everyone wasn't nice to me, but you always were." I went, "Really? Why wouldn't they be? Why aren't we just nice to everybody?"

Floyd Little, the Hall of Fame running back with Syracuse and the Denver Broncos, said the same thing. We had all those all-star football games after my senior year—Hula Bowl, the East-West Shrine Game in Atlanta, the College All-Star Game in Chicago. I was sitting around with Floyd one time and he said, "Us black guys always liked Steve because he hung around with us all the time." I said, "You guys are a lot more fun than those white dudes." This group included Floyd, Bubba Smith, Gene Washington (the one from Michigan State), Mel Farr, and others . . . They had fun.

When I played for the 49ers, on a few road trips I roomed with the other Gene Washington, the All-Pro wide receiver from Stanford. We had wonderful camaraderie for the nine years I was out there.

It seems crazy that we've hung on to some racial stereotypes even today. And some people just don't want to acknowledge that most African American athletes grow up disadvantaged. That has been especially true with college athletes. The hypocrisy of colleges' reaping millions of dollars from football and being reluctant to pay players a stipend to assist them and their families is just flat wrong.

I once made a statement that twenty-five years ago I was coaching at Duke making $125,000 a year and the players got a full scholarship. Then, when I was making $3.5 million a year, the players were still getting only a scholarship. So why weren't the players afforded the chance to improve the way the coaches and everybody else were improving their incomes?

I was proud to have pushed for SEC coaches to support cost-of-attendance stipends for athletes in support of the economically challenged families. We brought it up for the SEC football and basketball coaches to endorse. At one point we volunteered to pay the cost out of our coaches' salaries, and we asked others if they would do the same. There was quite a bit of support for that. So I decided to write a memo presenting them with a formula where we could grant college football and basketball players with $4,000 to $5,000 so they could live like first-class student-athletes.

I brought it up at the annual SEC meetings in Destin. My secretary Rita Boykin had it all printed up—about fifteen pages—and I sent one to all the coaches. I passed it around the table and said, "I'd like for all fourteen of us to sign this." Three or four of them said, "I'm not sure this will ever go through . . . I don't know . . ."

I said, "Well, I'm going to tell the media when we leave here all the coaches who signed and all the coaches who didn't." Still several of them didn't sign. Mark Richt of Georgia didn't. So I went and told the media who did and who didn't. The next year I had another proposal, pretty much the same thing—it was signed by every coach, fourteen to none. Coach Richt reported that a couple of players said, "Last time you didn't sign. How come you didn't sign that thing, Coach?"

With the amount of money football and basketball bring in now, I just felt it was time to reward the performers.

A lot of students come from families with average to superior incomes, but most of the football players come from low-income families.

They just don't have the money that the other students have. It would certainly help their parents with travel expenses—motel, gas, food, et cetera. I've always thought that was the right thing to do. Those players are bringing in the money for all of us; it's time to share.

Outgoing SEC commissioner Mike Slive was always in favor of a cost-of-attendance scholarship for the players. But the NCAA and the Power Five conferences really didn't move on it until January 2015, when they passed the first package of autonomous legislation with full cost-of-attendance scholarships by a vote of 79–1. Boston College was the 1.

That's a step in the right direction, but we have been slow in certain parts of the South to deal with discrimination issues and matters that were offensive to the black community. And in the case of flying the Confederate flag just outside the State House in Columbia, we even regressed. That flag wasn't raised there until 1961, but it took us more than fifty years to take it down.

Having that Confederate flag up was a detriment to our state. The universities could not hold NCAA tournaments or postseason tournaments in our state because of it. It was oppressive to African Americans. They don't like the flag. It represented slavery, the reason for the Civil War. Those who supported flying the Confederate flag thought it represented their heritage and their history and those brave souls who fought and gave their lives.

If anything's oppressive to people, however, we shouldn't have it. In the United States of America, the South is not a part of the old Confederacy anymore. So we needed to get it all together. When I was asked, I made this statement:

"My opinion is we don't need the Confederate flag at our Capitol. I don't really know anybody that wants it there, but I guess there are a lot of South Carolinians that do want it there.

"I realize I'm not supposed to get in the political arena as a football coach, but if anybody were ever to ask me about that Confederate flag, I would say we need to get rid of it. I've been told not to talk about that. But if anyone were ever to ask me about it, I certainly wish we could get rid of it."

I made that statement all the way back in 2007. Obviously, it sort of fell on deaf ears. But I was not going to go downtown and stand on the soapbox and make a crusade out of it. I made my statement and then it was up to those people in charge—the governors and the legislators—to do what they needed to do.

I didn't take all that much heat for it back in '07. But I guess it was sort of a shock to some people—"Hey, he said that? You can't talk about that! We don't talk about that!" It was like everybody was afraid to talk about it.

I think there was a wakeup call for our state in 2015 with the Charleston massacre. We all grieved about the terrible event that took the lives of nine church members. It rocked our state. Once again, that tragedy brought to the forefront the issue of the Confederate flag. Our whole coaching staff joined in the cause after the murder of the Reverend Clementa Pinckney of Mother Emanuel AME, and others.

Those mass shootings were terrible and depressed a lot of people. We had a person come in and talk to the entire athletic department about that and what to do (if you are ever in that situation). He said what I've always said the men have to do: You have to charge these guys even though one or two of you are going to go down. And we talked about that horrible day at Virginia Tech. That killer went into a room with about thirty-five kids in it. They all hid under their desks. And they all waited to take their bullet. He went up and down the row shooting them in the head. If the men had maybe charged him, he might have gotten one or two of them, but they would have overcome him.

For some reason, in America nobody talks about that. I don't understand why they don't. Because if that person's intent on killing everybody in the room, and you stand there and take it, he's going to get everybody. But five guys can certainly overcome a lone shooter. That's what you have to do.

On June 22, 2015, Governor Nikki Haley called for the Confederate flag to be removed. A day later we tweeted: "The South Carolina football team, players and coaches strongly support Governor Haley's decision to remove the flag from the Capitol."

That flag needed to come down.

It was removed on July 10, 2015.

PLAYER DISCIPLINE is always a tough one for coaches. I have a few policies that I enforce fairly and strictly. One of them pertains to domestic violence.

I think we've all learned a lot about domestic violence in the last several years. I personally didn't know a lot about it until I took the job at South Carolina. I got a call from the South Carolina Coalition Against Domestic Violence and Sexual Assault. And they told me that the state of South Carolina was No. 1, the worst in America on domestic violence. It's one of the charities I give some money to because it's something we've all got to be aware of.

With what happened in the NFL, I think people became quite aware that this obviously has been going on for many, many years. And you wonder why it took this long for somebody to speak up and say, "This is wrong—this is terribly wrong. And let's quit doing it." I believe we've made some strides toward cutting back domestic violence in our country.

I've had a rule that I tell the team every year: If you hit, slap, or punch a girl, you're finished as a South Carolina football player. And I've had to release two players. And once you get the message out clearly I don't think it will happen as much, if at all. Both of the incidences occurred in the off-season. It was evident right away that these two players did something they should not have done. Both of them admitted it.

Justice should be firm and swift, with no tolerance for that kind of thing on a team. You must follow the team rules as well as the rules that govern the game of football.

RULES ARE RULES. One rule in the NFL, however, seems a bit frivolous and I doubt most of us knew about it until Tom Brady became involved in what they called Deflategate. The footballs were slightly underinflated in the AFC championship New England–Indianapolis game in January 2015. Tom Brady had played sixteen years. Why has this not happened in other games involving New England and Bill Belichick? Most of their passing yards came in the second half, anyway, with a fully inflated football, but nobody seems to bring that up.

There have been college coaches who have maybe told their managers to "stick that needle in and take a little air out." But I don't think it happens much anywhere. What I see is some teams that use really old footballs. You can barely see the white stripes around some of those college balls. The rule is that "slightly used balls" are supposed to be put in play for games. But I saw some schools that used balls that looked five years old. And maybe they had balls that were easier to handle than others.

In every other sport we all use the same ball. Baseball, both sides use the same ball. Same in basketball. But in football the visiting team brings their own balls. And the manager handles them. It's just something a little different about football.

When I played, I liked the balls slightly used, but they didn't have to be real old. They were slippier earlier in the game. After the first quarter or so they started feeling better.

In the USFL, we had the head coaches/owners meeting before the season. We started talking about the USFL ball, which Wilson had made with USFL on it—very similar to the NFL ball.

I made the suggestion that we let the teams rub the balls down and get rid of that shiny finish the way colleges do—obviously because I played quarterback and all the quarterbacks like to get the feel of the ball.

George Allen, formerly of the Redskins and then coach of the Chicago Blitz, disagreed. "We didn't do that in the NFL," he said. "Why would we want to do it in the USFL?"

We hashed it around a little bit and I think it was Chuck Fairbanks— former Oklahoma, Colorado, and Patriots coach and then with the New Jersey Generals—who said: "Maybe Steve's got something there. Why do they rub them down in college? So they can hold on to them better. We don't want the ball slipping out of the guys' hands, like we see often in the NFL."

So they went ahead and passed a rule that you could rub them down like the colleges did. I think in life, just because one league does it one way doesn't mean it's the best way. We should always look at what's the best way to get the job done. What's the best way to create a better game? And rubbing down those footballs is definitely a better way. So the NFL does it now.

ONE SUBJECT that seems to be almost off limits for coaches anymore is spirituality. For one thing, they are limited in what they can say or do by policy. But a lot of us coaches will say, "God smiled on us." "We had good fortune." "We need to be thankful." "We were blessed today." And I think that's a way of us coaches or players saying we appreciate it—we thank God that He did smile on us. It's not to say the Lord didn't smile on the other team. There have been times when it didn't always go our way. Sometimes He smiles on the other team, if you want to look at it that way. It's just a way of saying you appreciate it and are thankful that some good things happened.

There is a common theme among the three Heisman Trophy winners from the University of Florida: Tim Tebow, Danny Wuerffel, and I are all sons of ministers. Just like my coach Ray Graves was. And it doesn't stop there. Urban Meyer's dad gave serious thought to becoming a Catholic priest as a young man, which is probably why Coach Meyer was named after Pope Urban.

Many coaches and players recognize that there is a higher power in charge of our lives. Everyone must decide for themselves about what part faith plays in football, even if we all may handle our faith in different ways.

I'm a Christian and I believe in Jesus Christ, just like my dad taught.

Dad actually tried to save just about everyone he met. He would ask, "Are you a Christian? Have you accepted Jesus Christ as your savior? Do you know that you are going to heaven?"

My dad had an invitation after every service. And sometimes on Wednesday night there were only about thirty people there, on just a small side of the church there in Johnson City. But he always concluded by saying: "If you feel like you need to rededicate your life, come forward and we'll talk about what you need to do." So 95 percent of the time he offered the invitation. Usually there would be one or two who came forward. And then occasionally he would have these revival services where he would visit other towns and cities. I didn't go to too many of those.

When I got into coaching, there were some coaches who sort of wore their religion on their sleeves because they felt it was right for them.

Over all the years, I can't remember missing a chapel service on Friday nights before Saturday games. For whatever reason, I felt like our chaplain was the team minister. He talked about what's in the Bible and what we all needed to do. I've always believed that you should let the preachers preach and the coaches coach. Some coaches think that with their position of influence they can also be a little bit of a preacher, which I'm not saying is wrong. That's fine if that's the way they want to do their job. This is the path I have chosen to do my job as a coach. Don't hide your faith, but don't push it on the players either.

Many players on teams we had at South Carolina in 2015 didn't want to attend chapel service as most of our teams had done in the past. We didn't make it mandatory, of course. Attendance was about 50 percent. I never preached to the kids or anything. Although it's hard to overlook the fact that our worst-attended services corresponded with our worst record in eleven football seasons.

In January 2016 when I spoke at the coaches' convention in San Antonio—one of my first official acts after resigning—I tried to explain that there's a different kind of athlete today: in some ways better, in some ways not. I spoke about faith, family, academics, and football. I talked about how God directs our path, and my path was a completely different and unique one.

Somehow faith played a big part in Gator football. The two greatest eras of Florida football were built around Danny Wuerffel and Tim Tebow—two sincere, strong, passionate Christian young men. They played during two of the best four- to five-year eras of Florida football ever. But things seem to have evolved differently and, as all the surveys show, college kids seem to be less expressive about their faith and don't seem to put much emphasis on organized meetings like chapel or church.

There's no doubt that sometimes God granted us favor. Without question, in 1996 when we won the national championship, we had Divine Intervention. How else do you explain how the things that we all needed to happen happened?

After we lost our last regular-season game to FSU that year we dropped to No. 5 in the country. For us to win the championship, as I previously said, things had to fall in line. Each of them was about fifty-fifty—the odds that they all would happen were 32–1. And yet they all happened—we won the national championship. There's got to be a reason for that.

I think I relied a lot on faith when I first arrived at Duke in 1980 when I took the job as offensive coordinator. While we were building a house in Durham, the builder said to me: "Boy, if you're going to coach football at Duke, you'd better get used to losing, because that's all they do in football." I said, "Well, we'll see." In the second year we had the first of a couple 6-5 records. But we refused to be held captive by that environment. You just have to say, "This is Duke football—and I'm part of it." And then you have to help change it.

We really had a lot of good players at Duke with wonderful attitudes. That Clemson game was a real blessing to us. And after winning the Clemson game, the closest regular-season winning margin for us was only nine points. We beat everybody pretty good. There weren't any flukes.

So for me it was always about the four F's—faith, family, football, and fitness.

THE FITNESS PART requires the commitment to a regular routine. Most coaches have some kind of routine these days, but some of them quit in the off-season. I think a lot of people believe you only need to work out just to break a sweat—walk around the block two or three times and say, "Well, I've exercised today."

I've read several books on fitness and I truly believe that the greatest Fountain of Youth out there is exercise. *Younger Next Year: Living Until Eighty as Though You're Fifty*, written by Chris Crowley and Henry S. Lodge, was given to me by Charles Waddell, deputy athletics director at South Carolina, and was read by a lot of people I know.

Crowley and Lodge, two internists, believe that working out six times a week is the key to good health. Someone who exercises and diets and who enjoys his family, friends, and work has a chance to live similarly at eighty as at fifty. I did six days of exercise during the season. In the off-season when I was traveling or playing golf, I could miss two or three days in a row. When Charles gave the book to me three or four years before I resigned, he said, "You're already working out six days a week!"

My workout routine is pretty consistent throughout the year. I have a goal. I don't just sit on the bike and say I worked out. And I truly believe that staying fit with a regular workout routine kept me going strong for thirty years. I highly recommend it for everyone.

My Head Ball Coach workout goes like this:

1. I do twenty to twenty-five minutes on a treadmill speed set on 41 with a 2.5 incline. That is a real fast walk. I wear an extra shirt or two to get a little extra sweat.
2. I ride eleven to fifteen minutes on a stationary bike with a

    resistance of 14 and keep the speed at 70 or better. In eleven minutes I should reach 115 RPMs.

3. I lift fifteen-pound hand weights—a few overheads and a few exercises, which my wife Jerri taught me to do.

4. I will do least five hundred sit-ups. I've put a big rubber ball under my back so it's not too difficult, and sometimes I do more.

Every now and then while I was exercising, I'd think of a new ball play or how to do something better. I usually watch TV. I have the remote and put it on all the ESPN channels. And I put it on CNN a lot. I like to know what's happening in the world. And, of course, the SEC Network. So when I'm exercising, I'm keeping up with what's happening in the world of sports and in the world beyond sports.

Sportswriter Josh Kendall of *The State* worked out with me on my seventieth birthday. Josh is a runner. The thing that runners have a problem with is that stationary bike. You put on a little resistance and you can get tired pedaling—it's like going uphill if you're not used to doing it.

We could all say we're too busy to exercise.

But it's something I like to do and I feel so much better after I do it.

You'd be surprised how many coaches don't work out during the season. They say, "I'm too busy." That's part of being a winner or loser. A loser's always too busy to do what's necessary. A winner always has time to do what's important.

Coaches have come a long way from the days of smoking unfiltered cigarettes, eating whatever was put down before them, and late-night drinking bouts. Coaches have learned other ways to counter stress. That's why I worked out, went to the beach, and played golf a lot in the off-season.

WHEN YOU'RE COACHING a program with integrity, no matter how hard you try to stay aboveboard, some people are going to take shots and try to bring you down and sully your reputation. They will tell lies, call you names, and, in general, try to discredit some of the things you stand for. One of their favorite things is to try to label you a cheater, and opposing fans will go to any lengths to promote that idea.

That's what happened to us in 1991 when our critics tried to make it sound like we had used subterfuge to gain access to Tennessee's playbook—which was laughable.

Ron Zook and Jack Sells became friends in 1986, when Zook worked as a defensive backs coach at Tennessee and Sells was a graduate assistant. Sells was later fired by Tennessee while Ron was on my staff at Florida.

Before the 1991 game, Sells had gone to a Kinko's store in Knoxville and faxed some pages to Zook showing some of the Vol's pass patterns. It was no big deal because we didn't benefit from it and we weren't going to change our game plan, anyway.

Doug Dickey was the Tennessee AD. He knew about it and he called me. He said he knew exactly what we were going to do: act like we're going to use them and then do something else entirely different. We laughed about it.

So after we beat them 35–18, on Monday morning I came in and Betty Ling of our administrative staff was crying. She said, "Coach, we're getting call after call. These people from Tennessee are calling us cheaters again."

And I said, "Betty, that's what they're supposed to do, because we kicked their tails Saturday. You didn't know that? When you beat somebody's butt and they don't like it, they'll call you names. So the only thing they can do now is call us cheaters because of that Jack Sells thing. I expected that!"

She said, "Really?"

I said, "Yeah! Laugh it off!"

That kind of stuff is overrated. I told the story about Jim Bates, a former Tennessee coach, having been on our staff the year before, and it certainly didn't help the Gators against Tennessee. We got beat 45–3.

Later Sells sued Kinko's, accusing them of violating his privacy, damaging his reputation, and destroying his career. Sells claimed one Tennessee fan punched him in the mouth in a Chattanooga bar and that he had been constantly harassed. So he dropped out of coaching completely. And he won the suit.

We just kidded about Jack getting a brand-new house somewhere and we forgot about the whole thing. Coaches can't linger too long on adversaries or pay much attention to the criticism—as long as they are doing things the right way.

Chapter 18

THE COACH, AND THOSE I HAVE KNOWN

THE COACH

And in those days, behold, there came through the gates of the campus a coach from far off, and it came to pass as the seasons went by he won games and championships in abundance.

And in that land where they used to be losers, and they used to spend their days adding to the alibi sheets, mightily were they astonished. They said one to the other: "How in the world doth he do it and how doth he have so much luck?"

And it came to pass that many were gathered in the corridors and a soothsayer came among them. And they spoke and questioned him, saying, "How is it that this coach has accomplished the impossible?"

Whereupon the soothsayer made the answer: "He of whom you speak is one fierce competitor. He riseth in the morning and goeth forth full of confidence. He complaineth not, neither doth he know despair. He maketh solid plans and doggedly doth he pursue them. While ye gather here and say one to the other, "Verily this is not a perfect situation," he hath convinced his people that nothing can stoppeth them. And when the eleventh hour cometh, he needeth no alibis. He knoweth his job inside and out, and they that would defeat him, they lose. Rivals say unto him "nay" when he cometh in, yet when he goeth forth he hath their names in the column that is marked "Victory!"

He taketh with him three angels: Enthusiasm, Determination, and Persistence, and worketh with a smile on his face. Verily I say unto you, go and do likewise.

—Author unknown

I've always tried to be like this coach. I even like the way "The Coach" is written—sort of a King James Version. I can't remember where it came from and don't know who wrote it, but I've kept a copy in my file all these years. I think it perfectly describes the plight of the coach who wants to be a champion.

We coaches, for the most part, are a committed bunch. We don't all get along all the time, but we mostly respect one another. And we each have friends and favorites among us.

Some of my favorites are basketball coaches.

People have told me in the past that I act a lot like a basketball coach, the way I am involved on the sideline, talking to players, coaches, and officials. My friends in Johnson City say I acted more like my basketball coach at Science Hill, Elvin Little, than any of my other coaches.

As I said, the one coach I've admired the most—football or basketball— is John Wooden. He wrote a book on his philosophy about coaching— how he treats players, what he says to players, about everything a coach should do. I found his philosophy fits with what I think and believe. I've taken some quotes from him, his philosophy, and I've put them on paper, and I've tried to follow them the best I could through my coaching career.

I've always supported our basketball coaches, male and female. At

Florida I was very good friends with Billy Donovan and have continued to stay in touch with him. I wasn't surprised to see him finally leave Florida for the NBA and, in fact, thought he might have done it before he finally took the Oklahoma City job.

Coach Dawn Staley is still one of my dear friends at South Carolina, and I am a big fan of the Lady Gamecocks. After I resigned and they gave me a role as "ambassador" for USC, I suggested I become the "ambassador" for women's hoops. They said they already had somebody who did that.

Former Tennessee coach Pat Summitt was a good friend. I loved the way she coached and was a big fan of hers. She was one of the best basketball coaches, men or women, that I've ever seen. We all mourned her loss in 2016.

At Duke I enjoyed my relationship with Coach Mike Krzyzewski, who has handled this aging thing gracefully. He is one year younger than me and looks like he is only fifty. He's got a youthful look about him. He just seems to handle stress better than most. Some basketball coaches do seem to survive the pressure better than football coaches. I think you will begin to see that the long-term stress on football coaches will motivate them to change their lifestyle, however.

Kentucky coach John Calipari and I talk a little bit now and then. After he won a game in Columbia one night, I called him. I figured he was on the airplane going back to Kentucky. I said, "Coach Cal, I am going to name you the most improved coach in one year. Not only did you guys win the game, but you didn't get thrown out. Congratulations."

He laughed a little bit. I said, "Are you back in Lexington yet?" He said, "Coach, I am in Florida. I took the school plane down here with my wife. We don't practice until Tuesday afternoon, so I am going to get away a little bit. I read in a book where you used to do that on open dates." I said, "You are right, I did."

So Coach Cal grabbed a little beach time in South Florida, got rejuvenated, and returned to the grind, coaching up his Wildcats successfully, as he always does.

I really like those head football coaches who take the hands-on approach to coaching their team and get directly involved in the game. A lot of times head coaches quit coaching and delegate everything. I don't know which way is the best—the best is whatever works for that head coach. I'm more in line with the ones who actively continue coaching as opposed to those who delegate.

A football coach I really admired was Bill Walsh of the San Francisco 49ers. Not only was he the coach during the 49ers' greatest run in history, but he also was a brilliant offensive coordinator, the quarterback coach, and play-caller. Over my years, I tried to emulate pretty much what he did. He probably multitasked better as a head coach than anybody's ever done it in the NFL.

Here are some other coaches I have admired.

BEAR BRYANT

Coach Bear Bryant is considered the No. 1 coach in the South, that's for sure. I have always remembered his "Three Rules for Coaching"—I sometimes cite them at coaching clinics when I'm asked to be the speaker. I actually spoke at the Alabama coaching clinic. And I said, "Let me close with Coach Bear Bryant's Three Rules for Coaching." I previously listed those rules in chapter four, "Winners and Losers." But his first one is worth mentioning again because it's so important:

Number 1: "Surround yourself with people that have a passion, a desire and an attitude that they cannot live without football." In other words, you have to be totally immersed in being a football coach.

On occasion I may have been accused of not "immersing myself" enough because I tried to get away from the grind and live a little bit of life. Truth be known, football was still always on my mind during the season and I was no less committed than the others. I just didn't want to go that route, or try to impress people by trying to "outwork" the others, so I did it differently—as did many of the legendary coaches, like Coach Bryant.

I like the story about a writer doing a piece on him one year as he was standing under the goalposts during warm-ups. He allowed the writer to sort of tag along during that game. The writer said, "Coach Bryant, your players don't look any bigger or faster than the other team's. What's your secret?" And Coach Bryant said, "Shhh! Don't tell them that! They believe they are!" I think that was the biggest thing for him: He was a master at getting the most out of his team.

JOE PATERNO

Joe Paterno is the winningest coach in FBS/NCAA college football, with 409 victories. Coach Paterno and I were good friends. I had always wanted to coach against him and we had that one game in the Citrus Bowl which we were fortunate enough to win. We spent some time together that week. I called him Coach Joe. But his players referred to him as just Joe. And that's what he wanted them to call him. In the South we always put a "Coach" in front of the person's name. We were at a press conference a couple days before the game when one of the media guys said to him, "Coach Spurrier calls you Coach Joe. You ever been called that before? What do you think of it?" He said, "Nah, I don't think I have ever been called Coach Joe. But I sort of like it!"

VINCE LOMBARDI

I believe Vince Lombardi is one of the all-time super coaches because of what he did and how he did it. He went to Green Bay in 1959 and took a team that hadn't posted a winning record in ten years—averaging under four wins a season—and with basically the same players, he turned them into champions. Coach Lombardi led the Packers to five NFL championships—two of them in Super Bowls I and II. He was one of only three coaches to win three NFL titles in a row in 1965, '66, and '67. He posted a record of 98-30-4 in Green Bay, including a 9-1 postseason record. He really emphasized that winning was not the important thing—"it's the only thing." I am pretty familiar with his quotes and some of his statements, and some of his books I really like.

One of Coach Lombardi's sayings is: When things are going good, you must stay on your players' butts to keep improving every single day. When things are going badly, you need to lighten up a bit. You just can't yell and scream at them every time when things are going bad. He was different. He was sort of an offensive line coach. Ran that Green Bay Packer sweep play. Somebody said he went to a clinic one time to hear Coach Lombardi and he talked for four hours on the Green Bay Sweep. How to block it against every defense.

BO SCHEMBECHLER

I certainly have a great admiration for Coach Bo Schembechler from Michigan. I met him only once or twice. His style of football, obviously, was very different. He had physical teams that ran the ball, threw the ball sometimes. I've already written about reading his book and how his quote "Running teams are tougher teams" stuck with me, as I learned after that game at Syracuse in 1990. Even though he never won a national championship, Coach Schembechler was a coach I greatly respected.

BILL BELICHICK

I've got to give Bill Belichick a lot of credit because he's got so many different players every year. He doesn't get the first pick any year. He gets close to the LAST pick. Winning consistently in the NFL is about coaching—and, of course, he's got Tom Brady. Everybody's got to have the solid guy at quarterback—and that's what he's got.

I don't know Coach Belichick that well but he's considered the best in the NFL. I think the one thing we all admire about the New England Patriots is not just that they've won four Super Bowls, but they've won their division thirteen out of sixteen years. That's real consistency in a coach and his team. It demonstrates what a tremendous coach and leader Bill Belichick is. Sometimes all the media talk about is how many Super Bowls a guy has won. When you look at his track record and what he has done year after year after year, that's really how you judge coaches.

MARTY SCHOTTENHEIMER

Another coach who was one of the best in the NFL and doesn't get a lot of recognition is Marty Schottenheimer, who won more games from 1990 to 1999 than any coach in the NFL. Not many people know that fact because he had some bad fortune in playoff games, and he never won a Super Bowl. I still think he was one of the all-time great coaches in the NFL.

AS FOR THE CURRENT best college coaches, certainly you'd have to put Nick Saban, Urban Meyer, and Bob Stoops in a special category. They are all super coaches.

NICK SABAN

He does an amazing job of winning championships. His win-loss record at Alabama is tremendous: 105-18 in nine seasons. He won the national championship at LSU and four of them at Alabama. Defensive-minded coach. Gets his guys playing at a very high level. He's maybe the best recruiter ever and usually gets the best players. I said that about him at SEC Media Days in 2014 and some people tried to make it sound like I was being coy. But Coach Saban admitted he agreed with me when we appeared on "ESPN Car Wash" in Bristol that year. And, I added, the team with the best players doesn't always win. But Coach Saban usually does.

BOBBY STOOPS

With Coach Stoops it's a little easier for me to comment since we worked together and he's one of my best friends in the business. So we have a long-standing relationship, and my son Steve Jr. is currently a member of his staff. He still has his condo in Crescent Beach, Florida, and I usually see him every July. I see him at the College Hall of Fame dinner every year. We talk every two or three weeks. I think all coaches need somebody they don't compete against to stay in touch with. I do want to point out that the seventeen-year longevity of Coach Stoops in this day and age is remarkable. And that Coach Stoops won more games at a major college (109) in his first ten years (between 1999 and 2008) than anybody. He's won nine Big Twelve championships in seventeen years. His first one was in 2002 and the last one was in 2015. That is what I call a consistent champion, year after year.

Postgame with Urban Meyer.

URBAN MEYER

He may be as good as anybody in big games—SEC and Big Ten championship games, national championship games. His record in four years at Ohio State is 50-4, and he's got two SECs, one Big Ten, and three national championships. He is the only coach to win national championships in two different conferences.

WE'RE ALL just coaches, trying to do it our way, as it was for me for thirty years.

As it says in "The Coach": "Whereupon the soothsayer made the answer: 'He of whom you speak is one fierce competitor. He riseth in the morning and goeth forth full of confidence . . . He maketh solid plans and doggedly doth he pursueth them . . .'"

Chapter 19

THINGS I PROBABLY SAID

Nobody who takes on anything big and tough can afford to be modest.

—Orson Welles

I've had my share of controversial quotes aired or published. But in talking to the media, I always strove for accuracy, clarity, and honesty. And sometimes a little fun. A few quotes attributed to me, however, I did not say. Most I did. And all the silly jokes and funny comments were in the off-season.

Over the years I've saved certain special comments for Clemson, Georgia, Tennessee, and FSU. And I always stood behind the quotes I actually made.

Probably my favorite quote was a comment I made on why South Carolina always preferred playing Georgia early in the season.

I said, "I sort of always liked playing them that second game because you could always count on them having two or three key players suspended." Their AD, Greg McGarity, who I knew when he was at Florida, remarked: "How can you be mad at him for saying that? It's the truth!" A few Bulldog fans even came up to me and said, "I like that one!" Apparently, even our rivals sometimes agreed with my comments about their teams.

A lot of this back and forth began my first year at Florida in response to some of the stuff said by Georgia fans and coaches. And it sort of carried over to South Carolina.

Clemson was a natural target while I was at South Carolina and enjoyed trading light jabs with Dabo Swinney. Dabo and I seemed to enjoy going back and forth. Clemson, of course, has nicknamed its Memorial Stadium Death Valley. So just to have a little fun, I was talking to the media one day when I suggested there were several stadiums with that name—one being LSU's in Baton Rouge.

I said, "Most of our guys have never been to Death Valley. That [LSU's] is the Death Valley, isn't it? Or is there another one? There's two of them? That's right, there's two Death Valleys. Was LSU the first one or the second one? They were first? Oh, okay."

Dabo fired back, saying for sure his stadium was "the original" Death Valley. And then he added: "I am pretty sure that is accurate, but I can see where he might have had a little confusion. Our guys have never been to USC. California is a long way from here. I can see where there might be a little confusion there—two Death Valleys and two USCs, but there is only one real one. That is classic Spurrier. When he is winning, you can say anything you want. He is one of the best."

One quote I did not make, but that was originally attributed to me following our 34–13 win over Clemson in 2011: Todd Ellis, our play-by-play announcer, was actually the one who said, "We aren't LSU and we aren't Alabama. But we sure ain't Clemson."

Unfortunately, that quote got picked up on our official Twitter account and it was assumed I said it.

Coach Swinney fired back: "They ain't Alabama. They ain't LSU. And they're certainly not Clemson. That's why Carolina's in Chapel Hill and USC's in California and the university in this state always has been, always will be Clemson . . . You can print that, tweet that, whatever."

Eventually my friend Dabo and I got that cleared up and now we can look back at it and laugh.

Then somehow Dabo and I got to talking about planets and he said about me: "He's from Pluto, and I'm from Mars."

And I responded: "Dabo probably thinks there's only, what, nine planets out there? I think I read where Pluto may not be considered one now."

Since I also don't believe in going off the record, everything I said for print or broadcast was often quite candid. My quotes were not contrived. Sometimes they were just spontaneous.

Other times in the off-season when I spoke to alumni groups and told jokes, they were meant to stir up a little fun, or in some cases use humor to point out a discrepancy or a serious issue. Such as the shoe scandal in Tallahassee during Florida State's national championship season in 1993 when agents were found to have bought more than $6,000 worth of shoes for Seminoles players.

At a Gator Club meeting the next year, I said: "You know what FSU stands for, don't you? Free Shoes University." That one stuck.

A lot of times us coaches would use humorous stuff to fire up our fan bases in the off-season. I just enjoyed commenting and joking about our opponents. And they told jokes on us and it never bothered me. Including Bobby Bowden! You'll never see me upset when somebody says something about us.

So just like my visor, my quotes were very much a part of who I am and how I coached.

Sometimes it was a case of reacting to a question. One day in Hoover, Alabama, during SEC Media Days 2014, I was asked about the newly created trophy that would go to the winner of the South Carolina–Texas A&M game. The award is a bronze sculpture of James Bonham, a South Carolina student who would become a hero at the Battle of the Alamo. And so I remarked: "I don't know. I was raised in Tennessee and we were always taught that Davy Crockett was the hero of the Alamo."

A little later, after reading the story of James Bonham, I added: "I'm sure this guy Bonham was a hero and did a lot of good."

Truthfully, I don't look back at what I said unless it's called to my attention. But the editors of this book asked me to go over the list of my quotes they dug out for verification. And here are the ones that I claim:

At SEC Media Days 2015 when I had been asked so many times about retiring, I opened with this remark to the media: "A lot of familiar faces out there. I would've figured a bunch of you guys would have retired by now."

On retirement: "Somebody said, 'Why are you still coaching?' I said, 'Well, I forgot to get fired, and I'm not going to cheat.' That's about the only way you lose your job: You get fired for losing or you cheat and then they get somebody else. I've not done any of those to any extent big-time, I guess."

On critics: "I know the critics are out there. That's why they're called 'critics.' They criticize everything. We gave them something to criticize [in 2014]."

On playing more than one quarterback: "I've been a coach to play two quarterbacks. You can win with two. Nothing in the rule book that says you have to play with one."

On managing players at my age, I made mention of Pope Francis, and it was one of my favorites: "They appointed this guy, and he's seventy-seven years old, and he's the leader of a billion people in the world. They call him the pope, and he replaced a guy that was eighty-five years old. So if he can be the leader of over a billion people worldwide, surely I can get eleven guys on the field."

An old joke I used many times at speaking engagements, about at a fire that burned twenty books at an Auburn University football dorm: "But the real tragedy was that fifteen hadn't been colored yet!"

To a photographer as our team posed in the Georgia Dome in December 1995 after winning our third of four consecutive SEC championships: "This is becoming our annual team picture."

A reporter asked who our punter Josh Korn was: "I'm not sure, but I think he's Jimmy Crack's brother."

Asked about a streaker who ran onto the field: "In my experience, I've learned women are better streakers."

Asked by Tennessee reporters how I felt being in "Big Orange Country": "I thought this was Vanderbilt country."

When Jadeveon Clowney got a speeding ticket: "I didn't know Jadeveon's car could go that fast. He doesn't have a pretty car like those FSU guys used to drive."

When the Gators were playing at Tennessee's newly refurbished Neyland Stadium facility, asked at halftime how loud it was: "It was really loud, possibly louder than the Swamp. And then the game started."

At a Gator Club meeting in Orlando in the summer of 1997 after Tennessee had played in the Citrus Bowl three straight years: "You can't spell Citrus Bowl without a UT in it."

After our kicker Josh Brown made a career-long forty-nine-yard field goal to beat Tennessee 16–15 at Neyland Stadium in 2005: "I've finally got a new line: 'God is smiling on the Gamecocks.'"

And finally, this next one is not my quote. It was a story written and told by writer Chris Harry, then with *The Tampa Tribune*. He and his wife had gone to the movies and their babysitter answered the phone when I called, for some reason I've forgotten. It went like this, according to Harry:

> She asked, "Is this Coach Spurrier? This is Christine. I'm Jeff Mitchell's girlfriend." [Mitchell was one of our best our offensive linemen.]
>
> "Jeff Mitchell's girlfriend?" I responded. "Jeff Mitchell jumped offsides today!"

I guess it's true. After all, we coaches take advantage of every teaching opportunity we can get!

Chapter 20

JERRI: MY HEAD BALL COACH

My Head Ball Coach, Jerri. We celebrated fifty years of marriage in 2016.

THE FAMILY

When I resigned at South Carolina, Jerri also resigned as the First Lady of South Carolina football. Stepping away from it wasn't all that easy, because her roots run deep in Columbia and the Gamecock football program. She clings to her memories but said initially it would take her a while to open up her scrapbook.

My memories have been her memories and vice versa. She could write her own book. As always, of course, she tried immediately to begin moving forward to the next chapter in our lives. But it's going to take a moment or two.

Jerri has been a natural, the perfect coach's wife, and she has loved every part of it. If you didn't know what a key role Jerri played in our football partnership, you'd have no idea how beloved she was by the players, coaches, and fans.

It takes patience and courage to be married to a football coach because of the volatile nature of the business.

Not only has she supported me at every turn in every job, but she has also been a Team Mom. She went to almost every practice at South Carolina, as she did almost everywhere I coached, spoke to every player she saw by name, and made it known how much she cared for them.

That's why I refer to her as my Head Ball Coach.

Once asked in an interview about her relationship with the players and what she said to them after practice, Jerri said: "I talk to them about their grades. I call their mothers. I go with them to their surgeries. I've offered to go see them when they get in trouble. I spend a lot of time listening to them, and that's like having a mother. And they know I feel that way. They know that if they need somebody that is not a coach—that somebody loves them. And I do."

The depth of her relationships and staunch support of the program showed up in big ways and in little ways—sometimes known only by the people she touched.

Someone sent me an account from garnetandblackattack.com, a Gamecocks fan website, that demonstrates how Jerri showed up in the life of a diehard fan one rainy night in Knoxville:

"Knoxville, 2009 . . . Halloween and South Carolina was losing to Tennessee on a cold and rainy night. It was a tough loss . . . Vol and Gamecock fans began to leave early to go celebrate or mourn the game . . . My family and I chose to stay . . . As I sat shivering in an emptying Neyland Stadium, a stranger came and wrapped a blanket around my shoulders and said, 'Hi. I know your frustration and we are probably going to lose . . . But it means a lot to this team . . . And staying for the whole game when you lose, makes it feel even better when you win' . . . The stranger was Jerri Spurrier."

THE WEDDING

The former Jerri Starr, a graduate of Fort Lauderdale High, already knew a lot about football when I met her.

We started dating as sophomores at Florida after meeting at the ATO (Alpha Tau Omega) fraternity house, where I was still a pledge and she was the fraternity's little sister. In between then and my senior year we had gone out with other people, but before my senior season at Florida, we started thinking of getting married. Since we didn't want to cause a disruption in the school year or football season, we thought we'd just have a small, private ceremony. My philosophy in life has always pretty much been that once you make up your mind to do something, then go do it! But we weren't exactly sure where to go or how to get married. I didn't have a ring yet, and certainly we hadn't thought about who would perform the ceremony.

We had several married players on our team. I was talking to my married friend Fred Goldsmith one night and discovered that he knew a lot about eloping. He said he and his wife had looked into it, but changed their minds.

"You want me to go with you?" asked Fred, who would eventually go into coaching and become the HBC at Slippery Rock, Rice, Duke, and Lenoir-Rhyne.

I said, "Yeah, come on along, in case I get lost or something." So off we went, driving up to Jacksonville, Highway 17, right on toward Folkston, Georgia. But somehow we ended up in Kingsland, Georgia. We got lost anyway.

I think I paid $10 for a tiny ring at either a pawnshop or a fishing tackle shop in Kingsland—Jerri says she thinks it was called The Tackle Box. In fact, Jerri still wears that ring today. She won't replace it, because it's her wedding ring. We were married at the Methodist church and got back in time for practice on a Tuesday.

We had told Coach Graves and my parents about our plans. My parents didn't know what to say. My mom was pretty easygoing. They loved Jerri. One of the best decisions I ever made was getting married to her. In addition to being a wonderful mom to Lisa, Amy, Steve Jr., and Scotty, and a loving wife, she has provided me with inspiration and wise counsel. Many of her opinions and decisions were very influential in my life as a player and a coach, in a big way.

The neatest thing is that because we married young, we were able to do so many things together. And having that last year at Florida as a married couple was special to us both.

Walking with Jerri on campus in 1966.

"The wonderful thing about it was sharing that whole year as husband and wife," she once said to a reporter. "I got to share the bowl games and the Heisman award ceremony. We still go back to the Heisman anniversary parties, and when I meet the wives of former winners most of them weren't there when their husbands won. It was a wonderful thing to share."

Since we were young parents, our kids sort of grew up with us and experienced a lot of things that we did. Lisa was there from the very first, being born in Gainesville. Then came Amy, Steve Jr., and Scotty. They have all been actively involved either as coaches or fans. Lisa (Spurrier King) and Amy (Moody) make as many of the games as possible and are totally committed to supporting our football team. Amy has sort of become our team historian and has done a wonderful job of keeping articles for our scrapbook. And Lisa has hardly missed a South Carolina game in recent years.

I was really blessed to work with my two sons as coaches at South Carolina.

Steve Jr. and I are about as close as a father and son could be—he's one of my two best pals in the world (Scotty is the other)—and it was comforting having him around. We've played golf together, had many dinners with his wife and children, spent weeks together at Crescent Beach every year, and coached together for seventeen years.

Steve Jr. has been around my teams since 1983, when he was a twelve-year-old ball boy with the Tampa Bay Bucs. He would come out and run routes with the receivers. When I went to Duke in 1987–1989 he ball-boyed all those games. He played at Duke, was on our Florida staff for five years before joining Bob Stoops's staff in 2000 when Oklahoma won a national championship, went with me to the Redskins, then spent a year with Mark Stoops in Arizona and came aboard when I started at South Carolina. Now he's back with the Sooners.

Steve was known as Stevie until he got to college and then sort of became Steve Jr. Sometimes people refer to his nickname, Bub. Having Steve Jr. on the staff for ten years as recruiting coordinator, wide receivers' coach, and co-offensive coordinator is the big reason I stayed as long as I did. I would oversee the run and pass game and almost always called the plays. However, Steve Jr. called the plays the entire game when we upset the Gators in the Swamp 23–20 in overtime in 2014.

As a ball boy or assistant coach, he was with our teams for twenty-three of the thirty years that I have been a head coach. Steve Jr. has seen just about all of it from a very close range—on the sideline spot or in a press box—and has contributed mightily to the success that his dad and team enjoyed. We have a wonderful picture together at Duke after we beat NC State 35–26—a victory that helped us almost clinch the ACC championship, which we won the next week.

At Duke from 1987 to 1989 as ball boy, Steve Jr. missed some road games while playing wide receiver for Northern High School on Friday nights. As a player at Duke, he earned a scholarship after coming in as a walk-on and also earned a starting wide receiver position his junior season.

Steve came to Florida with me as a graduate assistant coach in 1994. In his first three years as a GA at Florida, we won three SEC championships and one national championship. He thought this coaching gig was a piece of cake and almost always a whole lot of fun.

I am hoping and praying that he will get the chance to be a head coach someday, as I believe he will be super. I'm looking forward to someday soon watching one of his teams play.

I've really been proud of my younger son, Scotty, for the way he has grown as a coach, a father, and a husband. When Steve Jr. and I left South Carolina, Scotty was retained by Will Muschamp. Scotty loves coaching, loves everything associated with coaching, and I believe he has a bright future ahead of him.

I was already pulling for both the Gamecocks and the Sooners, but with my sons coaching for them I will be pulling even more passionately.

We've been fortunate, having our family so close to us all these years—a special treat for Jerri and me. As we were finishing up this book we were still pondering our future. We had a whole range of things to think about—full-time coaching not being one of them.

Through it all, Jerri has maintained a steady hand. In the summer of 2016 we celebrated fifty years of marriage in Daytona Beach with our four children and thirteen grandchildren and a large group of friends. I find it almost impossible now to think about how life would have been without her.

THE NEAR MISSES

Looking back on a half century of marriage, I sometimes marvel at how we have journeyed through all these years without any major tragedies. I think about some of the close calls and near misses and they make me shudder. I've had several instances where something really bad could have happened.

The first one happened when I was a little kid and I ran across the street without looking. A car came to a screeching halt. I got to the other side and a lady said, "Son, you could have been killed by that car. You've got to look both ways before you cross the street." For some reason, that was the first time I'd ever been told that: "You've got to look both ways." I can assure you I've looked both ways after that.

Another close call happened when I was a junior in high school. That summer I got a job out at the municipal golf course in Johnson City on the maintenance crew, mowing the fairways, watering the greens, whatever needed to be done. One day I'm on a tractor—I don't know anything about tractors—and I was on this big hill and decided I would coast straight down the hill to get to the bottom. So I was riding the brake. It was a steep, steep hill and that tractor started skidding and jumping around, and I held on for dear life and somehow I got to the bottom. The superintendent saw the skid marks on the side of the mountain and said,

"Boy, you could've died. That tractor could have flipped on you. You can't go straight down a mountain like that." I said, "Okay, I understand it now. I didn't understand it at the time." Ironically, a tractor turned over on him in the maintenance shed and killed him about a year or so later.

The next scary incident happened after my third or fourth year in the NFL, when we were living in Gainesville. Jerri and I were returning home late one night from a visit with our good friend and attorney Bill O'Neal, who had a house out on a lake near Melrose, approximately twenty-five miles outside of Gainesville. Jerri was driving at about two a.m. An approaching driver had fallen asleep at the wheel and come across on our side of the road. Jerri tried to avoid him on his side, causing a collision. I think our right headlight hit his right headlight, causing a spinning, glancing blow that prevented a total head-on collision. Neither the driver nor I were hurt seriously, but I did take a blast across my forehead. Jerri suffered lacerations and had some scars on her knees and chin that took a long time to heal up. That could have really been a disaster right there—a head-on collision. So we avoided that one. Another thank you, Lord.

And then twice I've been on airplanes, approaching a takeoff, when the pilot shut down the engines and said we were returning to the terminal. The first time it happened was when I was an assistant coach at Duke. We were recruiting in the Pittsburgh area and we had a midnight flight back to Durham and the pilot shut it down in rainy, kind-of-snowy weather, so we went back the next day.

The next time that happened was when we were on a golf trip to Ireland. We called it the Gator Golf Trip. A good friend put it together down in Gainesville; we took about twenty people over to Ireland and played those courses. We were returning from Shannon, Ireland, on one of those real big Delta jets that must have had four hundred or more people in it. And the pilot went roaring down the runway, and sure enough, right before liftoff, he slammed on the brakes, shut it down, and came on the PA system and he said, "We're returning to the terminal. This plane is no good." So we came back and spent another night in Ireland and then flew out the next day.

Right after the pilot shut it down, a flight attendant was walking by and I asked her, "Has this ever happened to you?" And she said, "No. This is the first time ever." And I started thinking that it had happened twice to me. So the Man Upstairs was watching out for all the people on that airplane.

So I avoided that—somebody was looking out for me. I know I've been blessed far beyond what I deserve. I know those instances could have turned out disastrously. But for some reason the Lord smiled on the Spurriers and we avoided possible serious injury and possibly even death.

There is such a fine line between failure and success, between life and death, depending on what path you take on that particular day. Choices we make are so critical, even if we don't realize how critical at the time. Which is why we need spiritual guidance.

Jobs I have taken or jobs I didn't take—who knows what was down that road?

I was asked about whether I came close to leaving South Carolina for Alabama when I appeared on *The Paul Finebaum Show* on the SEC Network in April 2016. I didn't bring it up and hadn't planned to talk about it, but since Paul already knew the circumstances and actually was contacted by Alabama athletic director Mal Moore about me at the time, there was no way I could avoid talking about it. I had just taken the job at South Carolina in 2005 and had been there one year. I told Mal, "I'm committed to these guys and this is where I'm going to finish up. Listen, I'm not going to come there. Hang with Coach Saban."

Coach Saban had already turned Alabama down and said he was staying at Miami. I said, "Go back to him. I think he'd rather be at Alabama than at Miami," because I had a two-year run in the NFL and sort of understood what he was going through in the pros versus college. Sure enough, Mal went back and convinced him he needed to come to Alabama.

I'm not saying that I facilitated the hiring of Nick Saban at Alabama. They maybe would have gotten together anyway. But it did happen. Finebaum asked me—after seeing what Coach Saban has accomplished—if I ever wondered if it could have been the same for me at Alabama. I replied, "No, I really don't. What he has done there is wonderful. I told him, 'You have another seven or eight years in you at Alabama, unless you lose three games in one season.' Coach Saban said, 'Oh, man, if we lose three in a season, I don't know what's going to happen around here.'"

As good a job as it is in Tuscaloosa, I think there are two better in the SEC. When asked about the best two jobs in the conference, I said, "I think Georgia and LSU are basically the best two. Nick Saban has made Alabama the best right now. But as far as recruiting advantages, LSU doesn't have much competition in their state, and Georgia pretty much should own their state there."

AS FRANK SINATRA sings in the song "My Way": "Regrets, I've had a few . . . but, then again, too few to mention . . ."

I, too, have had a few regrets—but I WILL mention them.

I regret somewhat that I could have done a little bit more during my college playing career to help our teams at Florida win the SEC. You realize later in life how important those championships are—the memories of a lifetime. You celebrate them every ten years when you have a reunion back at your school. We did not do that, and I wish I could have done a little bit more to help our team more in the '64, '65, and '66 seasons.

As far as being an NFL quarterback, I'll always wish I had invested more time in trying to be a good one, and I regret having been content being a backup for all those years—even if the pension checks for being vested ten years are so nice.

And finally, I now realize I should have stayed at Florida longer. Our 2001 team was outstanding—maybe as good as the '95 and '96 teams that went 12-1 and finished second and first in the nation. We didn't have a good game against Tennessee (in 2001). They ran the ball extremely well. I could have stayed another four or five years. And I have no doubt we would have kept winning.

People have often asked me exactly why I left Florida, even though I keep telling them because I wanted to coach in the NFL and that there was no rift between Jeremy Foley and myself. What did happen the day after the Orange Bowl win over Maryland in January 2002 was that after I invited him over, he arrived with a bottle of Dom Pérignon. We sat on the beach sipping champagne, celebrating our successes, recalling the good times together. Jeremy said in a 2016 article that our twelve-year ride together "was the time of my life." And I suppose I could say the same thing. Although I would never take anything away from the challenges and success I enjoyed immensely at South Carolina.

The decision to go to the Washington Redskins obviously didn't turn out too well. I probably could have gone to another team and maybe lasted a little longer. Still, I will always appreciate the good things that came out of that experience.

I used to think it was important to be able to say, "I never got fired." People almost look at you like they feel sorry for you after you get fired. I don't know why I used to always think that was important. Most coaches do get fired—that comes with the profession.

CRESCENT BEACH

By the time SEC Media Days 2016 rolled around I knew I'd start thinking more about another year without football. But after six months I was perfectly fine playing golf, visiting friends, and going to the beach—because that's my regular off-season routine.

Ever since I can remember, my parents would take our family—plus my uncles, aunts, and cousins (probably about two dozen people)—to a place near Myrtle Beach, South Carolina—usually Cherry Grove Beach, the northernmost South Carolina beach.

We would rent a house, three or four blocks from the ocean. If I was lucky, I'd sleep indoors on a sofa. Occasionally, I got the outdoor swing to sleep on. Fortunately, it was screened in, but it was always hot—about 80–85 degrees.

In 1965, when Jerri and I were juniors at the University of Florida, I asked someone where a nice beach was. I had a date with Jerri and we did not want to go to Daytona Beach. We both love the beach and were looking for a quiet place to ride some waves and do what you do at the beach. This person told me to go to Crescent Beach and how to get there. We would drive over from Gainesville and spend the day. Sometimes a good Gator friend would let us use his place there in the 1970s.

We drove on the beach for miles and maybe saw one or two tiny, small houses. It was mostly wild dunes—very high at that.

In 1994, I was in my fifth year coaching at Florida. We had bought two condominium units at the Coquina in 1986 and 1992. A piece of property from the ocean to the Matanzas River, which is also the Intracoastal Waterway, was on sale. Fortunately, I had enough money to buy the piece of land and I told Jerri, "If we ever have enough money, I'm going to build a really nice house on it."

Crescent Beach is on a Florida barrier island, and St. Augustine Beach joins it on the northern side of the island, called Anastasia. It has the highest dunes I've ever seen on a beach in Florida, and the beach at low tide could be 100 yards from the shoreline.

We started the house in 2006 and builder Winston Radford did a super job. We were in no hurry as I still had several years of coaching left. It was finished around 2012 and we now live there part-time.

Jerri and I have watched our children—and now our grandchildren—grow up and vacation at Crescent Beach since the 1970s. I've said many times that Crescent Beach is the best beach in the world and I'm blessed and fortunate to live there.

Also on the island is one of the best golf courses I've ever played. Marsh Creek Country Club is a challenging, beautiful golf course that has water and marsh in play on sixteen of the eighteen holes. You can't hit grounders or pop-ups at Marsh Creek. The pro, Cary Splane, is one of the best club pro golfers in the country. This is the course on which we filmed *Feherty* for the Golf Channel special in July of 2015.

So we go there often and never tire of all the natural beauty, good friends and wonderful amenities that Crescent Beach has to offer.

AS I SIT BACK and think about the wonderful journey of winning all those conference titles at Florida—or finishing in first place—I reflect on the fact that a streak really began at Duke in 1989 and carried over at Florida through 2000. And then I have to refer to that passage of "The Coach": "How is this possible?"

People ask me a lot about what it's like having a statue up at my alma mater. We were incredibly blessed at Florida: in the Ring of Honor, winning the Heisman, seven—yes, seven—SEC titles. Having that bronze likeness in front of the Swamp next to those of my Heisman-winning quarterback Danny Wuerffel and our friend and fellow Heisman winner Tim Tebow is a real honor. And now to have my name on the stadium and field . . . It causes me to repeat that phrase I have already used numerous times in this book: Thank you, Lord.

I was stunned when I received a call from Jeremy Foley just a few days before the start of summer 2016 to learn about the most special honor I have ever received: The University of Florida was going to announce the placing of my name on Ben Hill Griffin Stadium as Steve Spurrier–Florida Field, the Swamp. I remain humbled, thankful, and appreciative for that, and grateful for having been recruited and signed by the original "Bull Gator," Coach Ray Graves. I thought back to Coach Doug Dickey giving me a chance to break into coaching; for players like Danny Wuerffel and Shane Matthews; and how much fun we had playing in front of our fans there.

Aside from fifty years of marriage with Jerri, there were lots of football milestones in 2016, including the fiftieth anniversary of my winning the Heisman, the twentieth anniversary of our 1996 national championship Florida team, and the fiftieth anniversary of our winning Orange Bowl team.

I AM ALSO PROUD to be the winningest coach at South Carolina. When I got the job, that was my goal. I only had to win sixty-five games to do that. But I told everyone that, because I wanted Gamecock fans to know I was going to be there at least ten years.

It has been such a pleasure going back to Gainesville and Columbia, watching my old teams practice and play. Coach Jim McElwain has made me feel very much at home. And so has Coach Will Muschamp at South Carolina, where they were kind enough to put Jerri's name and mine on the new indoor practice facility.

All nice tributes—as is having your jersey numbers retired at your high school and college. However, I felt those numbers would live in perpetuity only if they were given to other players, so I asked both schools to un-retire them. And they've been worn by others.

I'M ALSO PROUD to say that Jerri and I have tried to live a life of continuing education. She went back and got her third college degree—this time in psychology from South Carolina. She even did her graduation walk in 2015 with some of the Gamecock football players who, of course, she knew. But she had to miss the official ceremonies because we were away at the Heisman Trophy dinner.

She told *The State*, the local newspaper: "I am very proud that I have my diploma. It's kind of wonderful for me that I have that. Now this is my school." And she added later, showing her degrees to a writer, "These are *my* trophies!"

On April 8, 2016, we visited Florida to pay tribute to Owen Holyoak, who was the chair at the College of Health and Human Development. I presented him with an award for service to his college. He had been instrumental in my getting a degree after ten years in the NFL, while I was an assistant at Duke. You must have your degree if you are a coach. So Dr. Holyoak was a key man in the life of the Spurriers.

So I came back for graduation at the O'Connell Center. While I was walking up to receive my degree, Jerri said she heard somebody say: "I didn't know Steve Spurrier had a son that old!"

Sometimes, when you choose to do things a little out of the ordinary, people get caught off guard and strange things can happen. But as I can attest to, it always seems to work out best in the end, over the long haul. It's called living life . . . a little differently.

Coach Spurrier did more than win a Heisman Trophy, a national championship, and a bunch of games. Coach Spurrier changed the culture of Florida athletics. We were an institution that always had a mantra of "wait 'til next year" and "wouldn't it be great to just win one championship." Coach changed all of that. The Gators won, won big, and won with swagger. As much as he impacted the football program, he changed the vibe in the entire athletic department.

—Jeremy Foley, Florida Director of Athletics

**With University of Florida Coach Jim McElwain
in front of my statue in Gainesville.**

AFTERWORD

As I wound down my days in Columbia, I felt very grateful that University of South Carolina President Harris Pastides and Athletics Director Ray Tanner allowed me to "resign" and not "retire," as I took up a role as consultant there. Without knowing what the best opportunity or challenge would be after South Carolina, I did not want to use the word "retire" because I wanted to stay active. Retirement was not an option.

All I knew was that I planned to finish writing this book and wait to see what opportunities arose. But I could never have foreseen the wonderful year that was ahead.

After my resignation from South Carolina, I was fortunate and blessed to receive a whole bunch of honors and awards—as well as an excellent job opportunity.

In June of 2016, Jeremy Foley called on behalf of the board of trustees for the University of Florida Athletic Association and said: "We are all set to put your name on Ben Hill Griffin Stadium. It's going to be called 'Steve Spurrier–Florida Field at Ben Hill Griffin Stadium.'"

I said, "You're kidding! Really?"

He said, "This is what we're going to do. You've earned it. Everyone wants to do it. So we'll have the official naming of the stadium at the opening game of the season when we play Massachusetts."

Of all the honors I've received, including winning the Heisman Trophy, the most overwhelming was having my name placed on the stadium here at the Swamp, where I played and coached for so many years. It will always be the greatest honor I ever receive as a player or coach.

At the same time, Jeremy, Coach Jim McElwain, and President Kent Fuchs were all onboard with me coming to Florida as an ambassador/consultant. That was an opportunity that Jerri and I jumped at.

They put me in an office up near the sports information department, close to Senior Associate Athletics Director of Football Steve McClain, and they gave me an administrative assistant, Jennifer Wagner.

I get a little bit involved in the football program, watching tape on occasion and making a few suggestions to Coach McElwain and Coach Nussmeier. But the rest is up to them. I don't get involved in coaching, which I shouldn't. But they are open to new ideas and suggestions.

So I have a job that I enjoy. It's not demanding. It's not stressful. And any way I can help my alma mater I am willing to do so.

I always thought when my coaching days were over we would return to the state of Florida. We had already built a nice house in Crescent Beach and, once there, we had been hoping to build a house in Gainesville, which we began doing in mid-2017. We're looking forward to having a lot of our family come and visit as they travel through Gainesville.

In December of 2017, I will be officially inducted into the College Football Hall of Fame as a coach. I had already been inducted as a player in 1986, so this will make me only the fourth person to be inducted in as both a player and a coach. The others were Amos Alonzo Stagg, Bobby Dodd, and Bowden Wyatt. It is a very nice tribute and one that I will always cherish.

I also deeply appreciate being honored in 2016 by the National College

Football Awards Association with the Contributions to College Football Award; in addition to having the Maxwell Football Club present me with the Reds Bagnell Award.

I've had the opportunity to do quite a bit of travel for speeches, book signings, and television and radio appearances since I left coaching, something I plan to continue. My message about the key to winning, as I have outlined in this book, is the byproduct of having good players who are focused and committed to goals. I also always emphasize that even when the players play well, sometimes we need help from a higher power above. That's just the way it was meant to be for us. And when those kinds of games are over, you say, "Thank you, Lord, for allowing this to happen," a whole bunch of times.

I began my new role at Florida on August 1, 2016, leading up to the first game of the season and maybe the busiest day of my life on September 3. Before the game, we had a book signing at the University of Florida Bookstore and I signed more than six hundred books. After that the University had a nice reception where I was able to invite some former players, coaches, family, and friends; followed by the ceremony for the naming of the field.

I was asked to dress up as Mr. Two Bits, the legendary cheerleader-superfan, the late George Edmondson of Tampa, who faithfully showed up to inspire Gator fans with his famous "Two Bits, Four Bits" cheers section to section from 1949 to 2008.

With both teams in the locker rooms, I was given a mic and made an acceptance speech for the honor of having my name on the field. I thanked a lot of people who were very instrumental in my life, including Coach Graves, who recruited and signed me as a player in 1963, and Bob Bryan, who hired me as coach in 1990. Then it was my turn to imitate the late Mr. Two Bits, which is something Florida does as a tradition for each home game. So I made it a point to come up with a little different routine.

Mr. Two Bits always wore a yellow shirt, orange and blue tie, and seersucker pants. He'd blow the whistle and hold up the sign for his "Two Bits,

Four Bits" cheer. So I put on a yellow T-shirt that had an orange and blue tie painted on it. I had seen Danny Wuerffel's video of his impersonation of Mr. Two Bits, which gave me a frame of reference.

I jumped around—"Two bits, four bits, six bits a dollar! All for the Gators stand up and holler!" So all the Gators stood up. And just as they did, I mimicked Usain Bolt shooting an arrow into the sky four times, at each side of the stadium.

Somebody asked, "Why'd you do that?"

And I said, "Because it's never been done before!" And it was sort of a little tribute to Bolt, too.

I have said it before and I repeat: Making the choice to attend the University of Florida in 1963 was maybe the best and biggest decision of my life. And it paved the way for me to meet and marry my future wife, Jerri.

Once again, I love that John Wooden quote: "We may not know where our paths lead, but we know they are being directed in some way." I have no doubt that has certainly been the case for me.

Go Gators!

Go Gamecocks!

Go Duke!

—Steve Spurrier

ACKNOWLEDGMENTS

Many hands provided assistance for writing this book, which actually was nearly twenty-three years in the making. The idea first popped up in 1993, but timing was an issue.

In August 2014 it took just one phone call to reignite the passion for a project between two good friends who had known each other for nearly fifty years—inspired, perhaps, by some advice we had read: "Tell your own story before someone tells it for you."

Through the guidance of Byrd Leavell of Waxman Leavell Literary Agency, a partnership was forged with Penguin Random House, Blue Rider Press, and editor Brant Rumble, whose shared vision with the authors and knowledge of Southern football proved invaluable.

We also owe many other people a big thanks.

- To Paul Finebaum for writing the foreword and keeping college football fans up to date on the book's progress through *The Paul Finebaum Show.*
- To special assistant Rita Boykin for her loyalty and dedication. She was the glue that held things together when everybody was traveling or apart. Rita's coordination and timely handling of the manuscript was highly professional and most appreciated.
- To John Fineran of Mishawaka, Indiana, whose suggestions, pre-editing, and research were invaluable.
- To Steve McClain and Jennifer Wagner from the University

of Florida Media Relations Department for providing photos and background information.

- To Chris Doering for digging deep into his family's film archives to double-check some key plays in one of our SEC championship games.

- To former *New York Times* sports editor Neil Amdur for his advice and perspective on book publishing . . . To Gator diehard and attorney Randy Briggs for his wise legal counsel . . . To Laura Novotny of Crescent Beach, Florida, for dutifully dispatching copies of the manuscript when the only other option was carrier pigeons . . . To Jeff Doubek for assistance in assimilating pre-publication material . . . To Tim and Mary Winter Teaster of Columbia, South Carolina, for their wonderful Gamecock hospitality . . . And to our longtime friend Norm Carlson for always being there when we need him.

—Steve Spurrier and Buddy Martin

APPENDIX

Steve Spurrier by the Numbers

CAREER COACHING RECORD THROUGH 2015

Duke: 20-13-1

Florida: 122-27-1

South Carolina (through part of 2015): 86-49

Overall: 275-130-2

College Overall: 228-89-2

Pro Overall: 47-41

SEC Overall: 205-71

Non-Major Conferences: 53-0

Bowl Record: 11-10

College Home Record: 132-27

Duke: 12-3

Florida: 68-5

South Carolina: 53-19

SPURRIER'S LAST TEN-PLUS YEARS AT SOUTH CAROLINA

Overall: 86-49

SEC: 44-40

Eastern Division: 29-21

Versus Florida: 5-5

Versus Tennessee: 5-5

Versus Georgia: 5-6

Versus Clemson: 6-4

Also beat Alabama, Nebraska, Michigan, Wisconsin, and Miami

PREVIOUS TEN YEARS AT SOUTH CAROLINA PRIOR TO SPURRIER'S ARRIVAL

Overall: 49-64

SEC: 28-51

Eastern Division: 18-33

Versus Florida: 0-10

Versus Tennessee: 0-10

Versus Georgia: 3-7

Versus Clemson: 2-8

RECORD VS. KEY OPPONENTS LAST FIVE-PLUS YEARS AT SOUTH CAROLINA, 2010–2014

Florida: 4-1

Georgia: 4-2

Clemson: 4-1

SEVEN-TIME CONFERENCE COACH OF THE YEAR

1988 ACC Coach of the Year

1989 ACC Coach of the Year

1990 SEC Coach of the Year

1995 SEC Coach of the Year

1996 SEC Coach of the Year

2005 SEC Coach of the Year

2010 SEC Coach of the Year

ABOUT THE AUTHORS

Steve Spurrier is a former football coach and player. He played at the University of Florida, where he won the Heisman Trophy in 1966. Spurrier played in the NFL for ten years and then worked as an assistant coach before becoming head coach of the USFL's Tampa Bay Bandits in 1983. He went on to coach at Duke University and then the University of Florida, where he led the Gators to six SEC Championships, as well as a National Championship in 1996. He coached the Washington Redskins from 2002 to 2003 and the University of South Carolina Gamecocks from 2005 to 2015. He was named SEC Coach of the Year seven times. He is now an ambassador and consultant for the University of Florida's athletic department.

Buddy Martin is a columnist for GridironNow.com and SouthernPigskin.com; a host for Southern Pigskin Radio Network; an Emmy-winning network TV journalist; and has won numerous awards as a sports editor/columnist for three major newspapers. He is the anchor of *Buddy Martin's Sports Page* on his hometown station, WOCA, in Ocala/North Central Florida. This is his seventh book.